# HEART-WORK

George Herbert and
the Protestant Ethic

# VOCATION

*Pascimur et patimur*

# HEART-WORK

## George Herbert and
## the Protestant Ethic

Cristina Malcolmson

Stanford University Press
Stanford, California   1999

Stanford University Press
Stanford, California

© 1999 by the Board of Trustees of the
Leland Stanford Junior University

Printed in the United States of America
CIP data appear at the end of the book

FRONTISPIECE: *(page ii)* A panel entitled
"Vocation" from the frontispiece of Richard
Brathwait's *The English Gentleman* (John
Haviland: London, 1630), C117.bb.8. By
permission of the British Library.

The image is characterized in "A Draught
of the *Frontispiece*": "VOCATION is
described in a grace, civill and demure
habit, a countenance constant and setled:
adjoyning to which Picture appeares
a ship with sailes displayed, while *Vocation*
fixeth his eye on a Globe, or a Marine Map:
under the feature are mattocks, sledges,
shovels, and other utensiles; from whence
he extracts this Motto; *Pascimur and Patimur*
[we are fed and we endure]."

*For my mother and father*

# Acknowledgments

This work is a contextual study, yet its primary debt is to the formalist critic Paul Alpers, whose brilliance in poetic analysis is matched only by the discerning generosity with which he engages historicist approaches. I am also grateful to the following people for their detailed reading and invaluable advice, as well as for their keen understanding of the early modern period: Richard Dutton, Margaret Ferguson, Sidney Gottlieb, Judith Haber, Eugene Hill, Lawrence Manley, and Don Wayne. My colleagues at Bates College—Steven Dillon, Sanford Freedman, and especially Lillian Nayder and Anne Thompson—have provided shrewd counsel as well as an atmosphere free for thought. For their perceptive reading of individual chapters, I thank Janet Adelman, Alan Bewell, Richard Burt, Joan Dayan, Deborah Dyson, Richard Halpern, Rebecca Laroche, Elena Levy-Navarro, Jonathan Post, Jeffrey Powers-Beck, Nancy Selleck, and Annie Smart. I am grateful to the librarians at the British Library, the Bodleian Library, and the Beineke Library, who always seemed to believe with me that there was still a great deal about the seventeenth century left to discover. I want to thank Helen Tartar, Kate Warne, and Ruth Steinberg at Stanford University Press for their wisdom and patience. I thank Edward Donald Kennedy for permission to reprint Chapter 1, which first appeared in *Studies in Philology* 85, spring 1988, pp. 245–66, and Sidney Gottlieb for permission to reprint Chapter 2, which first appeared in *George Herbert in the Nineties: Reflections and Reassessments*. Finally, Deborah Dyson, Jancy Limpert, Wilna Limpert, Inge Malcolmson, Leslie Malcolmson, Oliver Malcolmson, and Peter Malcolmson made me laugh as they reminded me of my duty.

*C.M.*

# Contents

# Illustrations

# HEART-WORK

George Herbert and
the Protestant Ethic

# Introduction

Richard Baxter wrote in 1681, "*Herbert* speaks *to God* like one that *really believeth a God*, and whose business in the world is most *with God. Heart-work* and *Heaven-work* make up his Books." Baxter stresses the devotionalism that, until recently, has been the focus of Herbert criticism. In this book, I hope to contribute to the changing of that focus by showing that, for Herbert, "heart-work" and "business in the world" were inextricably linked. I will argue that the Protestant doctrine of vocation was the principal source for Herbert's conception of self. Unlike modern critics, Baxter was quite aware of the relationship between piety and business in the world, since he preached the rules of the doctrine of vocation throughout his life. In fact, Max Weber uses Baxter's religious writing to illustrate that doctrine in *The Protestant Ethic and the Spirit of Capitalism*.[1]

When Baxter speaks of "heart-work," he refers to the Protestant devotional life initiated by the calling of God and defined as the "general" calling in the doctrine of vocation. In my title, I use the phrase in a different way, however, to refer to the link forged by that doctrine between the devotional heart and labor in the world associated with one's estate or profession, called the "particular" calling. The Protestant ethic included the rule that devotion emerge through what Weber described as "restless, continuous, systematic work in a worldly calling." As preachers taught this doctrine in their sermons, they constructed a new structure of self, in which heart and work were coordinated like soul and body. This new structure of self determined the organization of Herbert's *Temple*, as well as the model of selfhood offered in *The Country Parson*.

The model of identity is also represented in the frontispiece of this book. The image is itself one part of the frontispiece of Richard Brathwait's *The English Gentleman* (1630). Whereas the earnest central figure is surrounded by emblems of the particular calling: merchant sailing, navigation, mining, writing, and farming, the motto refers to the need for grace inherent to the general calling, or the Protestant devotional life. The motto "pascimur et patimur," or "we are fed (by God, the shepherd) and we endure," reminds Brathwait's upper-class audience that it is God who is ultimately responsible for one's survival and well-being.[2] Such a remarkable contrast between activity and passivity is characteristic of the language of the doctrine of vocation. Just as the central figure remains "constant and setled" by remembering his dependence on grace, so Protestant ministers used the "general" calling to refute individualism and to restrain the worldliness that they themselves had set free through their celebration of secular labor (see p. iv).

## I. VOCATION AND SUBJECTIVITY

In part because of Weber's critics, the Protestant doctrine of vocation has not been recognized as a major influence in the development of modern subjectivity.[3] If the division between home and work is the mark of the modern self, with its distinction between public and private realms, then the doctrine of vocation participated in this process of subject-formation by constructing a horizontal model in which devotionalism lay within and business without. This horizontal model was significantly at odds with the vertical system of status. Protestant ministers provided an early version of the modern subject, in which the terms *inward* and *outward* provided an alternative to the distinctions of social degree. On the other hand, while ministers formulated the categories of this early modern subjectivity, they also preached the dangers of individualism, whether religious or economic.[4] Our versions of privacy were anathema to them. Their solution for this danger was to establish a close connection between devotionalism and business in the world, a linking that attempted to preserve traditional models of "the common good."

Recent historians and literary critics of the early modern period have largely employed a theatrical model to illuminate the new conceptions of identity that developed between 1509 and 1660. According to these accounts, the growth of the court and the city undermined the traditional village community and replaced feudal norms of obligation and service with a mobile, improvising self, an "artificial person" identified not through kinship ties, status, or geographical location but through the ability of that person to take on the multiple social roles now available. These accounts imply that the experience of self as "persona" helped to initiate the disjuncture between social role and inner subjectivity.[5]

Such a history ignores the articulated connections between inward and outward "profession" made by the preachers of the doctrine of vocation. The theatrical model no doubt accurately reflects the powerful sense of social fluidity felt by many in the court and city, especially in the upper classes. But it cannot account for the experience of Protestants who understood this fluidity in terms of a religious doctrine. In fact, many Protestants of the "middling sort" labored in their callings in the very city where such theatricality was supposed to be the new norm.[6]

In this study, I hope to bring to light how determined Protestant ministers were to preserve the connection between devotion and business in the world, and how strong was the social pressure to force apart these two newly defined parts of the self. In 1603 William Perkins introduced the influential terms for the "general," or Christian, calling and the "particular," or secular, calling in order to tie godliness more firmly to social duty.[7] In doing so, he fully re-

vised the categories used fifty years earlier (in 1552) by Hugh Latimer. Latimer had defined the "general" calling as one's given
social estate and the "special" calling as the sudden call from God
to follow Christ in one's public life, for example, in the role of
preacher. Latimer, like Perkins, was interested in controlling such
sudden changes: he urged the godly to "tarry our vocation till God
call us."[8] Perkins, however, hoped to regulate such changes
through the link he forges between devotional life and social duty.
According to Perkins, this link, properly developed, protects those
who labor in the world from the covetousness that is "one of the
head and master sins of the world, and from it a sea of evils flow,
both into church and commonwealth." Such worldly desire would
overflow "the limit and compass" of one's divinely chosen social
estate. The remedy for this appetite is to employ the religious
qualities of holiness, constancy, obedience, and faith in order to
turn labor into sanctified action.[9] Sanderson clarifies the connection between religious and social employment in his use of Perkins's terms: "demean thy self in thy *particular* calling, as that thou
do nothing but what may stand with thy *general* calling. *Magistrate*, or *Minister*, or *Lawyer*, or *Merchant*, or *Artificer*, or whatever
other thou art, remember thou art withal a Christian." Since God
has called individuals to both callings:

> Do not think he hath called thee to *service* in the one, and to
> *Cosenage* in the other; to *Simplicity* in the one, and to *Dis-
> simulation* in the other; in a word, to an entire and universal
> *Obedience* in the one, and to any kind or degree of *Disobe-
> dience* in the other.[10]

Here, Sanderson insists on a correspondence between the two
callings that rules out not only hypocrisy but disobedience.

These formulations express the special urgency felt by ministers
during this period to control the effects of the theology of grace
and the doctrine of vocation. Each could lead to the disruption of
the social hierarchy, either through a new kind of godliness or an
increased worldliness. For these ministers, the sin of privacy, or
"private benefit," could take a religious or social form: transgres-

sion consisted in working in a way detrimental to the "common-wealth" or worshipping in a way that led to the neglect of one's social duties. To be "private" was not necessarily to be hidden from public view but to erode the delicate ethical tissue of hierarchical interdependence. As Thomas Adams puts it:

> This is an ambitious age of medlars; there are almost as many mindes as men, sects as Cities, Gospels as Gossips: as if they laboured the reducing of the old Chaos, and first informitie of things againe. . . . That by-word, Every man for himselfe, and God for us all, is uncharitable, ungodly; and impugneth directly the end of every good calling.[11]

For Adams, the "end of every good calling" includes the preservation of the traditional social order through the exclusion of ambition and profit-seeking individualism: "Every man for himselfe." But such social conformity is related to religious conformity as well; ambition is also spiritual and mental, and Adams fears a world with "as many mindes as men." Protestant ministers celebrated the direct connection between man and God and authorized in a new way labor in an occupation. At the same time, they tried to limit the effects of these doctrines by tying together their versions of godliness and worldliness, the inner Christian calling and the outward social estate, in order to preserve the traditional model of community.

I hope to show that Herbert's writing reveals not only his life-long attempt to link his devotion to his business, but also his suspicion that the doctrine of vocation was a form of individualism. In the original *Temple*, Herbert uses this doctrine to provide a justification for the acquisition of status and wealth. His later revisions erase such a justification as a form of pollution. The "self" that the revised *Temple* tries so mightily to defeat is the "private benefit" that Protestant ministers claimed was the major threat to the commonwealth.

I will argue that the doctrine of vocation is the fundamental principle shaping *The Temple* and Herbert's prose manual, *The Country Parson*. Both works coordinate the general calling of an inner Christian devotional life with the particular calling of a social role. It is clear that *The Country Parson* delineates Herbert's role as rural minister. But it may be less clear that "The Church-porch," the didactic poem with which *The Temple* begins, describes Herbert's original "calling" as a civic-minded gentleman. His transition from gentleman to rural minister is largely the story of his life. But both works are similar in their juxtaposition of an inward piety with an outward social estate. In both cases, Herbert uses a written form of self-representation to chart out for himself the nature of his contribution to the English nation, Protestantism, and "the common good."

Biographies of George Herbert have never satisfactorily explained why he begins his career as Public Orator at Cambridge University and concludes it as minister to a small country parish.[12] Critics who consider his life in any detail have assumed that he withdrew or was forced to withdraw from London, the court, parliament, and the active pursuit of a secular career. This volume includes an argument about why Herbert's plans for civic office and a prestigious church position evaporated and what effect this change in his life had on his poetry and prose.

I claim that the shape of Herbert's life was determined by his position as a client in the Protestant faction headed by William Herbert, Earl of Pembroke.[13] George Herbert entered public life as a representative of the Earl during a period when the Protestant faction opposed the Catholic-leaning programs of the monarchy and those of the royal favorite, the Duke of Buckingham. These factors—the Stuart alliances with Catholic nations and the increasing control of the Duke of Buckingham over royal patronage—severely restricted the preferment opportunities for Pembroke's clients. George Herbert's inability to obtain employment appropriate to his birth and education throughout the later 1620s cannot simply be the result of a personal disenchantment with the court, since his brothers Edward Herbert and Thomas Herbert suffered from the same difficulty. I believe that this problem was caused by the role of the Herbert brothers within the Protestant faction.

William Herbert, third Earl of Pembroke, is known to literary scholars as one of the "incomparable paire of brethren" to whom the First Folio of Shakespeare is dedicated, and as the patron to Ben Jonson, Samuel Daniel, and Michael Drayton. But historians speak of William Herbert as the leader of the Protestants within England and the principle opponent to Buckingham's power at court. As son of Mary Sidney Herbert and nephew to Sir Philip Sidney, William Herbert inherited the role of spokesman for the Protestant cause previously played by Leicester, Sidney, and Essex. Between King James's accession in 1603 and Pembroke's death in 1630, the Earl organized the resistance in court and in Parliament to the Stuart alliances with the Catholic nations. Pembroke controlled several seats in the Commons, and the men elected under his auspices were expected to back his policies. These men included George Herbert, who attended Parliament in 1624.

The members of the Protestant faction shared not only religious and political interests but also business ventures. They justified their financial investments as religious programs pursued for the good of the commonwealth. For them, the economic development of England was meant to accompany and was at times synonomous with the nation's mission as champion of the future of world Protestantism. They saw their engagement in overseas colonization, mining, and agricultural innovations as an investment in English Protestantism; they were in fact incipient capitalists. Their conflict with the Stuart monarchy before and during the Civil War was motivated both by differences in religion and by the court's interference with their financial ventures.

Scholars have noted that the concept of vocation is central to George Herbert's piety.[14] But they have not recognized that his use of the doctrine of vocation was part of his family's larger Protestant vision linking religion and enterprise. Like other Puritan and Anglican preachers, Herbert identified "idleness" as the major obstacle to the health and progress of the English state. He celebrated his family's financial projects as part of the Protestant Reformation at the same time that he evaluated his own life in terms of the professional offices identified by him as his religious duty.

The question of whether Herbert was a Protestant or an Anglo-Catholic has received a great deal of critical attention. Many have claimed that the emphasis on the relationship between grace and works is the central dynamic of Herbert's poetry.[15] My argument will provide further evidence that Herbert was a Reformation Protestant in his theology. I will also show that the members of his extended family were well known as Protestant activists. But their religion was not simply a matter of theology. For Herbert, the major works at issue are not religious acts of worship but the professional business required by his various positions. In *The Temple* and *The Country Parson*, Herbert weaves a connection between labor and grace, piety and employment.

This relationship between Herbert's religious lyrics and his engagement in society has been a crucial issue for recent critics. Michael Schoenfeldt has argued that Herbert's experience with courtiership infiltrates or contaminates his most devotional texts. On the other hand, Richard Strier claims that there is a marked and crucial split between the self-interest of "The Church-porch" and the anti-worldliness of "The Church." Debora Shuger notes the same contrast and argues that it represents a division in Herbert's experience of selfhood: the autonomous courtier and the dependent religious petitioner existed together uneasily. I will claim that the doctrine of vocation is the discourse by which English Protestants themselves understood the relationship between devotion and social role. Vocation required Herbert to coordinate his piety with his professional life, and *The Temple* is a record of Herbert's difficulty at doing so. His extensive revisions to that work, as well as his formulations of the problem in *The Country Parson*, reveal the need to unite "being" to "seeming." Therefore, his problems with worldliness were not simply the result of courtly experience and language but a dilemma shared by all Protestants, who were taught to maintain a devotional purity in the midst of their business in the world. Unlike the critics listed above, I place Herbert within the history of economic and social change and argue that his use of the doctrine of vocation determined his role in that history.[16]

Herbert began his career with a buoyant expectation of success as well as a pride in the technical skill needed to accomplish his various professional duties. His labor was not manual or commercial but intellectual: writing lectures and letters, delivering speeches and sermons, and writing the poetry that brought his considerable verbal ability to the notice of prospective patrons. Technique and craftsmanship were fundamental to Herbert's sense of self, and he considered his public persona to be one of his major works. His original vocation included the construction of the social image of gentility. Since Herbert did not receive an estate or a sufficient income through his upper-class family, his status as gentleman was more achieved than ascribed, and he himself considered it to be something made. The fashioning of his gentility included the strategic use of clothes, behavior, language, and knowledge to secure a reputation that would result in appropriate preferment.

The "Jordan" poems and associated allusions throughout Herbert's poetry treat the artifice of gentility explicitly and implicitly. Most of these poems are related to Herbert's pursuit of patronage within the circle of the Earl of Pembroke, and many of these poems refer obliquely to verses by the Earl's uncle, Sir Philip Sidney, as well as to Edward Herbert, Shakespeare, and the Earl himself. Through their witticisms about the plain style and about modes of upper-class language and behavior taken to excess, the poems attest to the "fiction" of gentility-making. Status is something made, and, the poems imply, often made up. The poems display, in part, Herbert's upper-class anxieties about labor and his desire to be free from its taint. Nevertheless, the poems also posit that the fiction of gentility can be religiously useful; like the fictions or figures of speech used generously throughout the poems, the art of gentility-making can be appropriate if accompanied by religious "truth." This association of the fiction of gentility and the truth of religion underlies the relationship, in *The Temple*, between the rules for social behavior in "The Church-porch" and the devotional lyrics in "The Church."

*The Country Parson* and revisions to *The Temple* demonstrate that, whereas gentility was one of Herbert's original "works," he later turned away from the pursuit of upper-class success. The "character" of holiness replaced the fashioning of gentility as the principle governing the shaping of the public persona, and the generative difference between status and piety was exchanged for a holiness "within" that was now expressed much more explicitly "without." *The Country Parson* is, in part, a rewriting of Herbert's original conception of this relationship between inside and outside, between the general and the particular calling, that was formulated in the first version of *The Temple*. This revision tries to pull the two callings together more tightly and to replace social artifice with a model of transparency, or "plainness."

The transition from gentility to holiness as the mark of Herbert's social image was accompanied by his move from Cambridge and London to the farmlands of Wiltshire. Although he had invoked the ideal of plainness in language long before, now it became a style of life. The pastoral genre, with its contrast between urban and rural, court and country, was used to counteract the status expectations associated with his earlier career. Revisions to *The Temple* affirm the pastoral ideal and attempt to exclude urban and courtly forms of ambition and artifice.

Raymond Williams identifies the appeal to nature in the pastoral as a mode of nostalgia for the feudal past and an escape from the history of the development of capitalism.[17] Herbert's "plain" style of life in the country elides his own experience of the artifice of courtly and urban performance. But his new mode of life does not exclude the link between religion and enterprise so important to his family's Protestantism. His poetic models of selfhood shift from images of social ascent to images of pastoral growth, metaphors that affirm the value of productivity and accomplishment as they "naturalize" labor into something spontaneous and necessarily genuine. The disturbing connection between workmanship and fiction disappears as the self is formulated as inherently "fruitful." Self-fashioning reappears as a divinely authorized form of growth.

I will argue that it is through Herbert's works and those of his family that we can trace the influence of and resistance to the new economic system emerging in seventeenth-century England. The conflict in Herbert's poetry and prose between ambitious works and unselfish productivity characterized the lives of the members of his family as well. The Herbert clan faced the religious and cultural stigma associated with profit-seeking, and they solved the problem in a way similar to Herbert's use of the pastoral. I consider this issue in terms of the family's program of gardening, through which they contemplated their economic ventures in England and America. I demonstrate that the family's gardens served as a medium through which they were able to "naturalize" expansion and commerce as the appropriate control of art over nature and as projects pursued from the common good. Both Herbert's poetry and the gardens of his richer relations erase "private benefit" or self-interest and celebrate economic enterprise as a form of improvement dedicated to the community.

This book supports but also qualifies Max Weber's thesis, presented in *The Protestant Ethic and the Spirit of Capitalism*, that the new religion fostered a new economic system. English Protestantism was a major influence in the development of new attitudes toward labor and investment. Weber's critics who consider religion and the early modern period primarily refute his claim that the Protestant work ethic and "the spirit of capitalism" were related to each other. They cite numerous attacks by Protestant ministers on the acquisitiveness for its own sake that Weber identified as the main characteristic of this spirit. Any comparison of seventeenth-century sermons and Benjamin Franklin's *Advice to a Young Tradesman*, quoted by Weber, would lead one to agree. Charles and Katherine George state that the "'spirit of capitalism' . . . simply does not exist in England before 1640."[18]

But these critiques are filled with telling and numerous qualifications. They acknowledge, as they must, that the Protestant sermons also include celebrations of the value of work; attacks on idleness; instructions on diligence, thrift, and the proper use of time; challenges to the status system; and justifications for the acquisition of wealth if not the active pursuit of it. The issue is not whether or not Weber was precisely right, but, rather, how can we account for the contradictory evidence in these sermons? If wealth is a blessing from God, why is it a sin to pointedly attempt to increase it? Weber's critics have not developed a mode of interpretation that allows them to evaluate the relationship between the old and the new. The contradictions in the doctrine of vocation reveal an ideology in transition.

The terms *dominant* and *emergent*, offered by Raymond Williams and used by Cultural Materialists, make it most possible to analyze the conflicts within the sermons on vocation.[19] For example, the justifications for acquiring wealth suggest an emerging acceptance of trade and commerce, but the attacks on profit-seeking sustain the traditional "moral economy."[20] Also, the horizontal model of the self hints at the division between public and private spheres, but the hortatory insistence that the two callings be bound together sustains the traditional order. I believe, with Williams, that interpretations of the doctrine of vocation will be more successful "if we develop modes of analysis which instead of reducing works to finished products, and activities to fixed positions, are capable of discerning, in good faith, [their] finite but significant openness."[21]

This book has been greatly influenced by the methodology of New Historicism and the work of its practitioners. Nevertheless, I have not found convincing New Historicist accounts of the relationship between sociopolitical forms of power and subjectivity. Usually, these explanations posit some form of mirroring, in which the social relationship is projected inwards.[22] Although I also at times use this model, I have found that it cannot explain the doctrine of vocation and its own extremely complex attempt to coordinate inward and outward experience. That attempt, I believe, is part of the process of historical change, and for this reason, the methodology of Cultural Materialism has been more useful to me.[23]

This book begins and ends with Herbert's experience in Wiltshire in order to first present his transition as a self-conscious transformation, and, in the last chapters, to discuss its ideological significance. In this Introduction, I lay out a history of the Herbert family that will explain my reading of George Herbert's life. This account is necessary to explain his difficulties with patronage and to clarify the role his family played in the Protestant movement.

Chapter 1, "*The Country Parson* and the Character of Social Identity," argues that after 1630 Herbert used the prose manual and the doctrine of vocation to transform his genteel lifestyle into a mode of self-presentation appropriate to his role as rural minister. In his "character" of holiness, Herbert constructs a coordination of inside motive and outside appearance whose "plain style" limits the performative quality of upper-class status. In the second chapter, "George Herbert and Coterie Verse," I return to the beginning of Herbert's career and consider the Herbert family circle as the context within which Herbert's poetics and his use of the "Jordan" allusions developed. This analysis should make more precise our understanding of what was upper-class and "courtly" about Herbert's life, since it is not clear that he ever entered the court. A major claim in this chapter is that Herbert's lyrics were not private but performed within the limited but significant circle of his extended family, which included his most important patrons. Therefore, his famous "sacred parody" should be considered in accounts of his pursuit of patronage.

In Chapter 3, "Gentility and Vocation in the Original *Temple*," I argue that vocation determines the order of Herbert's poetic collection as well as *The Country Parson*. In his first role as civic-minded gentleman, Herbert sought to preserve a connection between a spiritually constituted interior and a humanly constructed upper-class social role. The chapter traces out the revisions that disguised Herbert's original model for a mobile self, capable of social ascent but balanced in piety. These revisions also obscured the extent to which the original "Church" was a spiritual autobiography with several personal references to Herbert's life. Chapter 4, "*The Temple* Revised: 'Selfnesse' and Pollution," presents evidence that the revisions to manuscript *W* occurred after 1627. These revisions reveal an increased anxiety about a polluted self associated with performative gentility. Labor was not only a religious activity for Herbert, but also a status dilemma. Using anthropologist Mary Douglas's *Purity and Danger*, I argue that the purity of "The Church" was in part a solution to the problem of Herbert's anomalous social status between the upper and the laboring classes. The chapter claims that modern critical views have identified as Herbert's "self" what is really one part of this double-class position. Chapter 5, "The Character of Holiness in *The Temple*," examines the poems on transparency in the revised manuscript, which posit a purified social identity analogous to the "character" of holiness in *The Country Parson*. Like the prose manual, these poems undermine the original emphasis on a constructed social role and redefine it as an "expression" of a spiritual devotionalism.

In the sixth and seventh chapters, I consider the economic implications of Herbert's struggles with status. Chapter 6, "Pastoral, Vocation, and 'Private Benefit,'" interprets Herbert's images associated with the country or the pastoral genre as attempts to handle the problem of ambition while simultaneously authorizing growth and the improvement of the self. These images are discussed in relation to treatises and sermons on vocation, whose Protestant ethic includes the same contradiction between the requirement to work industriously and the demand to stay in one's social place. In these sermons, the "inward" Christian calling and the "outward" Christian calling are linked together to guard against individualistic versions of religion and secular engagement.

Chapter 7, "Religion and Enterprise in the Gardens of the Herbert Family," develops the approach of the previous chapter in terms of the issue of gardening. Gardens provided the Herbert family with powerful images of self-cultivation, as well as a means of contemplating their own ventures in America as moral rather than economic enterprises. Herbert's poem "Paradise" is discussed in relation to the gardens of his stepfather, John Danvers; those of his patrons at Wilton House, William and Philip Herbert; and the literature on Virginia, which uses the imagery of gardening to justify colonization as cultivation. These "gardens" coordinate the ideals of patriarchy with those of improvement; they subordinate self-interest to a project of expansion dedicated to the community.

In the Conclusion, "Modern Criticism and the Ideology of Sincerity," I argue that, through its horizontal structure of personal definition, *The Temple* contributed to the birth of the criteria by which it has been judged. The ideal of sincerity as the voice of the autonomous individual underlies the belief that Herbert's lyrics were private, and these assumptions have obscured from view the social milieu out of which the lyrics were generated, the importance of Herbert's extended family to his biography, and the social and economic ramifications of their Protestantism. Through its seventeenth-century discourse on the relationship between social role and devotion, the Protestant doctrine of vocation can free criticism from the modern myth of personality and clarify the role that *The Temple* has played in the history of subject-formation.

## II. HERBERT AND EMPLOYMENT

Herbert's employment history was largely the result of his engagement in the Protestant faction led by William Herbert, Earl of Pembroke. Many of the people in this faction also populated William Herbert's poetic coterie, which, I will argue in Chapter 2, was the context within which George Herbert initiated his career as a poet. Here, I want to demonstrate that, in several key cases, Pembroke or his associates either provided Herbert with employment or were responsible for his lack of it. In almost every case, Herbert will be found to be connected to a family and a faction that put him at odds with major patronage-brokers at court.

Biographers have not recognized George Herbert's position as a client to the Earl of Pembroke.[24] As a leader of the "anti-Spanish" alliance at court, Pembroke worked for the Protestant cause and the defeat of "Papism."[25] Along with Archbishop Abbot and Lucy, Countess of Bedford, Pembroke opposed King James's plans for an alliance with Spain and supported the interests of the King's daughter, the Queen of Bohemia:

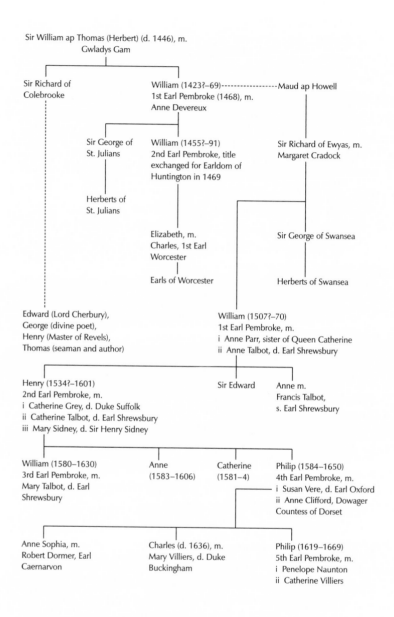

FIGURE 1. Family tree of the Herbert family. From Michael Brennan, *Literary Patronage in the English Renaissance: The Pembroke Family* (New York: Routledge, 1988), ix.

> This policy was based ultimately on the Protestant apocalyptical conception of history, within which the Bohemian revolution of 1618 and the acceptance of the Bohemian crown by the Elector Palatine were seen as the great revolution that would usher in the final struggle between the godly and the papal Antichrist. "The apparent way His providence hath opened to the ruine of the papacy," commented Sir Edward Herbert . . . ambassador in Paris in 1619.[26]

William Herbert and his clients were publicly associated with the goal of spreading the Protestant religion throughout the world. Pembroke was also an "adventurer" and an investor in the Virginia Company, as well as several other trade companies, and tried to protect the members of the Virginia Company against what they saw as their Spanish enemies and competitors.[27] But Pembroke was also a politician. He worked carefully to stay in power while he supported the interests of his cause. I hope to show that both his successes and his failures resulted in George Herbert's lack of preferment.

In 1670 Izaak Walton obscured from view Herbert's participation in the Protestant faction in order to present the poet as a High-Church Anglican Royalist.[28] William Herbert, the third Earl of Pembroke, is not mentioned as Herbert's patron, perhaps because such mention would have reminded readers that the fourth Earl, Philip, as well as Herbert's stepfather, John Danvers, were parliamentarians in the recent Civil War. Whereas Walton mentions King James, the Duke of Richmond, and the Marquis of Hamilton as Herbert's patrons, in fact, Hamilton was one of Pembroke's allies, and Pembroke had as clients Herbert and most of Herbert's relatives. John Danvers received several seats in Parliament through the Earl's influence and invested with the Earl and his brother in the Virginia Company. Henry Herbert, George's younger brother, received his position as Master of the Revels through Pembroke, Lord Chamberlain of the Royal Household between 1615 and 1626. Edward Herbert, George's elder brother, attended Parliament as Pembroke's client in 1604, and later represented the interests of the

Protestant faction on the Continent by opposing the Spanish marriage and supporting Bohemia, both before and after he was ambassador to France. Two more of George's brothers were probably associated with Protestantism: William died as a soldier fighting in the Low Countries, and Thomas commanded the ship that brought Prince Charles and Buckingham back from the Continent after the failure of the Spanish marriage. In seeking the position of Public Orator in 1619, George Herbert appealed for help to the third Earl, Danvers, and Benjamin Rudyerd, Pembroke's spokesman in the Commons. Herbert was elected in 1624 to a parliamentary seat that was within Pembroke's purview, and, in 1630, the Earl named George Herbert to the position of pastor of Bemerton and chaplain to the Earl's family estate at Wilton.[29]

Biographers differ in their interpretations of Herbert's record of employment. Some have insisted that his decision to join the church in 1624 was a conscious withdrawal from courtly life and that during the years before 1630 Herbert meditated on his worthiness to be a clergyman. This account is rather pious and idealistic, but actually far more satisfying than other interpretations because it can explain why Herbert received no prestigious position despite his impressive connections at court. Other critics believe that Herbert's unemployment was occasioned by a combination of court opposition, vaguely defined, and a new sense that high office would be undesirable.[30]

Herbert's biographers need to include in their calculations the histories of George's brothers Edward and Thomas, who also received little patronage after 1625 and complained about it loudly. Both had been visibly engaged in national affairs—Edward as ambassador to France between 1619 and 1624, and Thomas as the commander of the ship that brought Prince Charles and Buckingham back from Spain on October 5, 1623.[31] Three days later, the Public Orator of Cambridge, George Herbert, delivered a speech to Charles and Buckingham welcoming them home. The Herbert brothers had been conspicuously placed in prominent positions.

I believe that the members of George Herbert's immediate family were perceived as Pembroke's clients, given positions as a sign of favor to him, and neglected when the King and his associates wanted to show their displeasure. All of these clients were understood to be "anti-Spanish" and promoted when it served the interests of the royal leaders, particularly when they wanted to create some sort of factional balance. As Buckingham rose from obscurity to Earl (1617), and finally to Duke (1623), his conflicts with Pembroke over patronage became more heated, and Pembroke's clients received significantly fewer positions.

Pembroke and his group had introduced Buckingham to King James in the hopes of decreasing the power of the then current royal favorite, Robert Carr, Earl of Somerset, and the growing power of the Spanish faction. After Somerset's fall in 1615, James apparently intended to use Buckingham as an independent who would balance the factions in the court and protect the King against them. But Buckingham's links with the Spanish party grew, as did his jurisdiction over patronage. In 1618 and 1619, he and Pembroke publicly sparred over particular nominations. Pembroke's reputation and rank in the nobility made him unassailable personally, and he continued to serve on the Privy Council and as Lord Chamberlain. But Pembroke's opposition to the King's plans for an alliance with Spain and Buckingham's increasing control over royal patronage meant that, by 1621, Pembroke's influence with the King had declined sharply.[32]

Buckingham considered Pembroke to be a rival patronage-broker. When Sir Humphrey May applied simultaneously to Buckingham and Pembroke, Buckingham regarded this as double-dealing.[33] As Lord Chamberlain, Pembroke was in charge of appointments to numerous key offices in the household of the King, including positions in the royal chapel. But some have argued that by the early 1620s, Buckingham "had totally usurped Pembroke's nominating power for positions in the King's chapel." The two also clashed over appointments to the Privy Chamber and the King's musicians.[34]

Nevertheless, several of Pembroke's associates did receive positions before 1625. Edward Herbert was named as ambassador to France after a casual meeting with Buckingham in 1619.[35] In 1623, after some conflict apparently with Buckingham over the position of Master of the Revels, Pembroke was able to confer it on his relative, Henry Herbert. Buckingham appointed Thomas Herbert to be Captain of the Dreadnought in September 1625.[36] After 1625, however, nominations by Pembroke became far less frequent, and Edward, George, and Thomas received very little recognition from the court.[37]

In 1625 the Duke became convinced that the Earl and his faction were leading the opposition against him.[38] During the Parliament of 1626, the Pembroke connection tried to bring about Buckingham's impeachment in both houses, but Charles dissolved Parliament before they were successful.[39] Even before this, in early 1624, Pembroke opposed the plans of Buckingham and Charles to renounce the Spanish marriage and seek a Protestant-led crusade against the Spanish and in support of Bohemia, even though they now espoused Pembroke's views. In late 1623 and 1624, King James still hoped that the Spanish marriage would go forward, and Pembroke sided with the King. Many were shocked by Pembroke's position, and, in February 1624, the Venetian ambassador urged him to back Buckingham in order to oppose the Spanish. The ambassador wrote, "But I found him very set in his opinions, namely that they must consider internal foes before external ones."[40] By early 1624 Pembroke considered Buckingham to be an internal foe, and by 1625 Buckingham knew it.

The Duke struck back at Pembroke through his associates. The Lord Keeper John Williams was dismissed from office in October 1625 because of his alliance with Pembroke and in order to warn the Earl to stop working against Buckingham in Parliament. Williams had announced to Buckingham that "he was engaged with William, Earl of Pembroke, to labor the redress of the people's grievances." Roger Lockyer calls the dismissal of Williams "a demonstration of Buckingham's power—which was such, Kellie told Mar, 'that none could have made me believe if I had not seen it'—and of his willingness to punish these who betrayed his trust."[41]

This political situation can illuminate particular events in George Herbert's life. Much has been made of Herbert's anti-war speech, on October 8, 1623, to Buckingham and Charles. The speech has often been cited as a possible reason for their opposition to his preferment.[42] However, Jeffrey Powers-Beck has recently demonstrated that Herbert did not explicitly oppose Charles in the speech, since Charles's opinions were probably not yet formulated and certainly not public by October 8.[43] But Powers-Beck also admits that, by that time, Buckingham had identified himself as anti-Spanish and as "a presumptive leader of a pro-war faction."[44] Therefore, it is possible that, in his comments against war, Herbert represented Pembroke's view in opposition to Buckingham's pro-war stance and in favor of the King's pacifist position.[45] Despite those who argue that Herbert had a personal antipathy to war, the speech affirms that war is acceptable if King James commands it: "But it is not our duty to proclaim war; our most prudent king will timely foresee where he should lift up the standard . . . the same force which traversed Spain will, if need be, conquer it."[46] Pembroke was also more concerned to support the King against Buckingham than to take a particular stance on the war.[47] It is assumed by historians that Benjamin Rudyerd regularly spoke for his patron in the Commons.[48] If George Herbert did so in his Cambridge oration, then his reward from Pembroke may have been the seat in Parliament in 1624.

During this Parliament, Buckingham and Pembroke worked out a compromise and both houses supported the war plans of the Prince and the favorite. George Herbert attended this Parliament, but after the session ended in May 1624, he did not attend another. Amy Charles has shown that Herbert's ordination was sudden and did not go through normal channels. In November 1624 Herbert obtained a dispensation from Archbishop Abbot, so that he would not have to wait the usual year before ordination, and so that Bishop John Williams could ordain him rather than the bishop of his own diocese.[49] Such a rushed decision is curious, given Herbert's developing career, first as Public Orator, and next as member of Parliament. Buckingham's opposition to Pembroke had not yet become as strong as in 1625, nor had Pembroke's clients become the objects of Buckingham's wrath. What led Herbert to make this decision, and how does it relate to his position within the Pembroke faction?

Between the period of February and November 1624, several relatives of George Herbert felt the heat of factional struggles because of their connection with "the protestant interest."[50] Edward Herbert was recalled from France in April, probably so that Buckingham's agents could freely carry on negotiations for a marriage with the French princess.[51] In the same month, the debate on the Virginia Company was suddenly ended by King James, and in June the company was dissolved. The decision was seen by the members of the company, including George's stepfather, John Danvers, as a victory for the Spanish ambassadors and the Spanish party at court. The members of the company were so convinced that the monarchy was bent on misrepresenting them that they had their records copied in fear of their being confiscated and destroyed.[52]

Also in June, Henry Herbert, Master of the Revels and George's brother, licensed *A Game at Chess*, the famous satire that mercilessly spoofs the Spanish ambassador Gondomar and King James's pro-Spanish policy. Theater historian Richard Dutton speculates about whether or not Pembroke was behind the licensing of the play, which was terribly successful and opposed publicly the policy to which King James was still committed.[53] Henry was apparently examined by the Privy Council about his reasons for licensing the play. The consequences in this case seem not to have extended beyond such an examination; Pembroke wrote a letter in his defense, and Henry may have satisfied the King that the text he had licensed was not offensive.[54] Nevertheless, three of George Herbert's relatives had, in quick succession, felt the penalties of factional struggles at court.

The difficulties that Herbert's relatives faced in 1624 may have led Herbert to use ordination as a method of withdrawing from Parliament. On October 1, 1624, the session of Parliament scheduled for November 2 was canceled, but the same Parliament could have been recalled the following year. Herbert's permission from Archbishop Abbot was dated November 3.[55] Such a permission would ensure that, when Parliament finally did meet, Herbert would not have to attend. If Herbert did intend to avoid Parliament through ordination, he might still have had hopes for high ecclesiastical office but also a desire to avoid the factional struggles associated with Parliament that he had witnessed during the year.[56]

After the Parliament of 1624, Herbert did receive some positions and recognition. In December of 1624 he was given a sinecure at Montgomeryshire, and in 1626 he was made Canon and Deacon at Lincoln. But both of these positions came to him from Bishop John Williams, who, by 1625, was out of favor with the monarchy but nevertheless still capable of rewarding a fellow ally of Pembroke's.[57] It is interesting that in the same month that Herbert became Deacon at Lincoln, July of 1626, he delivered another speech before the Duke of Buckingham. This is curious because Herbert had not performed his duties as Public Orator since 1623. Significantly enough, it was also in the month of July that Buckingham was trying to patch up his quarrel with Pembroke through a marriage between Buckingham's daughter and Pembroke's brother's son. It seems likely that the Protestant alliance sensed some openness to Pembroke's interests in Buckingham and therefore presented to him once again their very talented orator who was also in great need of patronage.[58]

In 1627 Herbert received a gift from the court, but it was limited in a telling way. After the death of Herbert's mother in June, a volume was published in July containing John Donne's funeral sermon and Herbert's Latin poems, *Memoriae Matris Sacrum*. These poems lament the loss of his mother as a kind of patron, "my clan's / Especial guardian," and refer explicitly to Herbert's unemployment:

> I grow weak as I
> Press my studies—but that the days
> In vanity have gone, I will make no moan,
> No entombed Minerva whine for,
> No hopes that went too far. I will count
> My crude imaginings the sterile world's mistake,
> To which I leave its pallid stars and comets
> As if it had a right to them.[59]

This passage dramatizes Herbert's career in ways characteristic of *The Temple*. It alludes again to his mother as his special patron, as well as to her previous high hopes of his success. Publishing these verses with a sermon by Donne, dean of St. Paul's, reminded the public of Magdalene Herbert's household and her role as a sponsor for her family and talented associates like Donne. It is entirely relevant that two weeks after the poems were published, the Crown granted the manor of Ribbesford to Edward Herbert, George Herbert, and their cousin Thomas Lawley. The manor was worth £3,000, and the £1,000 that Herbert received from it gave him the freedom to marry.[60]

The grant is significant in two ways. First, it reveals that Charles and Buckingham realized that George and Edward Herbert needed special recognition after the loss of their mother, perhaps because of the ways in which they had been previously neglected. Second, the grant did not include court or ecclesiastical preferment for either of them. Although the grant expressed the monarchy's concern, it also expressed its unwillingness to place George or Edward in positions of responsibility. They were identified as Pembroke's men, and Charles's patronage was still determined by Buckingham.[61] It is possible that George Herbert saw this as a definitive answer from the Crown, and that, after this event, he saw a less prestigious position, like that at Bemerton, as a logical alternative.[62]

Pembroke died in 1630, but there is evidence that his faction continued into the Civil War period. Although revisionist historians have argued against long-term causes for the war, anti-revisionists have reasserted the importance of such claims, especially the religious and political opposition to the Stuart court among particular factions.[63] William Herbert's brother Philip, the fourth Earl of Pembroke, supported Parliament against King Charles, and George Herbert's stepfather, John Danvers, was a regicide. A pamphlet written by George Herbert's friend, Arthur Woodnoth, celebrated Danvers and "the parliament-interest," particularly in terms of the conflicts over the Virginia Company in Parliament during 1624 and before. The company had been associated with radical politics: the members were accused of starting a "Brownist republic" in Virginia, and the pamphlet represents King James as saying "the Virginia Company was a seminary to a seditious parliament."[64] The publication of the pamphlet in 1651 suggests that the interference of the Crown with the religious and economic projects of the company strengthened the parliamentarian sympathies of Danvers and perhaps the fourth Earl of Pembroke.

It is interesting that Nicholas Ferrar defended the Virginia Company in the 1624 Parliament by arguing that the King was hindering trade and commerce abroad.[65] However, Ferrar, like George Herbert, never attended another Parliament and withdrew from public life into the community of Little Gidding.[66] There was something very explosive about the political climate of 1624: it created both regicides and hermits out of members of the Protestant faction. George Herbert tried to walk a fine line between these extremes by remaining a public Protestant through his clerical responsibilities at Bemerton, but free from the conflict of Parliament. He remained a client of Pembroke, evident in his post in Bemerton and his poem, "A Parodie," but he also acquired an aversion to the patronage relationship. According to Ferrar, Herbert's dedications in *The Temple* were meant "to testify his independency upon all others."[67] Herbert himself wrote to Ferrar that he identified his friend as God's servant, "not considering you any other wayes, as neyther I myself desire to be considered" (p. 378). Both have the events of 1624 in mind when they refer to "independency." The factional strife they had experienced led them to seek other methods of self-definition than that of family or political association. Nevertheless, Herbert remained dependent on the patronage of Pembroke throughout his life.

# *One*

## *The Country Parson* and the Character of Social Identity

In 1618, when George Herbert was twenty-five years old, he wrote to his younger brother Henry in Paris and encouraged him to acquire as much Parisian sophistication as possible, "whether it be in knowledge, or in fashion, or in words." Clothes, speech, and demeanor should testify boldly to one's quality; a backwardness in dress or a loss of composure is unworthy of a gentleman, "and it is the part of a poor spirit to undervalue himself and blush" (366). Thirteen years later, at the age of thirty-eight, when he wrote to the wife of the fourth Earl of Pembroke, then residing at the court of Charles I, Herbert wrote as the country parson of a tiny parish: "In the mean time a Priests blessing, though it be none of the Court-stile, yet doubtless Madam, can do you no hurt: Wherefore the Lord make good the blessing of your Mother upon you" (377). Though it is courteous and rhetorically stylized, this "Priests blessing" is nevertheless offered specifically in opposition to the "Court-stile." The brave gentleman, adept at verbal elaboration, has not only been translated into the provincial priest, he calls attention to that provinciality and plainness and so stresses his alienation from the court in both language and identity. A year before Herbert wrote this letter, in 1630, he had begun to write *The Country Par-*

*son*, a text that codifies the mode of a rural minister, and so distinguishes Herbert from the "Court-stile" of his earlier years.[1]

The Country Parson has frequently been mined as a source of information on George Herbert's life, theories of style, and religious beliefs, but it has rarely been examined as a text in itself worthy of attention.[2] Although it seems at first to be simply a handbook, it is rather a self-portrait that reveals Herbert's methods of representing himself socially. This chapter will provide a "reading" of Herbert's life which assumes that the composition of The Country Parson was a major biographical event. The work should be interpreted as a literary instance of the achieving and fashioning of social identity necessary for a younger son of the gentry in the seventeenth century.[3] By placing The Country Parson at the center of the interpretive process rather than in the background, I hope to show the relationship between the artistry used by Herbert in his text and in his life, and to demonstrate how active a role writing could play in his construction of a social self.

Herbert's former acquaintances in the city and the university most likely interpreted his life as a failure. If we can believe Walton, a "Court-friend" tried to persuade Herbert against entering the priesthood because it was "too mean an employment and too much below his birth."[4] According to Barnabas Oley, another of Herbert's colleagues remarked that he "did not manage his brave parts to his best advantage and preferment, but lost himself in an humble way."[5] This comment speaks of the calculation and dexterity necessary for a younger son to acquire a social place appropriate to his family name and intellectual credentials. In this paradoxical situation, one works desperately to become what one already is, since status is ascribed by birth, and yet must be achieved through labor. There is no possibility of defining the self outside the system of status; a loss of rank is equivalent to a loss of self. This was a society in which the primary distinction enforced was that between those who were gentlemen and those who were not, and in which "both by law and common practice, every man was known not only by his name but by his rank."[6] In general, the clergy as a profession was at the time very low in social prestige, and the nobility and gentry steered their sons away from it. Apparently, only four near relations of peers entered orders between 1600 and 1660; Christopher Hill calls Herbert an "aristocratic eccentric" for his participation in the church.[7]

It is in this context that The Country Parson is written to reformulate the terms of social identity as exempt from the system of status. The text provides an alternate reading of Herbert's life in which "failure" is redefined as a willing renunciation of the role of an urban gentleman. The work identifies Herbert specifically with his post in the country and argues for the intrinsic dignity and value of his profession. The management referred to by Herbert's colleague is not discarded but recast into a form of self-presentation which claims to be free from the pursuit of advantage and preferment.

## I. THE CHARACTER OF HOLINESS

In his handbook, Herbert constructs a version of social identity that unites public performance and the inner life, "holiness" and self-presentation. He achieves this by modeling his text on the "character," a literary genre which claimed to teach its audience how to "read" men in society and how to "interpret" their actions as signs of their inner dispositions. Herbert's manual is a "character," a description of the social type of the Parson, but it also instructs ministers in the ability to conduct themselves according to the "character" of holiness, a stylistic mode of life, or a lifestyle that expresses the piety that motivates it (233). For Herbert, "character" referred directly to the process of public self-representation, since the word at this time meant inscription or likeness rather than personality or ethical makeup. To have a holy "character" was not to be spiritually minded but to make that spiritual-mindedness public.[8] Herbert's full title is The Country Parson; His Character and Rule of Holy Life not only because the manual is a verbal portrait of the Parson, but because it teaches parsons how to write out their holiness before the audience of their parishioners (227).

According to the character genre, the quality of human beings is inscribed in their social actions. The characters of Theophrastus, the Greek originator of the genre, are built on Aristotle's assumption that people are essentially social creatures and that they create and express themselves through their acts. English character writers, like Joseph Hall, modified this Aristotelian notion because, for them, inner disposition determined action; an individual's words and deeds were clues to the motives of the heart. Nevertheless, both Greek and English characters imply that behavior, like a verbal description, can be read as a sign of a person's disposition.[9]

Renaissance books on manners supported this connection between reading and the evaluation of individuals; for Erasmus in *De Civitate Morum Puerilium* the attitude of the soul can be deduced from a person's clothing.[10] Behavior or appearance was understood as a kind of language that one spoke consciously or unconsciously; etiquette and courtesy books explained how to compose the language of behavior persuasively, and the characters explained how to read it. The character and portrait popular in later seventeenth-century France have been described as constituting a "literature of worldliness"; English character sketches resonate with the activity not only of a developing court society, but an energetic, almost chaotic urban scene—the world of London, St. Paul's, and Ben Jonson's city comedies.[11] Like Jonson's comedies, the character evaluated the *dramatis personae* of this society and offered its readers a set of ethical and social criteria that would allow them to do the same.

In their characters of court and upper-class society, Thomas Overbury and John Earle instruct their readers to expect hypocrisy, superficiality, and deceit. Characters like "The Courtier," "A Fine Gentleman," and "An Intruder Into Favour" complicate their mode of representation by stressing that the marks and signs of gentility may not testify to a gentle nature. As with "The Dissembler," the "inquisitor must looke thorow his judgement, for to the eye only he is not visible." The clothes, speech, and demeanor of the gentry in this case do make the man: "A Gallant is one that was born and shapt for his cloathes; and if Adam had not falne, had lived to no purpose . . . his business is the street; his Stage the Court, and those places where a proper man is best showne." To observe "propriety" is to perform in the proper upper-class theaters, and, like "The Courtier," to care more for words than meaning and more for pronunciation than words. Most foolish are those who have bought the signs of gentility, like the "Upstart Country Knight," who has purchased a hawk, lace for his clothes, and a title.[12]

These characters suggest the extent to which gentility had become a matter of performance in the sixteenth and seventeenth centuries. This was a period of remarkable social mobility, in which merchants, yeomen, and their sons rose into the ranks of the elite through purchasing titles, heraldry, and country estates, or through attending the university and receiving the bounty of court favor.[13] Gentility, then, was not always the result of privileged birth but often of wealth and a certain style of life. As William Harrison put it in his *Description of England*: one must "bear the port, charge and countenance of a gentleman."[14] James's famous "inflation of honours," between 1603 and 1628, increased the numbers of "new men," the fears of the established elite about "intruders," and the pressures to demonstrate publicly one's claim to upper-class status.[15] The character genre, which arose in England during this period, attests to the effort expended by those who sought to be "genteel," as well as to the discomfort that such efforts caused in the society, since rank now appeared to be determined by wealth and external behavior rather than blood.

Much of the satiric force of the characters is conservative: beneath the witty exposure of the Gallant's fascination with clothes and the Upstart Country Knight's acquisition of hawk, lace, and title is a deep nostalgia for a stable social order whose signs of rank are not open to imitation or purchase.[16] But these portraits of court figures also display an anxiety about the ontological basis for gentility and an effort to penetrate beyond the theater of upper-class status to discover some alternate system for the measurement of merit: "A Wise Man is the truth of the true definition of a man, that is, a reasonable creature. . . . He understands things, not by their forme, but qualities."[17] The character writers show the disturbance of a culture whose social standard of personal evaluation has been upset and as yet replaced by nothing that is felt to be more reliable.

Herbert uses the genre of the character to structure *The Country Parson* because through it he can fashion a direct correspondence between inner disposition and social signs. This clarity, or "plainness," claims to dispel the interpretive confusion of court performance through grounding appearance in the "sacred" standard of holiness. Like a character writer, Herbert's Parson inscribes his holy character into the flux of experience, making his inner quality legible to his parishioners through his habitual words and deeds:

> The Countrey Parson is exceeding exact in his life, being holy, just, prudent, temperate, bold, grave in all his wayes. And because the two highest points of Life, wherein a Christian is most seen, are Patience, and Mortification; Patience in regard of afflictions, Mortification in regard of lusts and affections, and the stupifying and deading of all the clamorous powers of the soul, therefore he hath throughly studied these, that he may be an absolute Master and commander of himself, for all the purposes which God hath ordained him. Yet in these points he labours most in those things which are most apt to scandalize his Parish. (227)

The chapter "The Parson's Life" stresses the full control the parson must exert not only over himself, of whom he is "absolute Master and commander," but over the image he projects in the community. That rhetorical self-consciousness so important in both *The Courtier* and *The Prince* is used for religious purposes to insure that the churchman's authority will be firmly established in the minds of his parishioners.[18] His particular audience determines that appearance: his attention is given to those points "which are most apt to scandalize his Parish." Behavior in reference to money, drink and truth-telling are most critical, because if he fails in one of these areas, "he wil quickly be discovered, and disregarded" (228). Like nobility, or authority of any kind, holiness depends on the power to maintain an external appearance "in all his words and actions," to control and sustain an audience's impression, the success of which depends on externals. Herbert is both coolly aware of the need to perform and insistent on countering the potential for hypocrisy and the fragility of appearance by grounding authority on an internal holiness adamantly sincere and genuine: "The Parsons yea is yea, and nay nay; and his apparell plaine, but reverend, and clean, without spots, or dust, or smell; the purity of his mind breaking out and dilating it selfe even to his body, cloaths, and habitation" (228). Through the phrase "the purity of his mind," Herbert creates a figure whose speech, clothes, and manners signify within a behavioral "plain style." This plainness critiques aristocratic artificiality but shares with courtiers the purpose of establishing oneself as "reverend" or as projecting the authority delegated to the governing classes. Artificiality may be replaced by authenticity, but superiority remains a necessity:

> Because Luxury is a very visible sinne, the Parson is very carefull to avoid all the kinds thereof, but especially that of drinking, because it is the most popular vice; into which if he come, *he prostitutes himself* both to shame, and sin, and by having *fellowship, with the unfruitful works of darknesse*, he disableth himself of authority *to reprove them*: For sins make all equall, whom they finde together; and then they are worst, who ought to be best. (227)

In this passage, religious and social hierarchies intersect through the language of difference; authority depends on maintaining a proper distance between the ruler and the ruled. Herbert's insistence on temperance seems motivated in part by a class-based fear of the intimacy that might result between parson and people, and self-prostitution becomes not simply the sin of intemperance but the contamination that might stem from such exposure to those of lower status.[19] To be "plain" for Herbert was to adopt the simplicity and directness associated by his culture with country people, but it was not to be common. Although *The Country Parson* cannot strictly be defined as a literary pastoral, William Empson's definition of the genre still applies: the manual puts the complex into the simple by collapsing the interpretive confusion surrounding status distinctions

in the early seventeenth century into the simplicity of a clear difference between Parson and people, and as such, it reinvents the necessity for class distinctions and paternalistic government. The manual presents "a beautiful relationship between rich and poor," or, in
this case, between pastor and flock.[20] The "character" of holiness
replaces the "character" of gentility as the sign of authority, though
that authority operates along traditionally hierarchical lines.

In *The Country Parson*, Herbert marks his entrance into the order of the priesthood, explicitly separated from the laity by Anglican apologists. Richard Hooker defines this order and the power
conferred through ordination:

> The same power is in such not amiss both termed a kind of
> mark or character and acknowledged to be indelible. Minis-
> terial power is a mark of separation, because it severeth them
> that have it from other men, and maketh them a special *or-
> der* consecrated unto the service of the most High in things
> wherewith others may not meddle. Their difference therefore
> from other men is in that they are a distinct order.[21]

As in Hooker's statement, Herbert's *Country Parson* defends the
Anglican priesthood, under attack by the Puritans, whose model of
church government included the election of ministers by their con-
gregations and the elimination of the office of bishop.[22] Herbert's
poetry reveals that he believed devoutly in this special order; his
instructions to parsons to preserve their virtue so they may correct
their parishioners is motivated in part by his sense of the importance of the difference between clergy and laity. Nevertheless, this
Anglican distinction would also have had special social implications for this upper-class, university-trained minister placed in a
humble country parsonage surrounded by rural laborers during a
time when the "lesser" clergy was ranked just above the category
of yeoman on the system of status. Herbert may have understood
his transition from urban gentleman to country parson as primarily
a shift from a social to an ecclesiastical elite.[23]

It would be a mistake, however, to assume that Herbert's insistence on the difference between parson and people is a simple

justification of the Stuart principle of hierarchy in court and church. Herbert's "character" of holiness "marks" his difference from the laity, as Hooker points out, but the values of simplicity and directness that characterize this mode of self-presentation contradict the traditional correlation between hierarchical authority and high ceremony. By embracing his provincial country post and its "plain" style of life, Herbert divorces himself from "the Court-stile" not only of elegant courtiers, but of elegant bishops as well—like Bishop Laud, who was, at this time, cultivating the use of ceremony and the display of high status in his public appearances. Since Herbert died before Laud became Archbishop and the resistance to the court and the established church solidified, it is impossible to predict just what side Herbert would have favored in the Civil War. For him, the "crisis of confidence" in the ruling elite took form in a conversion from stylish gentleman to "plain" rural minister, whose hierarchical authority was to be grounded in his "holiness" rather than his class status, and in a reaction against the "port, charge and countenance" of gentility.[24]

Herbert's instructions to chaplains in noble houses verge on autobiography, since Herbert served as chaplain to his aristocratic cousin Philip Herbert, Earl of Pembroke:

> Before they are in Orders, they may be received for Companions, or discoursers; but after a man is once Minister, he cannot agree to come into any house, where he shall not exercise what he is, unless he forsake his plough and look back. Wherefore they are not to be over-submissive, and base, but to keep up with the Lord and Lady of the house, and to preserve a boldness with them and all, even so farre as reproofe to their very face, when occasion cals, but seasonably and discreetly. They who do not thus, while they remember their earthly Lord, do much forget their heavenly; they wrong the Priesthood, neglect their duty, and shall be so farre from that which they seek with their over-submissivenesse, and cringings, that they shall ever be despised. (226)

Ministers, whatever their class background, must "keep up with the Lord and Lady of the house" by asserting the eminence or at least the equality of their position through their demeanor and bold readiness to correct their hosts "to their very face." The office of a minister absolutely defines a man, to the exclusion of any role of companion or discourser; the nobility might prefer to receive their clergy in these latter roles, but they would restrict a parson or chaplain from exercising "what he is." "He is" nothing else than a priest, neither aristocrat nor commoner, neither family member nor discoursing scholar, though he enter the house of richer relations, like Pembroke's Wilton House.

As in the case of the prospective disciple rebuked by Christ in Luke (9:63), "looking back" means wavering between family allegiance and apostleship or confusing past identities with that absolutely defining role of minister. Herbert imagines that at ordination all other affiliations of a man are dropped like worn-out clothes, and his exclusive social identity becomes that bestowed by his vocation.

This passage is illustrative of *The Country Parson* in general. It is an attempt to eliminate class and familial identity for the sake of a vocation. This new identity is built in the image of the old; both share the need to project and establish social and personal authority. The genteel Herbert advises his younger brother to "be proud . . . it is part of a poor spirit to undervalue himself and blush" (366). The pastoral Herbert advises chaplains to "preserve a boldness" with the nobility, and to renounce "oversubmissivenesse, and cringings" (266). Both versions of identity demand the recognition and status that younger sons of the gentry had to acquire for themselves. Nevertheless, this pastoral version of social identity allows Herbert to obscure his dependence on Pembroke and to claim some measure of autonomy from his patron and cousin.[25] His value, he can then believe, stems not from bloodlines but from his profession and the industry it requires.

## II. THE NECESSITY OF A VOCATION

Herbert's reaction against his former life as an urban gentleman is echoed in a passage from *The Country Parson* that juxtaposes the system of status to the Protestant doctrine of vocation:

> Because Idleness is twofold, the one in having no calling, the
> other in walking carelesly in our calling, [the Parson] first rep-
> resents to every body the necessity of a vocation. . . . Now
> because the onely opposer to this Doctrine is the Gallant,
> who is witty enough to abuse both others, and himself, and
> who is ready to ask, if he shall mend shoos, or what shall he
> do? Therfore the Parson unmoved, sheweth, that *ingenuous
> and fit* imployment is never wanting to those that seek it.
> (274–75)

The dramatic confrontation of this passage mirrors the impulse of
the work in general to establish value in employment rather than
in family or class.[26] The seventeenth-century gentleman represented his high status through his fashionable dress, manners, and
sharp wit, or, as Herbert put it in his early letter to his brother, "in
knowledge, or in fashion, or in words" (366). In this passage, Herbert reduces these accoutrements to a self-centered, idle show, in
part through the term *gallant*, which, as it does in the characters,
satirizes this mode of gentility as self-interested theater. This display, argues Herbert implicitly, is insignificant, since man was originally built to work: "God hath placed . . . Reason in the soul, and
a hand in the Body, as ingagements of working: So that even
in Paradise man had a calling" (274). Only if this aristocrat can
employ himself in a worthwhile occupation can he discharge his
"debt to our Countrey" and account to God for the ability with
which he has been entrusted: "All are either to have a Calling, or
prepare for it" (275).

The Parson attacks Herbert's own "gallant" proclivities here, that
attraction to wit, fashion, and social rank recorded in "The Pearl"
and his early letters, and attacks as well the system of prestige that
reduced his position as clergyman to a menial and base occupation. "If he shall mend shoos, or what shall he do?" resonates with
the contempt shown by Herbert's former circle for his decision to
enter the ministry. In the text, the Parson is able to take aristocratic
derision "unmoved," and to claim to himself and to others that
hard work and "reasonable imployment" are natural to man, while
pride in one's social position is illegitimate.

Like the character genre, the doctrine of vocation allowed Herbert to tie the externals of social performance to an "authentic" spirituality. In "A Treatise of the Vocations," William Perkins distinguishes between God's invocation to the elected soul, or the general Christian calling, and an individual's particular occupation in society, but these, he asserts, must be joined like soul and body: "It is not sufficient for a man in the congregation and in common conversation to be a Christian, but in his very personal calling he must show himself to be so."[27] Work in the world was not only legitimate to Protestant divines, it was essential: "O then up and be doing: why stand ye all day Idle!" exhorted Anglican Robert Sanderson, Bishop of Lincoln. "In the church, he that cannot style himself by any other name than a Christian, doth indeed but usurp that too."[28] The visible proof that one is a Christian and elected is lacking, Sanderson argues, until one has a professional title as well as a religious reputation.

A Protestant, then, had to have two names—one, a "Christian," and the other, his occupational title, and these were to be joined like soul and body. An occupation was not simply a public role that one adopted during business hours and shed during private contemplation and prayer. Social performance was not disjunct and isolable from Christian essence; it was the means (and, according to Sanderson, the only means) by which personal holiness could be verified. In this doctrine, the "new man" emerged during business hours, perhaps even more than amidst private meditation.

The enormous amount of literature at this time encouraging commitment to a vocation and condemning idleness testifies to a shifting economic structure. Christopher Hill diagnoses the main problem of seventeenth-century society as the failure to use the full human resources of the country: "An ideology advocating regular systematic work was required if the country was to break through this vicious cycle to economic advance."[29] Historians disagree about the exact causal relationship between capitalism and the Protestant doctrine of the calling, but most see the two as interrelated.[30] In an age of nascent industrialism, nobility and gentry uninvolved in social duties as well as the vast number of wandering poor were sharply criticized as "drone bees," unproductive, parasitic loafers who lived off the labors of others.[31] Perkins, Herbert, and others refer to Christ's parable of the talents, in which the "slothful" and "unprofitable" servant who does not invest nor increase the money left him by his master is thrown into "the outer darkness."[32] It is in this context that Hal banishes Falstaff in *Henry IV, Part II* and that Milton laments "that one talent which is death to hide."[33] During the seventeenth century, the word "talent" acquired its meaning of a natural capacity for success in some department of mental or physical activity. Religious and economic factors cooperated during this period to produce a new ethic of work, in which the dignity of labor was stressed and trade received a sanctification unknown in the Middle Ages.

*The Country Parson* itself is evidence of the author's response to the work ethic and its values of industry and diligence.[34] In the preface, Herbert defines his pastoral task as feeding "my Flocke diligently and faithfully"; the purpose of writing *The Country Parson* is to foster hard work and his own best effort, since "it is a good strife to go as farre as we can" in pleasing God in one's occupation (224). Self-discipline motivates and structures the handbook, which records professional duties in an effort to insure they are remembered and performed effectively. The manual also provides an account of its author and shows in the careful descriptions of his activities that he has made something out of the talent, resources, and opportunity he has been given. Instead of demonstrating that he "lost himself in a humble way," the text testifies to the social and religious gains accrued through Herbert's investment of his abilities in his clerical work.

The Parson diligently pursues his occupation in his church, his home, in the homes of his parishioners, and when he travels, he "leaveth not his Ministry behind him" (250). If the Parson leaves his parish, it must be "a just occasion . . . which he diligently, and strictly weigheth" (250). In no conversation or social activity does he participate as an individual divorced from his clerical responsibilities, but "where ever he is," he "keeps Gods watch, that is, there is nothing spoken, or done in the Company where he is, but comes under his Test and censure" (252). Each day and each event requires the Parson's assiduous effort, but Sunday marks the high-point of his work week:

> The Countrey Parson, as soon as he awakes on Sunday morning, presently falls to work and seems to himselfe so as a Market-man is, when the Market day comes, or a shopkeeper, when customers use to come in. His thoughts are full of making the best of the day, and contriving it to his best gains. (235)

An efficient use of time, a concentrated, calculating application of thought, a spirited attention to profit and success—these qualities characterize the merchant engaged in business as well as any diligent man pursuing his vocation. Effective ministering is defined in this passage as a successful commercial transaction. The market-man or shopkeeper is consciously used by the Parson as a model for effective action, as he industriously seeks to increase his parishioners' spirituality as well as the dividends on his own invested talent.

Weber and Tawney have defined the work ethic of the religious shopkeeper and others motivated by the doctrine of vocation as "worldly asceticism," the secularization of the monastic life, the spiritualization of labor. The Protestant laborer is now responsible not only for the "individual meritorious acts" of a lay Catholic, but a consistent holiness that sanctifies and orders his work. According to Tawney:

> The labor which he idealizes is not simply a requirement imposed by nature, or a punishment for the sin of Adam. It is itself a kind of ascetic discipline, more rigorous than that demanded of any order of mendicants—a discipline imposed by the will of God, and to be undergone, not in solitude, but in the punctual discharge of secular duties.[35]

Weber credits Sebastian Franck with perceiving the central significance of the Reformation in the fact that "now every Christian had to be a monk all his life."[36]

The title of Herbert's work is *The Country Parson; His Character and Rule of Holy Life* in part because the text prescribes a disciplined mode of behavior that is similar to the "rule" observed by a monastic order.[37] This discipline requires not simply personal virtue but the diligent application of the Parson to his pastoral task. One of the central intentions of the text is to insure that the general and particular callings are linked together closely, that personal, inner holiness animates and becomes evident in the midst of daily work. The Parson's "Holy Life" forms itself not in solitude but in "the punctual discharge of secular duties."

In his book *Renaissance Self-Fashioning*, Stephen Greenblatt studies the figure of Thomas More, a man who lived in a cloister for four years, and who, in his multiple public duties, always maintained the privacy of a separate self, exempt from the demands of his public persona:

> More's sense of his own distinct identity is compounded of a highly social role, fashioned from his participation in a complex set of interlocking corporate bodies—law, parliament, court, city, church, family—and a secret reserve, a sense of life elsewhere, unrealized in public performance.[38]

His engagement in the world demanded "the maintaining of a calculated distance between his public persona and his inner self."[39] More perceived public life in the law courts or royal administration as a fiction, essentially unreal and disjunct from spiritual reality; secular life was a complicated but artificial drama that required the clever improvisation of a play-actor, who knew his stage, adapted himself to the play at hand, and performed his role neatly and appropriately.[40] This version of public life as fictional and essentially unreal, and of a public persona as an artifice to be dropped in moments of privacy, contrasts strikingly to Herbert's behavioral "plain style," in which each aspect of his life becomes a signifier for "the purity of his mind." This mode of identity participates in what Charles and Katherine George have called the Protestant "consecration of the world" and the sanctity that was now a "revelation more of the workshop than of the cloister."[41] Life was now a "business," and holiness was to realize itself in occupational activity. Vocation created a new sense of what constituted a public role and its relationship to the "real" inner self. Herbert's *Parson* welds together the purified, philosophical Hythloday and the politic More into one being, calculating and alert in relation to social dynamics but committed to revealing his religious spirit in the midst of them.

*The Country Parson* creates an identity out of a profession through the character genre, which links internality and appearance, inside and outside, ethical quality and visible behavior. This concept of social being is very different from the image of the play-actor that underlies Thomas More's engagement in secular life, although both are artful and based on a literary genre. Both are composed, or compositions, but the fictional quality of the theater is replaced by the ethical quality of the character. This structure of social identity includes an effort to limit its constructedness by defining itself as expression rather than fiction or artifice; it claims to exclude the theatrical by basing what is fabricated, the public image, on what is essential, the holiness within.

### III. "THE PARSON PREACHING"

The chapter "The Parson Preaching" reveals the pressure Herbert felt to identify with his vocation and to resist the influence of his former role as a status-conscious gentleman: "he procures attention by all possible art. . . . By these and other means the Parson procures attention; but the character of his Sermon is Holiness; he is not witty, or learned, or eloquent, but Holy" (232–33). The goal of the rhetorician to impress his audience through language and gesture is appropriated here for Christian purposes; however, the introductory "but" is a sharp warning against the unconsidered desire to procure attention, which may dissolve into showmanship, expand into hypocrisy, or veil an ambition for social prestige. The Parson cannot win his people through charisma, verbal agility, or a method of speaking that would identify him with the courtier or scholar: "he is not witty, or learned, or eloquent, but Holy." Again, the "but" signals the contrast between the talents of a worldly speaker and those of the minister, whose spirituality should guard against ambition and an urge for self-display. Herbert intends the phrase "the character of his sermon is Holiness," quoted above, to work as a surprise, radically to connect an invisible spirituality to an external, perceivable embodiment—the devotional is transformed into a rhetorical mode. This divine basis for the public persona is contrasted to the well-meaning but unenlightened tradition of classical rhetoric: "he is not witty, or learned, or eloquent, but Holy. A Character, that Hermogenes never dream'd of, and therefore he could give no precept thereof." These lines expose the classical world and its ideal of the urbane, powerful orator as ignorant of the demands of Christian spirituality; nevertheless, "holiness" becomes a particular style of speech, analogous to Hermogenes' seven "Characters" or "Ideas" of style described in his *Art of Rhetoric*.[42] Again, Herbert forcefully distinguishes between rhetorical skill and spirituality, the classical orator and the Christian minister, his former life and his present one, and yet he also welds them together, insisting that the spirit of Christianity can flow into language and rhetorical performance.

The rest of the passage is continuously strained by anxieties about such a project. The minister is not only to speak with feeling, since rhetoricians have argued that this "procures attention," but this feeling must come from the heart, "truly affecting, and cordially expressing all that we say; so that the auditors may plainly perceive that every word is hart-deep" (233). Here, Herbert attempts to break through the surfaces of social experience to a nearly immediate communication from heart to heart, a "plain," fully transparent speech that makes impossible all artificiality and misuse of language. But, as if to acknowledge that this transparent speech is impossible, the next precepts instruct the minister to call on God's power as a teacher; here, again, the explicit reason is that "such discourses shew very Holy," yet the apostrophes themselves place the power of efficacy in God's hands: "Oh Lord blesse my people, and teach them this point; or Oh my Master, on whose errand I come, let me hold my peace, and doe thou speak thy selfe" (233). Or from the Bible: "'*Oh that thou wouldst rent the Heavens, that thou wouldst come down.*' . . . '*Oh Lord, I know that the way of man is not in himself*'" (234). These instructions set up a dialectic in which the minister is alternately empowered as an artist and erased as an obstruction; the expression of holiness paradoxically requires a denial of the very human effort needed to produce it publicly: "let me hold my peace, and doe thou speak thy selfe."[43] The last precept gives the fullest voice to this distrust of the human speaker: "Lastly, by an urging of the presence, and majesty of God, by these, or such like speeches. Oh let us all take heed what we do, God sees us, he sees whether I speak as I ought, or you hear as you ought, he sees hearts, as we see faces" (234).

This statement warns parishioners about the dangers of disregarding God's spokesman. But it threatens parsons, and Herbert himself, with the dangers of self-fashioning. Only an omniscient God could see if a minister has linked the appearance of holiness to its essence, since social performances are not innately connected to inner states of mind and feeling and therefore can be manipulated by anyone skilled in the art of rhetoric. This unnerving intuition lies behind the dissonance in this section between optimistic instructions and cautionary examples, as well as the text's constant assertion that "seeming" be joined to "being."

The chapter "The Parson Preaching" demonstrates that Herbert's dilemmas with rhetoric went beyond poetic language into public self-presentation. To preach in the "character" of holiness distinguished Herbert from the wit, scholar, and courtier of his earlier life. This suggests that Herbert's poetic concern with style had much more to do with social identity than has been suspected. Those moments in the poetry when "the self" begins to weave itself into the sense and interfere with God's message echo the danger discussed above that the methods of the worldly speaker will corrupt the parson's language. The search in *The Temple* for a "plain" language, the uneasiness over "quaint words and trim invention," the consistent, often urgent preference for that which is truly rather than eloquently said, suggest that a good part of the en-

ergy in *The Temple*, as in *The Country Parson*, was invested in redeeming Herbert not only from the unregenerate self, but from the
"character" of gentility which had marked his original modes of
self-presentation.[44] *The Temple* can perhaps be read as another
text in which Herbert develops his new method of self-representation, or "character," of holiness.

*The Country Parson* was for Herbert "a Mark to aim at," an ideal-
ized figure beyond the author's own performance (224). He cast
the work in the form of a character sketch, with a "he" rather than
an "I" at the center of it, because that "he" was a man Herbert was
not yet internally, a man completely defined by his vocation. The
text was born in the disjunction between Herbert's need for clear,
identity-defining boundaries, and the inability of the hierarchical
class structure to provide them.[45]

Moving to the country also provided Herbert with a measure of
clarity, since he left behind the confusing social mobility and com-
mercialization of relationships in the city. Surrounded by the older
forms of manorialism that appeared to dominate in the country-
side, Herbert may have participated in what Raymond Williams, in
discussing the country-house poem, described as "an idealization
of feudal relations."[46] Herbert imagines authority according to paternalistic and therefore traditional models; like the country-house
"lord," the Parson cares for his people as a father, "as if he had be-
got his whole Parish" (250). The handbook implies that the benevolent, patriarchal Parson is an authentic social role, whereas the
pursuit of favor at court, presumably the work of the "Gallant," is
no vocation at all. Thus, Herbert extracts himself from the pressur-
ized competition of an urban and courtly career and no doubt es-
capes from his own ambition, evoked by the opportunities for social ascent in the city and his problematic status as younger son.
His country role fits him securely into one of the traditional "three
estates": aristocratic lord, tenant farmer, and parish priest.[47] The
natural unit of society becomes the parish; the city and court are
excluded as chaotic and unmanageable.

But Herbert's use of the country in his restructuring of identity cannot be satisfactorily explained as a nostalgic recovery of feudal, aristocratic, or traditional values. The Parson shares with the "new men" of the early modern city and court a consistent, self-conscious attention to the constructedness of identity, developed in every aspect of behavior and language. Herbert's "country" version of this self-fashioning was an attempt to live the plain style rather than "Court-stile," but it nevertheless required an art of self-presentation as elaborate as that detailed by the courtesy books of the time. Furthermore, this art of holiness was meant to be authentic to the extent that it held in check a sense of superiority based on family or class, and to the degree that it disrupted the power of the system of status to determine human value. As such, it made possible a modern emphasis on employment and labor as the source of the individual's social significance. Like the middle-class citizen handbook, and unlike the country-house poem, *The Country Parson* preaches the "gospel of work" and the Protestant ethic.[48]

For Herbert, social identity was an art, not only because his status as a younger son required that he achieve it, but because he understood it as a process of representation: the theory of identity implicit in *The Country Parson* is largely a theory of style. Herbert composed the representation, or "character" of holiness in his handbook, in his duties at Bemerton, and, it seems most likely, in his poetry as well. His poetic plain style, then, was an instance of a much larger personal program, *The Country Parson* a latent *ars poetica*.[49]

# *Two*

# George Herbert and
# Coterie Verse

In Chapters 3 through 7, I will argue that *The Temple* is as fully influenced by the doctrine of vocation as *The Country Parson*, and that this collection of poems is also a text in which Herbert fashions an identity alternate to his anomalous position within the hierarchical class structure. But before an analysis of *The Temple* can occur, some consideration of the relationship between Herbert's verse and his extended family is necessary. This chapter seeks to establish that Herbert's lyrics were from the outset conceived in terms of the Herbert family coterie and therefore played a significant role in his pursuit of preferment. An account of that family coterie will reveal a great deal about the original "profession" that Herbert claimed for himself, that of civic-minded gentleman. It will also set the stage for a discussion of his eventual revisions to the poetry and his adoption of the "character" of holiness.

When George Herbert announced his relationship to the English literary tradition, it was largely a family affair. His imitations of Sir Philip Sidney's poems, and of the sonnet sequence itself, were responses not only to a legendary literary figure but to a relative, the most famous member of the Sidney–Herbert clan. The family was known for its writers and patrons of the arts, but it was also recognized as a significant political and Protestant faction. Lawrence Stone characterizes a landed family as "a dense network of lineage and kin relationships," whose members were involved in "a reciprocal exchange of patronage, support and hospitality in return for attendance, deference, respect, advice and loyalty." George Herbert's decision to make good on Sidney's claim that one's lyric powers could best be dedicated to God, a credo that Sidney did not follow himself, was impelled by Herbert's sincere devotional commitment as well as the knowledge that, in order to maintain himself as a gentleman he needed the support of Sidney's nephew, William Herbert, the Earl of Pembroke.[1]

In this chapter, I will argue that what we call Herbert's sacred parody originated in a specific context of poetic debate popular among the Herbert clan as well as other literary coteries.[2] This contest in verse was an upper-class fashion as well as a convention that writers could learn and appropriate for their own purposes. To answer a poem was to request entrance into the upper-class circle that had produced it and to take on that coterie's air of gentility. The point of the debate was to demonstrate one's verbal skills, not to express a personal opinion, and writers often displayed their training in the universities and the Inns of Court by arguing on both sides of the question. The debate was competitive, not only because it took its cue from disputations in logic but because writers matched wits with friendly rivals or vied for the attention of prospective patrons. George Herbert's criticism of erotic love poetry was a more sustained version of the position taken by several poets. Sidney, Donne, Edward Herbert, Benjamin Rudyerd, and Shakespeare all argued for and against secular love, at times by renouncing it for sacred devotion. George Herbert entered the debate through his sacred parody, and "Jordan" was his emblem both before and after he gave up his plans for a secular career. In this essay, I will consider the devotional lyrics in *The Temple*, not as a set of private meditations but as part of Herbert's lifelong performance within the Herbert circle.[3]

## I. THE PUBLICATION OF HERBERT'S ENGLISH VERSE

Because of Herbert's upper-class status, he withheld most of his poetry from commercial publication during his lifetime.[4] I believe that he regularly presented his devotional lyrics to a select, elite group. Some critics have argued that Herbert's English lyrics were not known to others in any significant way until the publication of *The Temple* after his death in 1633. Underlying these arguments is the assumption that social performance within a patronage network and the expression of religious conviction are mutually exclusive. I plan to show that *The Temple* was conceived within the context of the Herbert family coterie and alluded continually to it; that George Herbert almost certainly sang or recited his religious lyrics in the family homes at Chelsea and in Wiltshire; and that it is possible that some of his manuscripts circulated.

Critical opinion has been divided on the question of the privacy of Herbert's verse. F. E. Hutchinson claims that Herbert's English poems must "have been circulated in manuscript, as he enjoyed some reputation as a poet many years before his death" (xxxix–xl). Rosemund Tuve argues that George Herbert's poem "A Parodie" was a musical imitation of William Herbert's "Soules Joy," and that both songs were meant to be performed during the musical entertainments at Wilton House: "A network of ties we are largely unaware of made poets answer each other's poems, try out each other's modes." She assumes that Herbert visited Pembroke's Wilton House regularly during his residence in Wiltshire (1628–1633) and urges us to realize that "Herbert as a poet could not have taken lightly such a kinsman's friendship."[5]

On the other hand, Amy Charles argues that George Herbert "was not generally known for his English poems" during his life because copies of the poems in commonplace books derive from printed versions published after his death. She admits that there may have been "small groups of amateur musicians (particularly in Salisbury) to whom he had perhaps sung some of his English lyrics," but she does not explicitly include his family in this group. Joseph

Summers states that Herbert "seems to have felt his 'love poems' to be in some ways too private to be generally read within his lifetime," and Summers attributes this to Herbert's conviction that

> an effect of sincerity was essential to the poems he wrote. . . . 'Sincerity' is likely to become a problem if one thinks of poems not primarily as constructions or social gestures but as true accounts of experience and as expressions of personal commitment.

For Summers, these expressions are not simple recordings of private experience but require "a suspicious mastery of rhetorical conventions." Nevertheless, such a view contrasts strikingly with Tuve's claim that "A Parodie" was written precisely as a social gesture intended for entertainments at Wilton.[6]

Charles and Summers discount the evidence that Hutchinson offers to support his claim that Herbert presented his religious poetry to others. In *The Translations of Certain Psalms into English Verse* (1625), Francis Bacon dedicates his volume to George Herbert because of his ability in religion and verse. Charles's comments imply that she believes that Bacon knew only Herbert's Latin verse:

> In the absence of any manuscript evidence of the circulation of Herbert's English poems during his lifetime, there is no ground for assuming that Bacon had read any of Herbert's English poems or that it was the English poems that led to his dedicating the translation of *Certaine Psalmes* (1625) to Herbert. Bacon's acknowledgment of Herbert's part in translating *The Advancement of Learning* into Latin refers to Herbert's fitness in "Divinitie, and Poesie," no more; the compliment could apply to English verse or to Latin verse, published or unpublished.[7]

Despite Charles's reasoning, there is more. Bacon's wording of his dedication suggests that he is referring not to Herbert's Latin poetry, but to his religious poetry, including the English lyrics:

> The paines, that it pleased you to take, about some of my Writings, I cannot forget: which did put me in minde, to ded-

icate to you, this poore Exercise of my sicknesse. Besides, it
being my manner for Dedications, to choose those that I hold
most fit for the Argument, I thought, that in respect of Divinitie, and Poesie, *met*, (whereof the one is the Matter, the other
the Stile of this little writing) I could not make better choice.[8]
[italics mine]

The phrase "Divinitie, and Poesie, met" suggests not two separate
skills, but rather Herbert's worth as a religious poet and his fitness
as a judge of sacred verse. Indeed, the "Argument" of Bacon's *Certaine Psalmes* is most like Herbert's religious poems in *The Temple*:
the Psalmist's personal experience of "Divinitie" versified into English. Both in "Matter" and "Style," Herbert's English devotional
poetry suits Bacon's description much more exactly than any of the
Latin poetry.[9]

Charles and Summers also do not consider the strong evidence
that Herbert composed music for his religious lyrics in order to perform them. Helen Wilcox gathers this evidence in "Herbert's Musical Contexts: From Countrey-Aires to Angels Musick."[10] Walton
states that Herbert "compos'd many *divine Hymns* and *Anthems*,
which he set and sung to his *lute* or *Viol*."[11] The anonymous author
of the preface to *Select Hymns, Taken out of Mr. Herbert's Temple*
(1697) implies that certain tunes were available for particular lyrics
before Herbert's death and that the tunes were sung in some public way: "Mr. Herbert's *Poems* have met with so general and de-
serv'd Acceptance" yet "few of them have been Sung since his
Death, the Tunes not being at the Command of ordinary Readers."[12] Aubrey's account of Herbert's life supports the view that
Herbert composed settings for his poems:

> When he was first maried he lived a yeare or better at Dan-
> tesey House. H. Allen, of Dantesey, was well acquainted with
> him, who has told me that he had a very good hand on the
> Lute, and that he sett his own Lyricks or sacred poems.[13]

H. Allen's testimony sounds like it is based on personal experience
and that he heard Herbert's "very good hand" play on his lute the
settings composed for the sacred poems. It is likely, in fact, that Her-

bert sang these poems just in the way Tuve suggests, before those people in the homes where he lived or visited—his mother's house in Chelsea and the three homes in Wiltshire, Dauntsey House, Bainton House, and Wilton House, the seat of the Earl of Pembroke. The Herberts at Chelsea and Wilton were themselves skilled at music and frequently arranged for musical performances at their houses. According to Aubrey, Herbert's stepfather set up an elaborate music room at Chelsea: "Sir John was a great lover of Musick. . . . The House is vaulted all underneath: which meliorates the sound of the Musique." Aubrey also reports that Francis Bacon was a frequent visitor to the house in Chelsea.[14] It is probable that Bacon and many others heard Herbert sing his sacred lyrics. Herbert's poem "The Posie" supports this view, since it refers to various kinds of "poesie," all of which are meant to be heard or read by others:

> This on my ring,
> This by my picture, in my book I write:
> Whether I sing,
> Or say, or dictate, this is my delight.
> (5–8)

The last two quoted lines refer to musical presentation, recitation, or dictation to a scribe, and all imply some kind of audience.[15]

In addition, the poems may also have been circulated in manuscript among a narrow circle of Herbert's family and friends. It is true that the commonplace books can prove that the work of a poet circulated, but they cannot prove conclusively that the poetry was kept private. There is no evidence for the circulation of "Upon Appleton House" by Marvell, yet it is more than likely that Thomas Fairfax received a copy of this poem.[16] The presentation of a copy of "A Parodie" to the Earl of Pembroke is equally probable. We have Herbert's first sonnets because Walton printed them in his biography; there is no manuscript or reference to them in commonplace books, although Herbert gave them to his mother in 1609. Therefore, copies of his poems could have been given to his family and close friends, and nevertheless not show up in contemporary commonplace books.[17]

In *Scribal Publication in Seventeenth-Century England*, Harold Love discusses a very limited form of circulation that would have been attractive to Herbert, given his aversion to print. In this case, a text is "communicated within a closed circle of readers on the understanding it is not allowed to go beyond the circle." One purpose for such limited circulation was to exclude the possibility that the text would appear in manuscript collections, and eventually, in print. Love refers to a situation that would have had special relevance for Herbert and his family: "Nashe in the 1590's seems to have been acting as an agent for the booksellers Richard Jones and Thomas Newman in obtaining scribally published texts by writers of the Sidney–Pembroke circle for unauthorized print publication."[18]

My argument is that Herbert's religious lyrics were known by his family and friends and that the genre of sacred parody used by Herbert in *The Temple* was a variation on the answer poem characteristic of poetic coteries. This context is explicitly visible in particular poems by Herbert: "The Answer," "The Posie," "A Parodie," "The Quip." I believe it influenced a great many of Herbert's religious lyrics, including the "Jordan" poems and the verses on mutual love between God and man. It is clear that Herbert did not want to be well known through his devotional poems: he did not allow his poems to circulate as widely as possible. Yet since the members of his family were his major patrons, it is essential to consider the possibility that Herbert's lyrics were composed with performance or circulation in mind. If they were presented even in a limited way, then the lyrics must be included in accounts of his pursuit of patronage.

## II. THE FAMILY DEBATE

William Herbert, Earl of Pembroke, socialized with his clients through the game of literary exchange, and writers sought to enter the circle through their offerings. Poetic contest marked family entertainments, the establishing of friendships, and the request for patronage. E. F. Hart has argued that the "answer-poem" thrived in the "rich cultural life" of the court and the exclusive communities of the country house. According to J. W. Saunders, a circle of amateur poets served as a "finishing school" by "preparing its members, through mutual competition and co-operation, for the service of the monarch." A wealthy, prestigious nobleman like Pembroke attracted a circle of "satellite" courtiers, who sought the rewards of court patronage through his influence. Henry Lawes composed music for the poems that were a social and musical recreation in William Herbert's household, and Lawes owed his position in the court to Pembroke. George Herbert originally intended to follow this path.[19]

The relationship between poetry and a public career can be clarified through a man very much like George Herbert, who sought Pembroke's support by writing verses against secular love. The poetic exchange between William Herbert and Benjamin Rudyerd signaled their friendly rivalry and social intimacy but veiled Rudyerd's dependence on Pembroke for his position in the court and Parliament. The poems collected and published in 1660 by John Donne's son were circulated earlier in manuscript form, and the title identifies the answer poem as the genre defining the exchange: *Poems Written by the Right Honorable William Earl of Pembroke Lord Steward of his Majesties Houshold. Whereof Many of which are answered by way of Repartee, by Sr Benjamin Ruddier, Knight.*[20] Poetic contest structures the "repartee" through a long series of poems debating love, poems that are debates in themselves, and William Herbert's version of the most answered poem of the time, Marlowe's "Passionate Shepherd to his Love."[21] This "genteel" performance also marks a political alliance between a Protestant "Earl" and a Protestant "Knight," Pembroke's spokesman in the Commons. As an educated younger son of the gentry, Rudyerd required Pembroke's patronage in order to receive the office of Surveyor of the Court of Wards and Liveries under King James, as well as for his seat in Parliament for the boroughs of Portsmouth and Wilton, under the purview of William Herbert.[22] The ritual of the answer poem helped Rudyerd secure his public position at the same time that it established a partial, temporary sense of equality with the Earl.

William Herbert, Benjamin Rudyerd, and John Donne were

members of the same coterie located in the Inns of Court in the 1590s, but Donne never seems to have became Pembroke's client.[23] Nevertheless, Donne played a significant role in the "repartee" that made up the volume by Rudyerd and Herbert. Donne's presence as a poet is strong enough in the collection that he was often identified in manuscripts as its author.[24] William Herbert's "Soules Joy" is a musical, simpler version of "Valediction: Forbidding Mourning":

> Soules joy, now I am gone,
> And you alone,
> (Which cannot be,
> Since I must leave my selfe with thee,
> And carry thee with me)
> Yet when unto our eyes
> Absence denyes
> Each others sight,
> And makes to us a constant night,
> When others change to light;
> *O give no way to griefe,*
> *But let beliefe*
> *Of mutuall love,*
> *This wonder to the vulgar prove*
> *Our bodyes, not wee move.*[25]

Both "Soules joy" and "Valediction: Forbidding Mourning" refer to the separation of the lovers, their spiritual union through mutual love, and their ascension above the "laity" or "vulgar." Donne's reputation determines our assumption that Pembroke's poem is an imitation of Donne; it is possible that the process of patronage led Donne to write his poem in answer to Pembroke in an attempt to secure a position similar to Rudyerd's.[26] Neither poet was the originator of this subject for verse: both poems, as well as Hoskyns's "Absence," are responses to Sidney's meditations on absence in *Astrophil and Stella.*[27] Authorial originality was not the goal for these writers, but rather skillful wit and sophisticated argument.

The writers within the Herbert circle vied with each other over the same conventions and genres that make up *The Temple*: imitations and parodies of Petrarchan verse, the valediction poem, the paradox, ditties, posies, the pastoral lyric, and the "echo" poem. Edward Herbert, as well as Shakespeare, wrote poems in praise of the dark lady. Both Edward Herbert's "Ode upon a Question Moved," and Donne's "The Exstacie" were responses to Sidney's "Eighth Song." Donne and Edward Herbert exchanged and answered each other's poems regularly: Donne's "The Progress of the Soul" (1601) influenced Edward Herbert's "State-Progress of Ill" (1608), which Donne answered in a verse letter in 1610. George Herbert's "Church Militant" resembles these poems. The relationship between Donne and Edward Herbert may have been more a matter of friendship than patronage; nevertheless, it is likely that Donne also imagined that the alliance might lead to further support from Edward's mother, Magdalene, or from her relative, Pembroke.[28]

George Herbert was influenced not only by the genres used in the Herbert circle; for this coterie, love poetry had always been tied to its renunciation. The contrast between secular and sacred love was a fully conventional aspect of poetic debate. Sidney wrote *Astrophil and Stella* and "Leave me, O Love." Donne argues for love in one poem and against it in the next; his religious poetry compares love for his mistress and for God. Edward Herbert uses the "Ditty" as a love poem six times in his volume of poems, but the first use, and the second poem in the collection, is addressed to God rather than a mistress. He also includes four "Echo" poems, the last of which redirects their previous romantic use into a sacred parody that exchanges a pastoral landscape for the inside of a church.[29] Again, we may assume that Edward imitates George, but this is simply because of our acceptance of the literary canon as it is formulated. It is possible that both George and Edward imitate other poets, like Benjamin Rudyerd.

The poetic repartee between Pembroke and Rudyerd may have provided a model for George Herbert's response to his patron's love poetry. Their poems include an exchange about the value of erotic love, in which Rudyerd argues against and Pembroke for it:

R: Base Love, the stain of Youth, the scorn of Age,
The folly of a Man, a Womans rage

. . .

P: Go on, and laugh at Loves commanding fire,
Till you cannot your scorched self retire.[30]

The contest is reminiscent of the debate about love held between
Musidorus and Pyrocles in Sidney's *Arcadia*. This debate shapes
the volume collecting their verse, since most of Rudyerd's contri-
butions repeat his original arguments against love. It is also interesting that the gentleman Rudyerd argues for restraint and the nobleman Herbert for erotic desire; Rudyerd and Herbert may be
playing the parts of humanist courtier and unruly prince. Rudyerd
instructs Herbert on the duties of the noble man through Rudyerd's
poetic renunciations of love and satires on women. The debate is
a playful but serious contest, according to this passage by Rudyerd:

Not like a skeptick equally distract,
Nor like a Sophister of sleights compact,
Nor to vie Wit (a vanity of youth)
Nor for the love of Victory, but Truth,
The lists again I enter, bold assur'd,
Within my Causes right, strongly immur'd.[31]

Despite this love of truth, the collection also contains an example
of Rudyerd's love poetry.[32] Apparently, Rudyerd was more interested in vying wit than he would admit in the passage quoted
above. This confirms that conviction was less important in this exchange than the display of verbal and argumentative skill.

The practice of rhetorical debate structured upper-class poetic
interchange during this period. The "answer" poem is the versified
equivalent of the disputed question used in Renaissance education.
Students were taught to generate elaborate and witty defenses for
opposing positions.[33] The practice of disputation was central to both
the grammar schools and the universities. At Westminster School
every Saturday, the students (including George Herbert between
1604 and 1608) would "declaim on a set original theme, and one
inveighs against another in speeches."[34] At Oxford and Cambridge,

such practices were even more widespread: disputations would occur every Monday, Wednesday, and Friday from one o'clock to
three o'clock, and they would also mark commencement exer-
cises.[35] The disputed question would also equip the prospective
lawyers at the Inns of Court for their careers and would underlay
many of the wit contests so popular there. At a Christmas festival at
the Middle Temple recorded by Benjamin Rudyerd, a "Tuff-taffeta
speech" was presented and immediately followed by a "Fustian answer," in which all figures of speech were used but nothing substantial was said.[36] Such comedy satirizes the students' education
but also emphasizes the extent to which verbal contest was a daily
practice in Renaissance schooling and entertainment.

### III. GEORGE HERBERT'S ANSWER

The disputed question and the Herbert family poetic contest structure the sonnets that George Herbert wrote the year he entered
Cambridge. They launched him into the poetic debate that characterized his family:

> My God, where is that ancient heat towards thee,
>    Wherewith whole showls of *Martyrs* once did burn,
>    Besides their other flames? Doth Poetry
> Wear *Venus* Livery? only serve her turn?
> Why are not *Sonnets* made of thee? and layes            5
>    Upon thine Altar burnt? Cannot thy love
>    Heighten a spirit to sound out thy praise
> As well as any she? Cannot thy *Dove*
> Out-strip their *Cupid* easily in flight?
>    Or, since thy wayes are deep, and still the same,      10
>    Will not a verse run smooth that bears thy name?
> Why doth that fire, which by thy power and might
>    Each breast does feel, no braver fuel choose
> Than that, which one day Worms may chance refuse?[37]

Like the answering speech in a disputation, this poem "inveighs"
against the love poetry of Sidney, William Herbert, Edward Herbert,
Donne, and Shakespeare. Like the "answer" poems of Benjamin
Rudyerd, it also requests attention for itself and its witty ability to

handle the issue. It seeks out that limited equality available to one
who answers well, no matter what the status of the participants. At
stake is not only the virtue of sacred rather than secular love poetry,
but the disputed question: should a man marry, or, is there any
virtue in women?[38] To simulate the debate, the poem pairs erotic
and religious analogues in order to reveal the primacy of the latter.
Like the competition between "thy *Dove*" (8) and "their *Cupid*" (9),
Herbert and his God "out-strip" (9) love poets and their women by
appropriating flames, altars, and passion, and restoring them to the
praise and worship of God. Although the poet announces his piety,
he also displays his own "adult" wit through his jokes about the secular poet's prostitution of his powers: "Doth Poetry / Wear *Venus*
Livery? only serve her turn? / Why are not *Sonnets* made of thee?
and layes / Upon thine Altar burnt? Cannot thy love / Heighten a
spirit to sound out thy praise / As well as any she?" (3–8). Herbert
"turns" a phrase here for the glory of God, but also to register his
verbal sophistication. The competitive display of wit is matched by
a strong antagonism against women, especially in the last lines,
when the love between man and woman is reduced to a misguided
attachment to decaying flesh: "Why doth that fire, which by thy
power and might / Each breast doth feel, no braver fuel choose /
Than that, which one day Worms may chance refuse?" (12–14).
This hostility against the female body is quite conventional in debates about love, especially within the Herbert circle. Edward Herbert's "To His Mistress for Her True Picture" is addressed to Death
and rebukes the speaker's attachment to earthly lovers in terms
reminiscent of Herbert's sonnets:

> And do not think, when I new beauties see,
> They can withdraw my settled love from thee.
> Flesh-beauty strikes me not at all, I know:
>    . . .
>
>    Be the nut brown,
> The loveliest colour which the flesh doth crown,
> I'll think it like a Nut—a fair outside,
> Within which worms and rottenness abide
>    . . . [39]

In Donne's elegy on "The Autumnal," traditionally assumed to be addressed to Herbert's mother Magdalene, he proves his skill in using the form of the paradox by praising an older woman more highly than a younger, but nevertheless the skull beneath the skin appears like a *memento mori*:

> No *Spring*, nor *Summer* beauty hath such grace,
>    As I have seen in one autumnall face
> 　　　　・ ・ ・
> But name not Winter-faces, whose skin's slacke;
>    Lanke, as an unthrifts purse; but a soules sacke;
> Whose eyes seeke light within, for all here's shade;
>    Whose mouthes are holes, rather worne out, than made
> 　　　　・ ・ ・
> Name not these living Deaths-heads unto mee
> 　　　　・ ・ ・ [40]

The display of wit and aggression against women in Herbert's early sonnets takes its cue from the renunciation of physical love characteristic of love poets during this period, and from the debate about women popular in the schools and pamphlets of the time.[41] Perhaps Herbert's sonnets express more actual conviction than those by other poets; nevertheless, they are just as fully coterie performances. Walter Ong has analyzed the agonistic quality of Renaissance education and remarked on its characteristic hostility and virulence.[42] The "answer" poem hides this hostility within its genteel wit, but the attempt to triumph and to achieve recognition remains the same.

The wit contest in an exchange of verses between Donne and Herbert reveals that religious poetry was as appropriate in coterie performance as secular verse. According to Helen Gardner, Donne wrote a Latin poem on his seal to Herbert, and Herbert replied in 1615, at the time of Donne's ordination and as Herbert was pursuing a successful academic career. Donne's poem alludes to shared religious interests, wishes Herbert well in his plans for secular preferment, and perhaps attempts to deepen an alliance with a young man who had better connections than Donne:

The Crosse (my seal at Baptism) spred below,
Does, by that form, into an Anchor grow.
Crosses grow Anchors; Bear, as thou shouldst do
Thy Crosse, and that Crosse grows an Anchor too

. . .

Under this little seal great gifts I send,
[Wishes], and prayers, pawns and fruits of a friend.
And may that Saint which rides in our great Seal,
To you, who bear his name, great bounties deal.[43]

According to Helen Gardner, the "great Seal" refers to "the George
that hangs from the Garter on the seated figure of the King on the
reverse of the Great Seal."[44] Donne associates George Herbert,
through his name, with the monarchy and identifies the King as the
source for Herbert's future preferment. This reference indicates
that Herbert's desires for high office were quite clear to those who
knew him. The poem also suggests that just as Donne bestows his
gift on Herbert, so he asks for some help with his influential relations. Herbert's reply acknowledges the alliance, but partially
through a display of wit that attempts to equal or perhaps surpass
Donne's own. Both poems play on the link between the cross and
the anchor, but Herbert's compact seven lines show up Donne's
more expansive twenty-two. Latin was, of course, Herbert's forte,
rather than Donne's:

Although the Crosse could not Christ here detain,
Though nail'd unto't, but he ascends again,
Nor yet thy eloquence here keep him still,
But onely while thou speak'st; This Anchor will.[45]

Witty and terse, the poem pins down its reworking of Donne's
conceit through its half-line on the anchor. The English translation,
perhaps by Herbert, praises Donne's preaching ability at the same
time that it suggests indirectly some conflict between Christ's word
and Donne's own. The poem clearly accepts Donne's good wishes
and connects the spiritual hope of the anchor with the firmness of
their friendship: "Let the world reel, we and all ours stand sure, /
This holy Cable's of all storms secure" (6–7). Yet the poem's re-

working of Donne's conceited style also displays the younger poet's ability to answer back, and to be more obscure and more condensed than Donne himself.[46]

"Jordan" (I) constructs itself as an entry into another wit battle, and its jaunty rhetorical questions are presented as if to imagined opponents:

> Who sayes that fictions onely and false hair
> Become a verse? Is there in truth no beautie?
> Is all good structure in a winding stair?
> May no lines passe, except they do their dutie
>     Not to a true but painted chair?
>
> (1–5)

Like Herbert's first sonnets, each rhetorical question is meant to score a point. The poem may honor truth rather than artifice; nevertheless each line spryly proves its verbal power through turning a phrase. This plain style will not be artless, since it uses metaphor (the "false hair" [1] of empty tropes), puns ("become" [2] as turn into or be appropriate to), and allegory (the "lines" [4] which bow before the chair of overly elaborate literary authority). The purification associated with the "Jordan" allusion does not require abjuring rhetorical figures but rather puts them into the service of religious truth. Wit, the poem claims, is most becoming in a sacred poem.

Like Herbert's first sonnets, this poem begins with questions and ends with a concluding answer. The last stanza stages an imaginary truce between the debaters:

> Shepherds are honest people; let them sing:
> Riddle who list, for me, and pull for Prime:
> I envie no mans nightingale or spring;
> Nor let them punish me with losse of rime,
>     Who plainly say, *My God, My King*.
>
> (11–15)

To each his own style, according to the speaker, but his words prove that the plain style he adopts will be as indirect as any other, though far more condensed and pointed than the pastoral allegory still practiced by a few. The words "pull for Prime" present a riddling figure for the very pastoral songs he debunks as pretentiously and superficially riddling: since the phrase comes from Primero and refers to drawing for the winning card, these poets are imagined as vying to produce the best pastoral poem, or version of *primavera*. The speaker appears to be less interested in contest: "I envie no mans nightingale or spring" (13); yet his last phrase again scores a point through its riddling ambiguity. Does *My God, My King* mean my God is my King, and therefore I abjure the court style? or does it mean that the speaker will praise both God and King, speak of religion and country, without the unwieldy self-protective artifice of pastoral allegory? Like the rest of the poem, the phrase pretends to be straightforward, but it outwits those who think plainness is equivalent to simplemindedness.

"Jordan" (I) is one of several poems by Herbert that answer or imitate Sidney. We should recognize that such imitations were written with a family history in mind. By the time Herbert was born, Sidney had become mythical as a soldier, scholar, and poet, but he was also Herbert's distant relative and the uncle of William Herbert. Sidney's status as an author and his "martyr's death" for the Protestant cause on the Continent led writers to invoke his name when they wished to obtain patronage from members of his family, especially his nephews William and Philip Herbert, or to encourage the Herberts to act as leaders of the Protestant faction in the English court. Daniel Featly wrote to William Herbert, "Of our faith, you and your family have always been a principle defender and protector." In a dedicatory sonnet to Philip Herbert in his translation of *The Iliad*, Chapman wrote:

> There runs a blood, fair Earl, through your clear veins
> That well entitles you to all things noble;
> Which still the living Sydnian soul maintains,
> And your name's ancient noblesse doth redouble.

Mary Sidney Herbert commissioned a life of Sidney from William Herbert's tutor in order to inspire her son to follow the example of her brother. George Herbert's brother Edward followed Sidney's example and entered the Protestant wars on the Continent.[47] Ben

Jonson's poetry contains several allusions to Sidney, often with an eye toward the patronage of Sidney's descendants.[48]

George Herbert's interest in Sidney is evident in the thematic, verbal, and technical echoes of *Astrophil and Stella* in *The Temple*. Sidney's translations of the Psalms and his religious songs and sonnets provided Herbert with an example for his own poetry.[49] But when Herbert takes up Sidney as a model, it is with the intention of placing himself within the family line of poets, and with a special zeal to correct Sidney's priorities. Herbert seems to have noticed the ambiguous position of religious poetry in *An Apology for Poetry*. Religious verse is named as "the chief, both in antiquity and excellency," but nevertheless it is left out of the discussion of the imaginative literature that is Sidney's chief interest. In his first discussion of lyric, he curiously mentions only the praise of heroic deeds, and in his second, he again gestures toward the priority of religious verse, but his deeper interest in love poetry and the expression of *energia* becomes immediately apparent.[50] Sidney takes up the position of poetic reformer, but such reform does not extend to a censure of love poetry even though his celebration of divine verse suggests that it will:

> Lord, if He gave us so good minds, how well it might be employed, and with how heavenly fruit, both private and public, in singing the praises of the immortal beauty, the immortal goodness of that God who giveth us hands to write and wits to conceive; of which we might want words, but never matter; of which we could turn our eyes to nothing, but we should ever have new-budding occasions.[51]

Sidney briefly imagines devoting his lyrical powers exclusively to religion, and intimates that "minds," "hands," "wits," and "eyes" created by God could best be dedicated to His service. Herbert picks up what is left as a suggestion in Sidney and turns it into a poetic career:

> then shall our brain
> All her invention on thine Altar lay
>
> . . .
>
> All knees shall bow to thee; all wits shall rise
> And praise him who did make and mend our eies
>
> ("Love" [II], 6–7, 11–12)

### IV. "A PARODIE"

Herbert originally intended to identify himself through the family debate as the "Herbert" who wrote lyric poetry exclusively about sacred love that was nevertheless just as witty and inventive, or perhaps more so, than the verses by other members of the family. But several poems in *The Temple* testify to a change over time in his attitude toward the answer poem and his relationship to the family debate. This new attitude did not result in a withdrawal from that debate; one of Herbert's late poems is an answer to Pembroke's poem "Soules Joy" quoted above. But the tone and the placement of the poem in *The Temple* reveal that Herbert approached such a contest in a new way later in his life. "A Parodie" uses the methods of the answer poem to evoke the spiritual communion between God and the soul rather than between human lovers:

> Souls joy, when thou art gone,
>         And I alone,
>         Which cannot be,
> Because thou dost abide with me,
>         And I depend on thee;
>
> Yet when thou dost suppresse
>         The cheerfulnesse
>         Of thy abode,
> And in my powers not stirre abroad,
>         But leave me to my load:
>
> O what a damp and shade
>         Doth me invade!
>         No stormie night
> Can so afflict or so affright,
>         As thy eclipsed light
>                 . . .
>
>                 (1–15)

Given the association of Pembroke's verse with the poetry of John Donne and Edward Herbert, all of whom considered "mutual love," it is clear that George Herbert's famous and compelling representations of spiritual intimacy owe more to his family circle than has previously been noticed. "A Parodie" responds not only to Pembroke's "Soules Joy"; it takes its position in a complex of poems including Sidney's meditations on absence, Hoskyn's "Absence," Donne's "Valediction: Forbidding Mourning" and "The Exstacie," and Edward Herbert's "Ode upon a Question Moved."[52]

Although "A Parodie," like the poems of Rudyerd, rebukes Pembroke's fascination with the erotic, the tone of aggressive contest characteristic of Herbert's early poems and the form of the parody in general is absent here.[53] The speaker interestingly takes on the role of the woman in the valediction poem and confesses the grief and sense of separation felt by the one who is left behind.[54] The significance of this careful avoidance of contentiousness can be clarified by the poem that precedes "A Parodie" in *The Temple*.[55] "The Posie" considers the very kind of wit contest inherent to the Herbert family ritual of answering. The poem does not renounce such verbal battles but suggests that they must be entered with a different spirit:

> Let wits contest,
> And with their words and posies windows fill:
> *Lesse then the least*
> *Of all thy mercies*, is my posie still.
>
> This on my ring,                                     5
> This by my picture, in my book I write:
> Whether I sing,
> Or say, or dictate, this is my delight.
>
> Invention rest,
> Comparisons go play, wit use thy will:               10
> *Lesse then the least*
> *Of all Gods mercies*, is my posie still.

A posie was a short motto engraved on windows or imprinted on personal objects like rings and books, which often represented an intimate relationship or expressed a secret about an individual. Pembroke and Rudyerd composed posies; Edward Herbert's posie "In a Glass Window for Inconstancy" may have been answered by Donne's "Valediction: Of my Name in the Window." Like the device, or *impresa*, the posie was a public symbol for a private or personal experience.[56]

George Herbert's "The Posie" is autobiographical because it refers to the ritual of the answer poem enacted by "A Parodie," which follows it. The motto in the poem has also been identified by Nicholas Ferrar as Herbert's own: "We conclude all with his own Motto, with which he used to conclude all things that might seem to tend any way to his own honour; *Lesse then the least of Gods mercies*" (pp. 4–5). The humility of the motto may suggest the renunciation of rituals of honor: Ferrar's account suggests instead that it allowed Herbert to participate in them while preserving a sense of religious integrity. The poem does not renounce poetry or its social rituals: "Whether I sing, / Or say, or dictate, this is my delight" (7–8).

Most critics have recognized that the motto in the poem would have special significance for Herbert; it is spoken by Jacob: "I am not worthy of the least of all the mercies, and of all the truth, which thou hast shewed unto thy servant; for with my staff I passed over this Jordan" (Genesis 32:10).[57] "Jordan" was the personal "device" which represented for Herbert the purification of ambition, especially ambition associated with literary creation.[58] But critics have not noticed that the next words of Jacob are equally important: "Deliver me, I pray thee, from the hand of my brother, from the hand of Esau" (Genesis 32:11). Jacob speaks these words after he has been informed of the approaching troops of his relative, with whom he has competed for the "honors" of the family literally from birth, and now he asks for divine help in this troublesome encounter. We might remember as well that Jacob's meeting with Esau is preceded by his wrestling with the angel of God, during which he is given the new name of Israel: "For as a prince hast thou power with God and with men, and hast prevailed" (Genesis 32:28).

The motto "lesse then the least of all Gods mercies" conferred on the poet a double identity, which allowed him to be both a Herbert and something else. In his contests with and "parodies" of his family relations and their client-poets, Herbert could hint at that devotional identity, that new name, in a public, but distanced way. The "temple" within preserved a separate area in the self, a space ideally purified of family rivalry and personal ambition.[59] It was both a protective and a disciplinary enclosure, since it required that "comparisons go play" (10), that is, that poetic imitation, including the use of similes, be free from the impulse to triumph over another. It demanded that "invention rest" (9), that imaginative creativity be less important than the truth, and that the "finding out" of topics occur without the disquiet of personal ambition. Similarly, the motto "is my posie still" because it did not change despite the social need for cleverness and because it provided a measure of stillness or quiet in the midst of public rivalry. Again, "The Posie" does not imply that Herbert gave up singing or reciting the lyrics before an audience. Like a "posie" that represented an intimate relationship, the poems referred in public to a personal devotional experience.

The sequence of both Herbert manuscripts of *The Temple* testify to the crucial role that the answer poem played in Herbert's literary career. When he revised the earlier *W* manuscript into the later *B* manuscript, he replaced one example of coterie verse with another. Near the end of the sequence, before the group on "last things" that ends "The Church," Herbert placed "A Parodie," his most focused answer to William Herbert, in the original position of "Invention," his most focused answer to Sir Philip Sidney.[60] The significant and analogous positions of the two poems were gestures toward the family literary circle. This revision demonstrates that the Sidney–Herbert coterie was fundamental to the original project of *The Temple* and that it remained so throughout Herbert's life.

The modern assumption that religious verse can only be sincere when it is private misrepresents the role of poetry in the seventeenth century and interferes with our understanding of the social context of Herbert's verse. For the Herbert coterie, poetry was a social ritual evoked by and participating in an upper-class world that included evenings of entertainment and the exchange of verse, as well as the forging of political alliances and client-patron relations. What we have identified as literary aspects of the verse—the use of wit, allusions to other poets like Sidney, the critique of erotic poetry—should be reassessed as social gestures. Herbert's engagement in social ritual does not make his poetry any less religious than previously imagined, but perhaps less modern.

# Three

## Gentility and Vocation in the Original *Temple*

**A**lthough the Sidney–Herbert coterie and its social rituals remained influential throughout George Herbert's life, he significantly altered the structure of selfhood implicit in *The Temple*. This chapter seeks to make visible that original plan. *The Temple* created a double identity from the outset: the later revisions attempt to transform a contrast between an inward holiness and an external gentility into a coordination between holiness and its outward expression.

The original *Temple* was built on a contrast between a social identity constructed by the "cunning workman" and the reborn spiritual man unpolluted by the "workmans tool." This structure of selfhood was no crass materialism but a rather elegant, although at times contradictory, coordination of piety and the pursuit of social advancement. It linked together the particular calling of the gentleman and the general calling of a Christian. Herbert's goal in the original *W* manuscript was religious sanctification as well as an improvement in his social and economic condition meant to benefit others. The "Jordan" allusions were intended to preserve the purity of the heart in the midst of the acquisition of wealth.

The *B* manuscript, which I believe begins after 1627, represents a conversion away from the goal of social ascent.[1] Its revisions erase both a desire to achieve social success and an emphasis on a renewed spiritual identity. These are the two focal points of the emerging modern self: the introspection of the inner man and the ability to shape one's social being according to one's desire. Its organization may seem to ensure that "outside" social experience is insignificant, but it actually affirms that one has the flexibility to take on any social role:

> If thou art nothing, think what thou wouldst bee
> Hee that desires is more then halfe ye way.
> But if thou coole, then take some shame to thee
> Desire and shame, will make thy labour, play
>
>             . . .
>
> ("The Church-porch," stanza 16 in *W*, cut in *B*)

The excited prospect of creating one's social identity is edited out of *The Temple* because Herbert came to feel that this goal was not a form of piety but of individualism, as Thomas Adams suggests in his *Temple*, a sermon written in 1624:

> So, of all Idolatries, God deliver us from a superstitious worship of our selves. Some have Idolized their Princes, some their Mistresses, some their Manufactures; but they are innumerable that have Idolized themselves. He is a rare man that hath no Idol, no little god in a boxe, no especiall sinne in his heart, to which he gives uxorious and affectionate Indulgence.[2]

Herbert changed the structure of *The Temple* so that it did not coordinate a central inner piety with an external social ascent, because such a structure began to seem like an invention devised for his own good rather than for the church, a cunning work whose clever connections between inside and outside constructed not the temple of God but a "little god in a boxe." As he moved to the rural community of Bemerton, he turned away from the construction of gentility to the "character" of holiness and pastoral images of the self, models that seemed less polluted by "the workmans tool."

Recent analyses of the relationship between "The Church-porch" and "The Church" have focused on Herbert's conception of his social role, but they have not considered how the doctrine of vocation influenced the relationship between these two parts of *The Temple* nor how his extensive revisions changed this relationship.[3] Richard Strier has called attention to the contrast between the Baconian opportunism of the introductory poem and the anti-worldliness of the lyrics. His account suggests that this contrast reflects a change in Herbert's perspective over time:

> It is deeply characteristic of 'The Church-Porch' that 'cunning' should be a positive term in its lexicon. . . . I have argued elsewhere that Herbert's major lyrics exhibit an extreme sensitivity to and revulsion from prudential and self-enhancing considerations. I suspect that Herbert's later revulsion from such considerations is inversely related to the prominence of such considerations in 'The Church-Porch' and in the life which this poem both reflects and manifests.[4]

On the other hand, Deborah Shuger argues that such a discontinuity was not a matter of time, but characteristic of lived experience for Herbert and others influenced by the doctrine of dual persons as formulated by Martin Luther and William Perkins:

> In 'The Church-Porch' the self is autonomous, ethical, and social; in 'The Church,' dependent, passive, and private. . . . [In Perkins's analysis of the dual persons] we have a clear distinction between a private self ('a person of mine own self'), which is nevertheless 'under' Christ, and a public, social self ('a person in respect of another'), which is constituted by its role or 'office' within a hierarchical sociopolitical order. . . . The spiritual and social are seen as equally obligatory but also essentially separate realms.[5]

Both of these accounts suggest nuanced readings of *The Temple* as autobiography, but neither considers William Perkins's coordination of "the double person" in *A Treatise of the Vocations, or Callings of Men*. Here, Perkins links the general calling "common to all men as they are Christian" and the particular calling "arising out of that distinction that God makes between man and man." Perkins speaks heatedly about the need to be a Christian as one practices one's social role:

> For wheresoever these two callings are severed, whatsoever
> is in shew, there is nothing in substance. . . . For though they
> be indowed with excellent gifts, and be able to speak well,
> conceive prayer, and with some reverence to heare the word,
> and receive the Sacraments, yet if they practice not the du-
> ties of godliness within their own callings, all is but hypocrisie.
> And therefore, unlesse they repent, the greater their gifts are,
> the more shal they make to their deeper condemnation at
> the day of judgment.[6]

I do not intend to show that *The Temple* seamlessly weaves together the general and the particular calling. Rather, I hope to
demonstrate that Herbert originally sought to hold together the
genteel lifestyle and religious holiness through the doctrine of vocation and that *The Temple* is a record of his difficulty at doing so.
I agree with Strier that there was a change in Herbert's perspective,
but that it occurred not with the initial plan for "The Church," but
with the revisions made to the *W* manuscript. The ideal of plainness in *The Country Parson* was the solution Herbert developed to
tie works and grace together into a more coherent unity. Holiness
replaces gentility as the principle for social performance in *The
Country Parson* in part because the contrast between the two inherent to the original *Temple* began to seem, as Perkins suggests,
like hypocrisy.

"Jordan" includes a complex of images that Herbert used to represent his commitment to sacred verse and the importance of humility in literary creation. But the idea also underlies the relationship
of "The Church-porch" to "The Church." The poetic sequence is
built on a contrast between the crafted gentility designed by a
gifted young man turned "cunning workman" and a divinely inspired piety untouched by any "workmans tool."[7] These references
to the workman allude not only to Herbert's status as a younger son
whose social position was his own achievement but also to specific
Biblical passages that describe proper and improper modes of
craftsmanship. Herbert's use of these allusions suggests that from

the outset of his career he regarded gentility not as an essence but as the result of work—the construction of a style of life through the handling of clothes, behavior, language, and the forging of personal alliances that could bring preferment.[8] The "Jordan" allusions attempted to sanctify that work through a link with divinely derived identity and to purify it from the taint of self-interest.

In "The Church-porch," the young man's social life is to be characterized by religious virtue: the poem opens with instructions on chastity, temperance, and honesty. But this virtue is accompanied by an avid concern for social success. The young man uses his conversational skills to improve his reputation, to win his audience, to manipulate people and situations for his own benefit:

> Slight not the smallest losse, whether it be
> In love or honour: take account of all;
> Shine like the sunne in every corner: see
> Whether thy stocke of credit swell, or fall.
> Who say, I care not, those I give for lost,
> And to instruct them, will not quit the cost.
>
> Scorn no mans love, though of a mean degree;
> Love is a present for a mightie king.
> Much lesse make any one thy enemie.
> As gunnes destroy, so may a little sling.
> The cunning workman never doth refuse
> The meanest tool, that he may chance to use.[9]
>
> (343–54)

The clever upper-class young man is a "cunning workman" (353) because he carves out his own reputation, or his "honor" (343), through the use of wit, intelligence, and the careful manipulation of his social relationships so that they may increase his "stocke of credit" (346), and in order that they may result not so much in companionship as prosperity. As Strier argues, Herbert's young man is Baconian in his attention to social appearances.[10] He uses people of mean degree just as David used a sling, because his "work" requires controlling his public image. Inside, however, in "The Church," this kind of self-fashioning is inappropriate:

A broken *A L T A R*, Lord, thy servant reares,
Made of a heart, and cemented with teares;
  Whose parts are as thy hand did frame;
  No workmans tool hath touch'd the same.

("The Altar," 1–4)

An emphasis on the craft of the "workmans tool," the shaping of social situations and the social self, is dropped, according to the poem, within the spiritual realm. The "cunning workman" must give up his capacity to fashion appearances when speaking to his "Maker." Workmanship is not ruled out, as the highly crafted "ALTAR" makes clear, but it cannot influence the process of sanctification. Divinely derived devotion within and a fashioned gentility without: this is the original structure of *The Temple*. That structure is temporal as well as spatial; that is, the work promises a transformative process by which the "young man" is turned into a devout servant of the Lord. Herbert intended to construct a bridge between gentility and devotion. But the work also makes possible, as Shuger points out, a lived division between social and sacred: gentleman on the outside, godly petitioner on the inside.

The contrast between the "cunning workman" in "The Church-porch" and the inefficacy of the "workmans tool" (4) in "The Altar" alludes to a set of Biblical passages associated with "Jordan." In several passages, the Israelites are told that, after they cross the Jordan, they must rear an altar of unhewn stone, "for if thou lift up thy tool upon it, thou hast polluted it" (Exodus 20:25). This altar is intended to turn the Israelites away from the worship of idols, the "gods of silver" and the "gods of gold" (Exodus 20:23) that must be purged from the promised land. This prohibition protects them from the workman's tool that devises graven images used by Aaron to carve the golden calf (Exodus 32:4) and, later in the Old Testament, used by the people to create false idols:

> For the customs of the people are vain: for one cutteth a tree out of the forest, the work of the hands of the workman, with the axe. They deck it with silver and with gold; they fasten it with nails and with hammers, that it move not. . . . Be not

afraid of them; for they cannot do evil, neither also is it in
them to do good . . . they are all the work of cunning men.
(Jeremiah 10:3–5, 9)

Here, "cunning" is a suspicious use of craft that substitutes artificial
idols for real divinity: "He seeketh unto him a cunning workman to
prepare a graven image" (Isaiah 40:20). On the other hand, the
word "cunning" is also used in the Bible to refer to inspired creativity, especially when used in building the Church. In Exodus 31
and 35, Moses is instructed to choose a "cunning workman" to
craft the elaborate ornament for the tabernacle that will house the
Ark of the Covenant. This "cunning" is not associated with deceit
but with technical skill received through divine inspiration:

> And the Lord spake unto Moses, saying, See, I have called by
> name Bezaleel the son of Uri, the son of Hur, of the tribe of
> Judah: And I have filled him with the spirit of God, in wis-
> dom, and in understanding, and in knowledge, and in all
> manner of workmanship, To devise cunning works, to work
> in gold, and in silver, and in brass, And in cutting of stones, to
> set them, and in carving of timber, to work in all manner of
> workmanship. (Exodus 31:1–4)

The phrases "cunning workman" or "a man cunning to work in
gold, and in silver" are repeated positively in the verses on the
construction of Solomon's temple: "Send me now therefore a man
cunning to work in gold, and in silver . . . and that can skill to grave
with the cunning men that are with me in Judah" (2 Chronicles
2:7). Therefore, the word "cunning" in the Bible can refer either to
technical skill used to create false gods, or to that same skill used
ingeniously to build the temple of God.

This is the contrast between proper and improper uses of craftsmanship that underlies Herbert's "Jordan" poems, as well as the relationship between "The Church-porch" and "The Church." These
Biblical passages suggest that Herbert thought that the construction
of an upper-class persona could result in an excessively contrived
"graven" image, or it could contribute to the building of the national
Church. The "Jordan" marked the difference between holy and pol-

luted forms of crafted gentility. For Herbert, the gentry lifestyle was like metaphor—something made by human hands but legitimate when grounded in religious truth. "Jordan" (I) suggests that metaphor is illuminating when representing "truth," but an empty "fiction" when excessively contrived or used to display oneself. In the poem, the metaphors used to describe ostentatious language—the "false hair" of the courtier, the "winding stair" of the country-house owner, the "painted chair" of secular authority—refer simultaneously to a style of language and a style of upper-class life taken to extremes. In "Jordan" (II), the use of brilliant verbal technique turns from sacred praise into a decking and curling that crafts the upperclass writer into a false god woven out of "quaint words, and trim invention." The arts of gentility, like literary technique, could at times illuminate religious "truth"; at other times, it created idols.

For Herbert, the doctrine of vocation originally provided a religious basis for the "cunning work" of performative gentility. Sermons and texts on the subject have some difficulty reconciling vocation with prevailing definitions of upper-class status because of the traditional association between gentility and leisure. Nevertheless, Protestants find a compromise: all must work, but class distinctions will remain through the difference between "the sweat of either *brow* or *braine*," according to Thomas Adams, or "divers sorts of labours, some of the minde, and some of the body . . . " as it is put in the *Homilies* (1623).[11] Richard Brathwait includes a sixty-page chapter on vocation, one of his eight constitutive categories that make up *The English Gentleman* (1630):

> None are less exempted from a Calling than great men. . . . I do not hence conclude, that all are to intend the *Plough*, or betake themselves to *Manuall* Trades. . . . No, I am not so stupid, as not to apprehend how severall places or offices are deputed to sundrie men.[12]

These writers differ on whether or not the professions should be grouped with the mind or the body: whereas the Homilies link the upper-class office of "governing the common weale publicaly" with the ministry, the law, and teaching, Sanderson seems to connect "the *Husbandman, Merchant, Lawyer, Minister*" with "*Manual*, and *Servile*, and *Mechanick* Trades and Arts . . . for men of lower condition."[13] Nevertheless, all preach "the Necessity of a Vocation," as both Brathwait and Herbert put it.[14]

The opponent to this doctrine is the idle "gallant," who appears repeatedly in this literature as the aristocrat who contributes nothing to the commonwealth. Donne attacks the gallant in "To Mr. Tilman after he had taken orders" through his satirical association of the lazy gentry with "dressing, mistressing, and complement." Herbert quotes this line in "The Church-porch" and *The Country Parson*.[15] Both echo the sermons on vocation, which unleash their harshest criticism on this figure:

> But for our (*meer* or *parcel*) *Gallants*, who live in no settled course of life, but spend half the *day* in *sleeping,* half the night in *gaming,* and the rest of their time in other *Pleasures* and *Vanities,* to as little purpose as they can devise; as if they were born for nothing else but to eat and drink, and snort and sport; who are spruce and trim as the *Lilies* (*Salomon in all his royalty was not cloathed like one of these;*) yet they neither *sow,* nor *reap,* nor carry into the Barn, they neither *labour* nor *spin,* nor do any thing else for the good of humane society.[16]

Brathwait becomes as impassioned as Sanderson about "these gilded gallants":

> These imagine it a labour sufficient, a *Vocation* for their *state* and *degree* equivalent, to spend the whole Morne till the Mid-day in tricking, trimming, painting, and purfling, studying rather to *Die* will, then *Live* well. These are they who beautifie themselves for the Stage, to become deluding *Spectacles* to the unbounded affections of *Youth.*[17]

Brathwait imagines these upper-class slackers as wasting the morning in "purfling," or decorating the edges of their clothes with ornamental borders in preparation for their attendance at the theater in the afternoon, where they will sit on the stage to see the performance but also to be seen by the audience. The inevitable connection between idleness and the figure of the gallant rebukes gentry contempt for the laboring classes, but also hides the immense amount of work required to maintain this kind of appearance. One wonders whether the gallant isn't actually another version of the courtier, who wants to be seen not just for the sake of vanity but to obtain the patronage he requires. Donne's attendance at the theater and Herbert's early interest in fashion suggest that their pursuit of patronage often involved them in activities quite similar to "dressing, mistressing, and complement." Vocation provided both with a protection against the claim of superficiality, as well as the upperclass aversion to labor. Their "cunning work" would not be merely decorative but would contribute to "the good of humane society."

Herbert's advice for the promising young man in "The Churchporch" redefines gentility according to the doctrine of vocation. He recasts the upper-class life so that it will include not only a "brave" and "glorious" appearance but also professional activity:

> Flie idlenesse, which yet thou canst not flie
> By dressing, mistressing, and complement.
> If those take up thy day, the sunne will crie
> Against thee: for his light was onely lent.
>    God gave thy soul brave wings; put not those feathers
>    Into a bed, to sleep out all ill weathers.
>
> Art thou a Magistrate? then be severe:
> If studious, copie fair, what time hath blurr'd;
> Redeem truth from his jawes: if souldier,
> Chase brave employments with a naked sword
>    Throughout the world. Fool not: for all may have,
>    If they dare try, a glorious life, or grave.
>
> O England! full of sinne, but most of sloth;
> Spit out thy flegme, and fill thy brest with glorie:
> Thy Gentrie bleats, as if thy native cloth
> Transfus'd a sheepishnesse into thy storie:
>    Not that they all are so; but that the most
>    Are gone to grasse, and in the pasture lost
>        . . .
>
> Some great estates provide, but doe not breed
> A mast'ring minde; so both are lost thereby
>        . . .

(79–96, 103–4)

Herbert replaces leisure with active employment as the defining feature of gentility. Gallants who deck themselves with extravagant clothes, courtly flattery, and fashionable affairs (80) are like cunning workmen who create false gods. The gentility they produce may seem impressive, but it actually disguises an inner "sloth" (91), which is incapable of expressing authentic authority. Leisure is not a mark of quality, but a sin, interfering with the progress of the commonwealth. But the moral commitment to work turns into an inner "glory" (90) and an outer "glorious life" (92) intended to attract the young gallant. The stylistics of gentility are grounded on the Protestant ethic but not discarded.[18] The landowner must teach his son the mastery (104) that is now located in the mind rather than the estate, but this mastery is still the mark of status-authority and superiority. This process continues throughout the poem; clothes, gaming, conversation, honor and reputation are all considered, in part to warn against fixation on these externals, but never to suggest that these aspects of gentry lifestyle are trivial or expendable.[19]

Nevertheless, the poem is intent on contrasting these externals with the internal qualities of the upper-class man and on translating that internality from social into religious terms.[20] Here, Herbert provides the link between the particular and general calling that Perkins demands. The contrast between the "great estate" and "mast'ring minde" of lines 103–4 reoccurs in the comparison of the value of clothes with demonstrable "worth" (181–82), and the difference between boldness in talk and "substantial worth" (209) or "solid bravery" (208) in conversation. By the end of the poem, this contrast has shifted to a comparison between the attention paid to a gentleman's clothes and that paid to his spiritual state: "Thy clothes being fast, but thy soul loose about thee" (414). Herbert harks back to this theme of clothing as a superficial aspect of gentility, but now with a different emphasis: "Dresse and undresse thy soul: mark the decay / And growth of it" (453–54). Like a church-porch, the poem leads the reader away from the secular to the sacred, to a more religious understanding of what is internal and substantial. In the line quoted above, the secular indeed is defined as a kind of clothing that needs to be removed so that the soul can be spiritually "dressed," a pun that refers to both clothing and religious correction. Unlike the workmanship of gentility, the soul is defined in terms of a creation of nature: "mark the decay / And growth of it." The poem builds the upper-class man in terms of a difference between outside and inside in order to redefine that inside according to the spirituality of "The Church."[21]

The difference is analogous to the distinctions made by "The Church-porch" between a status-conscious social life and the holiness required in church:

> When once thy foot enters the church, be bare.
> God is more there, then thou: for thou are there
> Onely by his permission. Then beware,
> And make thy self all reverence and fear.
>     Kneeling ne're spoil'd silk stocking: quit thy state.
>     All equall are within the churches gate
>         . . .
>
> Let vain or busie thoughts have there no part:
> Bring not thy plough, thy plots, thy pleasures thither.
> Christ purg'd his temple; so must thou thy heart.
> All worldly thoughts are but theeves met together
>     To couzin thee. Look to thy actions well:
>     For churches are either our heav'n or hell.
>                                   (403–8, 421–26)

The social promise of the young man, which the provisos of "The Church-porch" are meant to support and help realize, must nevertheless be forgotten when in church. Outside, active engagement in social plots and plans is encouraged: "Let thy minde still be bent, still plotting where, / And when, and how the business may be done" (337–38). Inside, these efforts must be stilled: "Let vain or busie thought have no part" (421). This line carefully includes both worldly elements it has previously legitimized as socially beneficial and those it has censored as "vain" whether in church or out: "Keep all thy native good, and naturalize / All forrain of that name, but scorn their ill: Embrace their activeness, not vanities" (361-63). This distinction between acceptable and unacceptable forms of the active, worldly life disappears within the church, where all secular endeavor and calculation are transgressive: "Christ purg'd his temple; so must thou thy heart" (423). To enter the church building described in "The Church-porch" is like entering the inner sanctum of *The Temple* itself: "Avoid, Profaneness; come not here: / Nothing but holy, pure, and cleare" (25).

Richard Strier has criticized "The Church-porch" for its "unpleasantly egoistic and calculating opportunism" and for its continual appeal to self-interest.[22] I am arguing that Herbert did eventually become uneasy about the forms of opportunistic, crafted gentility authorized by "The Church-porch." But it is important to recognize to what an extent such self-interest and craft were required for a younger son of the gentry. "The Church-porch" may start with the estate provided to the landowner's heir, but the primary subject is the work of the verbally skilled gentleman without land. His stock did not consist in a fund of money or an estate but in the talents and skills he could develop, as well as the good opinion of others who could help him to secure an office. Protecting one's reputation was necessary for the survival of a gentleman dependent on preferment. "The Church-porch" also provides some religious limits for the worldliness it prescribes: "A grain of glorie mixt with humbleness / Cures both a fever and lethargicknesse" (335–36). Both glory and humility seem dangerous as ideals in themselves, since alone they would lead to the extremes either of feverish ambition or, the worst sin for the younger son, doing nothing.[23]

It is the younger son's necessary self-interest and attentiveness to honor that the inner realm of "The Church" casts out as impure. Herbert's interior is very much like that of Thomas Adams, whose sermon *The Temple* was delivered and published in August 1624, three or four months before Herbert was ordained. Like other typological accounts of Solomon's Temple, the sermon maps out a structure in which the heart within is purged of the temptations without: "The Holy place is the sanctified mind, that which S. Paul calls the *Inner Man*. . . . Here is the *Altar* for sacrifice, the contrite heart: the beast to be slain is not found among our heards, but among our affections."[24] Adams refers also to the idols that must be purged from the temple: "There be three maine Idols among us; Vaine pleasure, vaine Honour, and Riches."[25] This list is remarkably similar to the one in Herbert's "Frailtie":

> Lord, in my silence how do I despise
> What upon trust
> Is styled *honour, riches,* or *fair eyes;*
> But is *fair dust!*
>
> (1–4)

The speaker of "Frailtie" despises honour, although the teacher of "The Church-porch" has urged its readers to guard their "stocke of credit": "Slight not the smallest losse, whether it be / In love or honour: . . . / Who say, I care not, those I give for lost; / And to instruct them, will not quit the cost" (343–48). Here is the contradictory division that Shuger has pointed out, between a concern for status in society and a reaction against it in devotion. As the young gentleman takes account of all in his social engagements, he declares "I care not" in his prayers.

Such explicit contrasts have led some critics to assume that "The Church-porch" is an early work and that poems like "Frailtie" represent a later anti-worldliness on Herbert's part.[26] But this approach flattens out the strangeness and historical significance of Herbert's original structure. He was putting into writing and into practice the doctrines of the "dual persons" and of vocation, both of which included contradictory attitudes toward status and hierarchy. In his social calling as a gentleman, he was to insist on "that distinction that God makes between man and man." In his devotional life, he was to know himself in terms of a calling "common to all men as they are Christian."[27] The teaching within vocation that he bind the two callings together required that he remember the sense of Christian community while he preserved his "distinction" from others, but this would be a demanding task. The two attitudes toward status would be experienced as especially contradictory by a younger son, required to build up and establish a gentility that was exposed as fallacious from a devotional perspective. I am arguing that the "character" of holiness was, in part, a solution to this contradiction, since the devotional and social could be unified in a more coordinated way.

In both the original and the revised *Temple*, the opening sequence of "The Church" is a drama in which grace is explicitly opposed to works, not only in the general religious sense of works done to obtain salvation, but in the very particular sense of works done to establish one's social status. The young man of "early hopes" and high "rate and price" finds that his abilities and promise in no way make him a "treasure," but that he is in fact spiritually impoverished.[28] His only real hope for salvation is to turn away from his own craftsmanship, his worldly tendency to shape his deeds and himself into cunning works.

The first poem of the sequence on Good Friday, "The Altar" implicitly contrasts labor expended to establish one's upper-class status and works done to build the temple of God. The poem parodies an anonymous poem in Francis Davison's *Poetical Rhapsody* (1602) and a dedicatory poem by Josuah Sylvester which prefaced his translation of du Bartas's *Divine Weeks and Works* (1605 edition). Both of these poems are built in the shape of an altar, and both use the shape for secular purposes. The anonymous poet "rears" an altar to "Disdain," which has freed him from the "sacrifice" that love requires. Through this allusion, Herbert evokes the love poetry that could usher a writer into an upper-class or courtly circle. The dedication is another crucial ritual for those seeking preferment; Sylvester dedicates his work to King James, and, though he is aware of the religious meaning of the altar, he concludes that he will give unto "Caesar what belongs to Caesar." This gift is described as a "sacrifice" of "my self, my service, witt, and art, / With all the sinnews of a loyall harte."[29]

Herbert's "Altar" protests that Sylvester has given unto Caesar exactly what belongs to God, the heart, and Sylvester consequently constructs a graven image of the king as a false god.[30] High status is to be considered in social performance; in devotion, deference to mistress, aristocrat, or king is idolatry:

> A broken A L T A R, Lord, thy servant reares,
> Made of a heart, and cemented with teares;
>    Whose parts are as thy hand did frame;
>    No workmans tool hath touch'd the same.
>       A  H E A R T  alone                                    5
>       Is   such   a   stone,
>       As    nothing   but
>       Thy pow'r doth cut.
>       Wherefore each part
>       Of  my  hard  heart                                    10
>       Meets in this frame,
>       To praise thy Name.
>    That, if I chance to hold my peace,
>    These stones to praise thee may not cease.
> O let thy blessed S A C R I F I C E be mine,                15
> And  sanctifie  this  A L T A R  to  be  thine.

The altar of the heart is the spiritual, inward counterpart to the physical altar built with unhewn stones by the Israelites or the altar in Solomon's Temple. This contrast between the internal and external also underlies the distinction in *The Temple* between the inward and outward man. Sylvester's dedication is misguided because he promises to sacrifice himself utterly to earthly authority. As Luther says of the spiritual realm, "no one has power over the soul except God."[31] Loyalty to one's social superiors is acceptable in worldly affairs, but not in the sinews of the heart or the spiritual realm, where all are equal under the rule of Christ.

Although "no workmans tool" has touched the heart, the poem is like a stone hewn and intricately engraved through the techniques of the pattern poem. The spectacle of poetic labor is paradoxical, given the reference to the unhewn stones by "Jordan," and some critics have dismissed the poem as an act of self-display that is corrected by the following poems in the sequence.[32] But the aesthetics of the poem are based on the allusions to "the cunning workman" in the Bible. The instrument used to cut or engrave is polluting when there is a danger of idolatry. Nevertheless, the temple of God requires craftsmanship, and the speaker of the poem uses his skill to announce God's power: "That, if I chance to hold my peace, / These stones to praise thee may not cease" (13–14). The poet carves out the stones of the poem as God cuts the heart: "A H E A R T alone / Is such a stone, / As nothing but / Thy pow'r doth cut" (5–8). Only a heart is hard enough to resist all human efforts and to yield to grace alone; other stones, like physical rocks and language, can be shaped by the power of the human hand. Herbert coordinates grace and works by cutting the lines of his poem from four feet (3–4) to two feet (5–12). This creates the pattern of the visible image as a sign of God's effect on the heart. Although God's hand "did frame" (3) the parts of the heart, the poet creates "this frame" (11), the poem. The pattern poem is an authorized work of artfulness like the building of Solomon's Temple: "And I have filled him with the spirit of God . . . to devise cunning works."[33]

Herbert's choice of Sylvester and Davison as the subjects for his sacred parody has autobiographical resonance. Francis Davison dedicates his *Poetic Rhapsody* to Herbert's patron, William Herbert, Earl of Pembroke, and Sylvester includes a dedicatory poem to William Herbert as well.[34] Also relevant is the dedication to Pembroke by his chaplain William Dickinson in 1619, "All my offerings . . . by a deep obligation do owe themselves to your altar, where long since I have made a dedication of myself."[35] Herbert chooses not to dedicate his works to the head of his extended family, the leader of the faction in which he had been engaged, or to the central member of the family group exchanging lyric poetry. His refusal to worship his patron as a god is linked with his refusal to worship a mistress as a goddess, since it was the love poems of Pembroke and his circle that Herbert had been "answering" from the age of seventeen. The final couplet of "The Altar" uses the rhyme of "mine" and "thine" to evoke the intimate relationship between God and man in the Protestant religion and to reinvent as sacred the mutual love celebrated in the Herbert family circle, like the following passage by William Herbert: "For I ame soe wholy thine / As in least sort to bee mine."[36]

The antagonism to patronage in "The Altar," and the emphasis on the inner man in "The Church," do not prove that the poems in *The Temple* were private or withheld from presentation to Herbert's family, including Pembroke's circle. The issue in "The Altar" is not privacy but loyalty. It is quite likely that Herbert imagined Pembroke as a reader of "The Altar," which both displays Herbert's skill and asserts his primary dedication to God. As I argued above, the grace which is the subject of that poem does not rule out the use of the "cunning works" of literary technique. The poems are not transcriptions of Herbert's actual prayers to God. Rather, the artfulness of the poems acknowledges a public, outward dimension to the inward communion they represent. Therefore, the spiritual devotion registered in "The Altar" does not exclude an engagement in the social rituals of the poetic coteries. It does suggest that Herbert believed from the outset of his public life that his first loyalty was to God rather than to any patron.

It would also be inaccurate to assume that by the time Herbert wrote "The Church" he had renounced the craft of controlling one's social image taught by "The Church-porch." A group of Latin poems called *Lucus* were written around the time of Herbert's ordination, and these include both poems on the altar of the heart (especially "Reasonable sacrifice") and poems on ethical problems dealt with in "The Church-porch."[37] Verses on "Avarice," "On the proud man," "On the glutton" suggest that the altar of the inner man had to be coordinated with proper conduct in the world. The poem "On vainglory" shows that devotion and proper conduct did not exclude a concern for reputation:

> Don't let your fame be loose, don't suck it in too much;
> Be moderate in what you do. If glory
> Leads the column, rein it in; if it
> Lags behind, let it loose
>    . . .

(15–18)

This poem repeats the teaching in "The Church-porch" on glory and humility, which "cures both a fever and lethargickness" (336). Apparently, altars of the heart and secular fame went together, at least around 1624. Whether "The Church" was initiated before Herbert was ordained or after, it was meant to preserve a religious spirit in the midst of public activity:

> Who with a greedy spirit sucks
> Idle rumor, and after huffing glories chases,
> Puts the essential joy beyond his reach,
> And dissipates it among as many heads
> As there are in the common crowd.
> Pull yourself together, shift for yourself,
> And bind with a tighter knot
> The loads of life, till you are self-contained.
>
> ("On vainglory," 1–8)

The original *Temple* pulls together devotion and achievement and provides the "tighter knot" (7) that contains the self and binds together the general and particular callings of a Christian.

Several critics have demonstrated that "The Thanksgiving," in the opening sequence of "The Church," confronts the speaker with the Protestant doctrine of salvation by grace alone, not by works.[38] But it has not been noticed that the works at issue are in part those listed in "The Church-porch" as fundamental to the vocation of a gentleman. The speaker's meditation on the crucifixion in "The Sacrifice" has left him confused and disturbed about his proper response to it. He decides to worship Christ through the offering of a beautifully crafted human life. As in "The Altar," the speaker affirms that he will dedicate himself to Christ rather than any human monarch.[39] But he cannot give up the "workmans tool," the skills used to craft his poetry and himself:

> Oh King of grief! (a title strange, yet true,
>     To thee of all kings onely due)
> Oh King of wounds! how shall I grieve for thee,
>     Who in all grief preventest me?
> Shall I weep blood? why, thou hast wept such store
>     That all thy body was one doore.

> Shall I be scourged, flouted, boxed, sold?
>     'Tis but to tell the tale is told.
> *My God, my God, why dost thou part from me?*
>     Was such a grief as cannot be.
> Shall I then sing, skipping thy dolefull storie,
>     And side with thy triumphant glorie?
> Shall thy strokes be my stroking? thorns, my flower?
>     Thy rod, my posie? crosse, my bower?
> But how then shall I imitate thee, and
>     Copie thy fair, though bloody hand?
>
>                     (1–16)

The speaker's desire to imitate Christ is not superficial. The phrase "bloody hand" (16) acknowledges the lived suffering of Christ and suggests that words are not enough. Lines 11–14 contrast the power of the Crucifixion with the inefficacy of literary works: "Thy rod, my posie?" Yet the reference to imitating Christ also casts devotion as analogous to a form of literary labor: "But how then shall I imitate thee, and / Copie thy fair, though bloody hand? (15–16). Here, writing and living become analogous, and the speaker imagines his own imitation in literary terms, that is, as requiring the craft and competitive test of skill involved in answering a well-known poem. Just as members of the Herbert circle answered the poems of established authors like Sidney and Marlowe, so the speaker answers Christ with the works of a gentleman listed in "The Churchporch," through his dedication of riches, honor, and sexuality to religious purposes:

> Surely I will revenge me on thy love,
>     And trie who shall victorious prove.
> If thou dost give me wealth; I will restore
>     All back unto thee by the poore.
> If thou dost give me honour, men shall see,
>     The honour doth belong to thee.
> I will not marry; or, if she be mine,
>     She and her children shall be thine.
> My bosome friend, if he blaspheme thy Name,
>     I will tear thence his love and fame.
>
>                     (17–26)

Wealth, honour, sexuality: these are the idols of the heart that must be cast out, according to Thomas Adams's sermon *The Temple*. Herbert's poem "Frailtie" identifies *"honour, riches,* or *fair eyes"* (3) as particular temptations, and these along with friendship are central topics for ethical instruction in "The Church-porch." It is interesting that the words "mine" and "thine" emerge again as referring to spiritualized affection: "I will not marry; or, if she be mine, / She and her children shall be thine" (23–24). In "The Thanksgiving," Herbert dramatizes the young gentleman of "The Church-porch," performing as he would in the schools, in an upper-class family, or in seventeenth-century society. But the poem suggests that the young man is brandishing these aspects of gentility to avoid confronting the terrible mystery of the Crucifixion and its provision of the grace necessary for salvation according to Reformation Protestantism. To dedicate these aspects of gentility to Christ may seem to cast them out of the heart, but a new false god is established in their place:

> Or what if we doe not set up Idols in these Temples . . . while we make gods of ourselves: while we dresse altars and erect shrines to our owne braines, and kisse our own hands for the good they have done us? If we attribute something to our selves, how is *Christ al in all* with us?[40]

Herbert's poem acts to level the pretensions of the young man, his belief that his dedication of wealth, honor, and sexuality to religious purposes determines his merit, since they mean nothing to God.

"The Thanksgiving" is an effort to cast out the tools and works of gentility that pollute the soul, or the temple of God, partly because they create a false sense of superiority and partly because they are humanly derived and therefore suspicious. The verbal dexterity taught in the schools and encouraged in "The Church-porch" is practiced here as the young man lists his promised gifts, but the poem exposes the utter inability of that skill to contribute to salvation: "As for thy passion—But of that anon, / When with the other I done" (29–30). To cover the subject mentally and verbally is the young man's goal, but the agony of Christ is not understood through a competitive verbal display. Hesitation and awkwardness, rather than eloquence, are required: "Then for thy passion—I will do that— / Alas, my God, I know not what" (49–50).

The poem specifically considers the version of verbal dexterity that we know as sacred parody, and that Herbert had developed since 1609 in his family circle:

> My musicke shall finde thee, and ev'ry string
>     Shall have his attribute to sing;
> That all together may accord in thee,
>     And prove one God, one harmonie.
> If thou shalt give me wit, it shall appeare,
>     If thou hast giv'n it me, 'tis here.
> Nay, I will read thy book, and never move
>     Till I have found therein thy love;
> Thy art of love, which I'le turn back on thee,
>     O my deare Saviour, Victorie!
>
> (39–48)

The passage focuses on literary invention as the finding out of topics or arguments. The writer of *The Temple* takes on the New Testament as his literary model: "My musicke shall finde thee . . . / I will read thy book, and never move / Till I have found therein thy love" (39, 45–46). What he discovers there becomes ammunition in this literary contest with Christ, and it appears as wit: "Thy art of love, which I'le turn back on thee" (47). The phrase "thy art of love" reinvents the New Testament into an answer, a sacred parody of Ovid's text. The wit of the young man so developed in "The Church-porch" becomes synonymous with the wit of George Herbert who could so easily "turn" a phrase from secular to sacred purposes. The love of Christ is recast as a technique, an art that can be learned and imitated like a verbal practice. The young man makes his own work, *The Temple*, an answer to the New Testament: "If thou shalt give me wit, it shall appeare, / If thou hast giv'n it me, 'tis here. / Nay, I will read thy book . . . / . . . which I'le turn back on thee, / O my deare Saviour, Victorie!" (43–45, 47–48).

The self-irony here is indirect but strong. The fallacy of works-righteousness is evoked through the speaker's attempt to use the practice of literary invention and poetic answering to capture in his own writing something comparable to the religious meaning of the life and death of Christ. The imitation of Christ as a model for behavior and writing is exposed as absurd.[41]

"The Thanksgiving" revises a Latin poem probably written in 1618 in which the autobiographical implications are much more explicit. "On the concurrence of a birthday and Good Friday" considers the fact that Herbert's birthday and Good Friday were regularly quite close together and sometimes on the same day:

> Christ, when you die, I am born.
> One little hour fixed
> My intellect to limbs, you to the Cross.
> O me, born with a fate
> So unlike God's! Christ, why give me
> The life which you deny yourself?
> Surely I will die with you: take up the life
> That you yourself pay no attention to—
> Unless the kind you give is
> The kind you had.
> If you bequeath it, Christ, to me
> By your doleful death, that death to me
> Will turn to double life:
> When I sanctified through you
> On my very day of birth, Good Friday then,
> Just as old as I, will flow
> Into every fibre of my being.[42]

The dating of the poem suggests that Herbert's dedication to Christ occurred rather early in his secular career when he was just taking on his prestigious positions at Cambridge. This evidence would undermine any account of a simple turn from worldliness to godliness. The poem is similar to "The Thanksgiving" in its desire to imitate Christ and in its hesitant recognition that the speaker is naive about what such a life would include: "Unless the kind you give is / The kind you had" (9–10). It reveals that the opening sequence of "The Church" dramatizes not only the Crucifixion of Christ and the entrance into the church of an individual member, but also the day in the church calendar when Herbert's natural birth and the possibility of his spiritual rebirth seemed to coincide.[43] "On my very day of birth" (16) refers to both the natural man and the new man reborn through the sanctification of Christ. The opening sequence of "The Church" also juxtaposes Herbert as young gentleman born into a prestigious family ("born with a fate / So unlike God's!" [4–5]) and the potential emergence of the new man when the grace of the Crucifixion will "flow / Into every fibre of my being" (16–17). But in *The Temple*, the young man knows himself not so much in terms of his high birth as in his upper-class works. The opening sequence of "The Church" replaces an achieved gentility with an ascribed sanctification through grace alone.

This relationship between grace and works, an unpolluted ascribed internality and a constructed upper-class persona, was significantly obscured by Herbert's revisions.[44] The earlier *W* manuscript refers much more explicitly to the spiritual rebirth of the speaker:

> Yet though my flours be lost, they say
> A hart can never come too late.
> Teach it to sing thy praise, this day,
> And then this day, my life shall date.
> ("Easter," 9–12 in *W*)[45]

These lines restate Herbert's Latin poem "On the concurrence of a birthday and Good Friday": "When I am sanctified through you / On my very day of birth, Good Friday then, / Just as old as I, will flow / Into every fibre of my being" (14–17). The *W* manuscript identifies Easter rather than Good Friday as the day of the spiritual rebirth; nevertheless, it calls attention to the contrast between one's human birth and the sanctified self, a contrast that may have occurred to Herbert on each of his birthdays. The poem in the later *B* version is greatly revised and the ending much less personal:

> Can there be any day but this,
> Though many sunnes to shine endeavour?
> We count three hundred, but we misse:
> There is but one, and that one ever.
>
>             ("Easter," 27–30 in *B*)

In *B*, Christ's exclusive position as the Son of God eclipses the individual rebirth of the speaker, and the emphasis on the day of the Resurrection obscures any human birthday.[46]

The final version of *The Temple* not only elides the emergence of the spiritual "new man" but also the construction of the social "new man." "The Church-porch" appears without this stanza:

> If thou art nothing, think what thou wouldst bee
> Hee that desires is more then halfe ye way.
> But if thou coole, then take some shame to thee
> Desire and shame, will make thy labour, play:
>     This is Earth's language, for if Heaven come in,
>     Thou hast run all thy race, ere thou beginn.
>
>             ("The Church-porch," stanza 16 in *W*)

Here is the energy of the "cunning workman" building his social identity from "nothing" through his desire and skill. This energy is joined with the anti-worldliness of "The Church," in which labour is not grace, the activities of earth only a prelude to heaven. This stanza represents the coordination of the particular calling of the gentleman and the general calling of the Christian that was the *W* manuscript. It also voices the uneasiness of this attempted coordination; notice how Heaven suddenly overshadows the talk of labour and ambition, dismissed here as "Earth's language."

Whereas the *W* manuscript looks forward to the success of the speaker's works, the *B* manuscript edits out several references to the expectation that his social position will improve through the acquisition of wealth and a higher status. "Employment" (II) originally implied that grace would result in ascent: "Then would I mount up instantly / And by degrees / On men dropp blessings as I fly" (23–25). "Employment" (I) included these last lines: "Lord that I may the Sunns perfection gaine / Give me his speed" (23–24). Herbert wrote a poem originally named "Perfection," now known as "The Elixir," which represented as well a personal ascent that wavered between the sacred and the spiritual:

> All may of thee partake:
> Nothing can be so low
> Which with his tincture (for thy sake)
> Will not to Heaven grow.
>
> (13–16)

In the *B* manuscript, the images of upward mobility in the "Employment" poems and "Perfection" are replaced with much more humble requests. The ideal in "The Elixir" shifts from "Perfection" to purity:

> All may of thee partake:
> Nothing can be so mean,
> Which with his tincture (for thy sake)
> Will not grow bright and clean.
>
> (13–16)

The poem relinquishes perfection and high status for an ideal of purity that includes the cleansing of the original desire to succeed voiced so explicitly in the *W* manuscript.

The poem "Submission" in the *B* manuscript acknowledges obliquely the crucial changes made to the original *Temple*:

> Were it not better to bestow
> Some place and power on me?
> Then should thy praises with me grow,
> And share in my degree.
>
> But when I thus dispute and grieve,
> I do resume my sight,
> And pilfring what I once did give,
> Disseize thee of thy right.
>
> How know I, if thou shouldst me raise,
> That I should then raise thee?
> Perhaps great places and thy praise
> Do not so well agree.
>
> ("Submission," not in *W*, 5–16)

This poem summarizes the original model of the self represented in the excluded *W* verses: mobile in rank, accumulating in value and substance through the acquisition of money and honor. The poem acknowledges obliquely that Herbert spoke for himself in the verse revised out of "The Church-porch": "If thou art nothing, think what thou wouldst bee." The original *Temple* imagines what Herbert might be through his use of the strategies of self-fashioning, and voices his desire to "mount up" socially. The revisions, which exclude references to the social and the spiritual "new man," suggest that, for Herbert, the original *Temple* began to appear not as an improvement of his Master's talents for the good of the commonwealth, but rather a desire for acquisition for its own sake.

# Four

## The Temple Revised: "Selfnesse" and Pollution

*Elder* [brother]: Have you gone all this while to school, and don't know what a gentleman is?

*Younger* [brother]: I am mighty willing to learn, especially of my elder brother.

*Elder*: Why then your elder brother may teach you. I take him to be a gentleman that has the blood of a gentleman in his veins. Nothing can be a gentleman but the son of a gentleman.

*Younger*: And virtue, parts, sence, breeding, or religion, have no share in it.

*Elder*: Not at all. They may constitute a good man, if you will, but not a gentleman. He may be the D . . . if he will, he is still a gentleman.

*Younger*: Well then let me be the good man, and you shall be the gentleman. But I tell you, Sir Thomas has a thousand good things in him, and above all I take him to be that good man too; for he is a very religious gentleman.

*Elder*: Very good then; he would have made a good parson, it may be, or a bishop; but what's that to a gentleman?

Here the minister put in, tho' modestly too: "Sir," says he, "I hope you will allow a clergy-man may be a gentleman."

*Elder*: What do I touch your cloth too, Doctor? I don't allow it I assure you. A parson a gentleman? No, I assure you I allow no tradesmen to be gentlemen.

> Then the chaplain spoke: "That's too hard, Sir," sayes he, "upon our cloth. I hope you don't call us tradesmen neither."
> *Elder brother*: Not tradesmen? why, what are you? Is it not your business to work for your bread and is not that your trade? Is not the pulpit your shop, and is not this your apron, Mr Book Beater?—

This passage from *The Compleat English Gentleman* by Daniel Defoe is part of the writer's plan to redefine gentility as a matter of merit rather than birth. The uneducated elder brother voices a benighted class contempt for those who work for a living, a contempt that the younger brother sees through automatically, given his dependence on labor and achievement. Defoe's younger brother so appealingly mirrors Herbert that it is tempting to place *The Temple* within a process of social change by which gentility was transformed into a set of achievable qualities, that is, "vertue, parts, sence, breeding, or religion." Yet if this is so, then it is also true that Herbert can be seen in the class-anxiety of the minister and the chaplain who react against the elder brother's peremptory exclusion of them from the ruling elite. The upper classes often grouped the lower clergy with commoners, and, for the minister and the chaplain in this passage, if not for Defoe, to be associated with tradesmen is an assault on their honor. Notice that, for the elder brother, since the parson is not a gentleman, he is a tradesman.[1]

I have argued that in 1627 Herbert gave up the pursuit of high office, both secular and ecclesiastical, because the grant given by Charles I to George and Edward Herbert following their mother's death in that year included no position of employment.[2] Donne had predicted in 1615 that Herbert would receive royal patronage.[3] By 1627, it would have been clear that the Catholic-leaning Stuart king and his favorite, Buckingham, were unwilling to offer George the rewards of preferment, especially given his participation in the Protestant Herbert faction. I will argue in this chapter that the revisions to *The Temple* began soon after this date, that they veil the original structure of identity that authorized social mobility through its performative gentility "without" and its poverty of spirit "within," and that the revised *Temple* tries to purify itself of a "selfnesse" associated perjoratively both with high status and profit-seeking. Purity had always been a goal of "The Church" in its use of Jordan imagery and in its antipathy to the polluting possibilities of human craft in "The Altar." Nevertheless, purity gains a new urgency in the revisions and the added poems, as the text attempts to wash its author clean of the desire for promotion voiced in the original *Temple*.

The self that the revised *Temple* tries to purge has social as well as religious meaning. It is significant that the threat to spirituality was always the "workmans tool." This Biblical phrase is used by Herbert in "The Altar" to refer explicitly to salvation by works rather than grace. But the phrase also evokes the threat of association with manual labor, a taint that, according to tradition, was anathema to the upper classes. Herbert openly attacks this sense of taint in "The Church-porch," but I believe that he felt it himself nevertheless, especially when the lack of preferment opened him up so much more fully to the loss of gentry status through downward mobility.[4] In *Purity and Danger*, Mary Douglas informs us that a sense of pollution is often the result when categories of mental or social order are transgressed. Herbert tried to cleanse himself from a kind of labor that he associated with the commercial and laboring classes, but which he actually used in his pursuit of upper-class status. As many critics have shown, the gentleman without an estate is himself a mixture of status positions: an upper-class style of life as well as the labor needed to secure patronage and employment.[5]

Herbert's place within the system of status was always anomalous; he was neither established gentleman nor tradesman. Mary Douglas comments on this issue: "There are several ways of treating anomalies. Negatively we can ignore, just not perceive them, or perceiving we can condemn. Positively we can deliberately confront the anomaly and try to create a new pattern of reality in which it has a place."[6] To some extent, the revised *Temple* condemns that very part of Herbert existing between the gentleman and the tradesman, the part that fashioned gentility as a commodity. As Herbert put it in an early letter to his brother, "Be proud . . .

by setting a just price of your qualities" (366). This chapter will detail the plan of the revised *Temple* to reject this polluting "selfnesse." But, in fact, both versions of *The Temple* provided "a new pattern of reality" in which Herbert had a place, despite the confusion of the status system. Therefore, a resolution of the contradictory dual class position inhabited by Herbert is a systematic purpose of "The Church" from the outset; purification from the taint of this mixture simply becomes more pressing with the revisions.

It would be a mistake to see either version of *The Temple* as an attempt to recover the permanent gentility denied to Herbert because of the birth order and his standing as younger son.[7] The fear of pollution voiced throughout *The Temple* is an anxiety about "works," but the solution was not the reassertion of the status system. *The Temple* creates something new in its interpretation of gentility as fictional and in its use of vocation, including the juxtaposition of the particular and general callings. The holiness within is not a religious alternative to pure gentry blood; it provides religious grounds for Herbert's insight that gentility was a matter of performance, not blood.

Although the revised *Temple* battles a disturbing "selfnesse," the solution is not a loss of self. This view, widely held by Herbert critics in a variety of ways, is actually quite similar to the claim that Herbert recovers his untainted gentry status through *The Temple*. Both take as self what is really an aspect of ideology: the dominant belief that high quality is innate to gentry and nobility versus the emerging ideology of achievement or merit. Herbert's experience on the margins of gentility brought him in contact with both aspects. It is this kind of combination that generated the need for purity in "The Church."[8]

The new version of the self in the later *B* manuscript is the "character" of holiness—a coordination between the holiness within and its expression without, a model of transparency that contends with the original set of differences between inside and out that first structured *The Temple*. In his revisions and in *The Country Parson*, Herbert follows the lead of those Protestant divines preaching on vocation who actively argued against dividing the two callings. The solution was to ensure that "whatsoever thou art, remember thou art a Christian."[9] The original *Temple* attempted to link together courtiership and holiness, and to provide a pathway from gentility to the Church. But the revisions to *The Temple* suggest that Herbert came to feel that his original structure of inward purity and outward social ascension was just as polluted by "selfnesse" as a fully secular version of courtiership. The revisions and *The Country Parson* try to tie the two callings so closely together that the holiness within appears explicitly without. The later *B* manuscript, the lyric sequence that we now read as "The Church," should be considered in association with *The Country Parson*, since that work also tries to cleanse itself from a "witty, or learned, or eloquent" self intent on promotion, and to replace it with an inner purity of mind "breaking out" into social appearances.[10]

It is significant that, although "The Church-porch" never urges its reader to take up Herbert's own vocation as minister, he nevertheless retains the poem as part of *The Temple*. Perhaps the opening poem became not so much self-instruction or autobiography for Herbert, but rather an introductory moral lesson for other upper-class readers. But we might speculate that, despite the insistence on the vocation of a minister in his handbook, the gentility in "The Church-porch" and the character of holiness in *The Country Parson* represented alternate social roles adopted by Herbert at different times during the years after 1627. If so, then the conflict between these two models of performance would be even more powerfully felt during the later years.

## I. "AFFLICTION" (I) AND THE DATING OF THE REVISIONS

A probable dating of the revisions to the *W* manuscript can be suggested through the poem "Affliction" (I), which is part of the earlier *W* group. It includes wording and images also used in Latin verses written by Herbert after the death of his mother in 1627. The language of the English poem is more impersonal than the Latin verses; this suggests that the English poem generalized upon a situation that had occurred in the past. If "Affliction" (I) followed *Memoriae Matris Sacrum*, then the revisions to the *W* manuscript and the new poems in the *B* manuscript were added during or after 1627.[11]

The Latin verses refer specifically to the death of Magdalene Herbert through the vivid image of the storm that the son now confronts without the protection of his mother:

> Dum librata suis haeret radicibus ilex
>> Nescia vulturnis cedere, firma manet.
> Post ubi crudelem sentit diuisa securem,
>> Quò placet oblato, mortua fertur, hero:
> Arbor & ipse inuersa vocer: dúmque insitus almae
>> Assideo Matri, robore vinco cedros.
> Nunc sorti pateo, expositus sine matre procellis,
>> Lubricus, & superans mobilitate salum.
> Tu radix, tu petra mihi firmissima, Mater
>>> . . .

> [The well-poised oak remains strong and fixed,
> Unbinding nothing to the wind,
> As long as it holds tight to its root.
> Later when, split, it feels the savage axe,
> That time then its superior has come,
> It is, dead, carted off.
> I would be known for tree cut down,
> Though, when grafted to my mother's richness
> I cleave to her, I am more vigorous than cedars.
> Now bare to chance, without a mother,
> To storms defenseless, mercurial,
> More fluid than the open sea, am I.
> Root and staunchest rock you are to me, my mother
>> . . . ][12]

Herbert works with the simile of the oak tree in the fourth book of the *Aeneid,* but reinvents Aeneas's resilience in the face of Dido's storm into a form of masculinity that dissolves at the loss of its "mother root," as Herbert puts it in "The Flower."[13] This root had provided a foundation for the son, but also a protective set of boundaries: "Nunc sorti pateo, expositus sine matre procellis" [Now I lie open to chance; without a mother, I am exposed to storms].[14]

The stanza from "Affliction" (I) refers only to unidentified "friends" who have died. It uses the same image of the storm, but its more distanced language suggests that the death of the mother has been developed into a general sense of loss:

> When I got health, thou took'st away my life,
>     And more; for my friends die:
> My mirth and edge was lost; a blunted knife
>     Was of more use then I.
> Thus thinne and lean without a fence or friend,
> I was blown through with ev'ry storm and winde.
>
>                        (31–36)

Both Magdalene Herbert's son in *Memoriae Matris Sacrum* and the speaker in "Affliction" (I) define themselves as "to storms defenseless," but the English poem broadens the cause: "for my friends die" (32). Both verses define the self as impotent and vulnerable without its protective source: "I would be known for tree cut down, / Though when grafted to my mother's richness / I cleave to her, I am more vigorous than cedars"; "My mirth and edge was lost; a blunted knife / Was of more use than I" (33–34). In both poems, "friends" provide the support and strength necessary for the speaker's performative ability. But "Affliction" (I) impersonalizes the situation in order to refer to several sources of grief and, perhaps, to dilute the intense filial emotions confessed in the Latin poem written so soon after Magdalene Herbert's death.

In the later *B* manuscript, "Affliction" (I) is given a new, crucial position in *The Temple*, as if it had come to represent for Herbert the alternate focus of the collection now replacing the original model. In the earlier *W*, "Affliction" (I) is one of several poems that consider the relationship between the speaker's spirituality and his social experience: "Church-monuments," "Frailtie," "Content," "Poetry" (later the "Quiddity), "Affliction" (I), and "Humilitie."[15] In the later manuscript, "Affliction" (I) is lifted out of this sequence, whereas the other poems remain in proximity to each other, and "Affliction" (I) is now placed soon after the opening sequence that moves from Good Friday to Easter. In the later *B* manuscript, after the poems on Easter and baptism, a new sequence begins that re-asserts the fallen nature of the penitent despite baptism. The order of "Nature," "Sinne," "Affliction" (I), "Repentance," and "Faith" clarifies that this member of the Christian church is no saint, and refocuses attention on the need for repeated self-examination.[16]

"Affliction" (I) characterizes the speaker's life in terms suggestive of the original structure of *The Temple*: the fruits of the social "new man" and the spiritual "new man" were at first conjoined and simultaneously satisfying. This balance between heaven and earth is replaced by a period of frustration, a "cross-bias" which forces the speaker to give up his original upper-class expectations:

> When first thou didst entice to thee my heart,
>       I thought the service brave:
> So many joyes I writ down for my part,
>       Besides what I might have
> Out of my stock of naturall delights,
> Augmented with thy gracious benefits.
>
> I looked on thy furniture so fine,
>       And made it fine to me:
> Thy glorious houshold-stuffe did me entwine,
>       And 'tice me unto thee.
> Such starres I counted mine: both heav'n and earth
> Payd me my wages in a world of mirth
>       . . .
>
> Whereas my birth and spirit rather took
>       The way that takes the town;
> Thou didst betray me to a ling'ring book,
>       And wrap me in a gown.
> I was entangled in a world of strife,
> Before I had the power to change my life.
>
>                      (1–12, 37–42)

Just as the original "Church-porch" urged the young man to "think what thou wouldst bee / Hee that desires is more then halfe ye way," so the speaker in "Affliction" (I) expected his pursuit of status and his religious devotion to provide mutual support: "both heav'n and earth / Payd me my wages in a world of mirth" (11–12). Yet this "world of mirth" is replaced by "a world of strife" (41), in which the speaker's "birth and spirit" (37), which "took / The way that takes the town" (37–38), is obstructed in its great expectations. The gentry lifestyle no longer cooperates with spirituality. God requires absolute commitment but provides no rewards: "Thus doth thy power crosse-bias me, not making / Thine own gift good, yet me from my wayes taking" (53–54). Here, the recognition of the inadequacy of gentle birth to meet the demands of spirituality results in a frustrating impasse, since it now appears that God demands the speaker's entire identity, leaving no room for "the way that takes the town" (38). The "gown" (40), religious study or preparation for the ministry, demands the speaker's full concentration, although with no clear employment in sight.

The relationship between "Affliction" (I) and Herbert's biography is illuminated by one of the sources for the poem, Sidney's sonnet #61 in *Astrophil and Stella*. Herbert's imitation of this writer, so powerfully linked to his family's poetic lineage, suggests that again Herbert writes about himself within a consciousness of the family circle. But now, instead of the witty, competitive "sacred parody" of the early sonnets and of "Jordan" (I), he dramatizes a more humbling piety.

In the Sidney poem, Stella teaches Astrophil that he must renounce his erotic desire for her and accept instead her virtuous direction of his heart and his life:

> But this at last is her sweet breath'd defence:
> That who indeed infelt affection beares,
> So captives to his Saint both soule and sence,
> That wholly hers, all selfnesse he forbeares,
> Thence his desires he learnes, his live's course thence.
> Now since her chast mind hates this love in me,
> With chastned mind, I straight must shew that she
> Shall quickly me from what she hates remove.
> O Doctor *Cupid*, thou for me reply,
> Driv'n else to graunt by Angel's sophistrie,
> That I love not, without I leave to love.
>
> (Sidney, 4–14)[17]

Lines 5–8 in this sonnet are difficult but crucial for Herbert's poem. Stella tells Astrophil that her true lover would dedicate to her "both soule and sence," and would therefore lose all power to govern himself or to choose what direction his life will take, since she will dictate to him what his desires should be: ". . . all selfnesse he forbeares, / Thence his desires he learnes his live's course thence."[18] Loving in this poem has a double definition: "true" dedication or self-interested erotic passion: "That I love not, without I leave to love" (Sidney, 14). In "Affliction" (I), the speaker's desire for success may not be erotic, but it is just as passionate and urgent, just as filled with this mysterious element of "selfnesse": "Therefore my sudden soul caught at the place, / And made her youth and fiercenesse seek thy face" (7–8). Like Astrophil, he is being taught to receive not only his "live's course," but his desires themselves from his Master. The speaker struggles between the punitive sense that his affliction is a "purge" (51) for his original hopes and the experiential knowledge of frustration and inadequacy:

> Now I am here, what thou wilt do with me
>     None of my books will show:
> I reade, and sigh, and wish I were a tree;
>     For sure then I should grow
> To fruit or shade: at least some bird would trust
> Her houshold to me, and I should be just.
>
> Yet, though thou troublest me, I must be meek;
>     In weakness must be stout.
> Well, I will change the service, and go seek
>     Some other master out.
> Ah my deare God! though I am clean forgot,
> Let me not love thee, if I love thee not.
>
>                (55–66)

The two types of love in "Affliction" (I) are less clear than those in Sidney's sonnet #61: Herbert's last line could simply mean, If I don't love you, leave me alone.[19] But the allusion to Sidney suggests instead a dilemma about the relationship between desire and devotion, as well as a mystery about the heart, which can include both the purest "infelt affection" (Sidney, 5) and hidden ambitions. The speaker admits at the end of the poem that he does not know what his motives for devotion really are: whether pure affection ("Ah my deare God!" [65]), or a deep desire for self-fulfillment ("Well, I will change the service, and go seek / Some other master out" [63–64]). This affliction is so debilitating because it, like Stella, attacks the speaker's desire for self-control and autonomy—his "selfnesse." The image of the tree appears here, as it does in so many Herbert poems, because it solves the problem of the conflicting demands of this God, who requires "service" but denies his servants that initiative necessary for imaginative and creative achievement. The tree produces "fruit or shade" (59) without calculation or strategy, without the lust for recognition.[20] Interestingly enough, it would also provide the stability lost through the "savage axe"[21] and the overthrown "fence" ("Affliction" [1], line 35). The vigor and keenness that this speaker received from his "friends," and Herbert from his mother, is turned here into an imagined fruitful productivity that would refrain from challenging divine authority. But such a solution is only a dream in this poem, which ends with a destabilizing ambiguity about personal motives.

The poem that precedes "Affliction" (I) in the *B* manuscript was also lifted out of its original position in *W* and placed after the Easter and baptism poems and within the sequence on the continuing need for repentance. "Sinne" (I) emphasizes the instability of the penitent's spirituality and, like "Affliction" (I), directs attention toward the private motives of the heart:

> Lord, with what care hast thou begirt us round!
>   Parents first season us; then schoolmasters
>   Deliver us to laws; they send us bound
> To rules of reason, holy messengers,
> Pulpits and Sundayes, sorrow dogging sinne,      5
>   Afflictions sorted, anguish of all sizes,
>   Fine nets and stratagems to catch us in,
> Bibles laid open, millions of surprises,
> Blessings beforehand, tyes of gratefulnesse,
>   The sound of glorie ringing in our eares:      10

> Without, our shame; within, our consciences;
> Angels and grace, eternall hopes and fears.
> Yet all these fences and their whole aray
> One cunning bosome-sinne blows quite away.

Herbert uses one of Sidney's favorite structures for the sonnet: the first twelve or thirteen lines build an edifice of significance, and a final line or couplet suddenly and thoroughly demolishes it.[22] The discipline of family, school, and church dissolves before the power of internal sin. Through his revisions, Herbert calls attention to the shared image of the "fence" in "Sinne" (I), "Yet all these fences and their whole aray / One cunning bosome-sinne blows quite away" (13–14), and in "Affliction" (I), "Thus thinne and lean without a fence or friend / I was blown through with ev'ry storm or winde" (35–36). But the poems differ on what shatters this defense, an external event like the death of friends or an inner defect defined as "one cunning bosome-sinne" (14). The arranger of *The Temple* considers both the heartfelt complaints of "Affliction" (I) and the possibility that personal sin is responsible for the suffering detailed in that poem. He also adds the word "cunning" to the original ending of "Sinne" (I): "Yet all these fences with one bosome sinn / Are blowne away, as if they nere had bin" (13–14 in *W*). The "cunning bosome-sinne" of the later manuscript brings back into view the "cunning workman" of "The Church-porch" and the Biblical passages on building the church or a false idol. But now this knowledge that wavers between expert skill and crafty artifice is found within, not without, in the motives of the heart. "Sinne" (I) suggests that the "cunning bosome-sinne" of "Affliction" (I) is the fierce "selfnesse" of ambition, a desire for achievement that seems dedicated but is not. Such a desire can disrupt even the most elaborately conceived models of discipline, like the original structure of *The Temple*: "Without, our shame; within, our consciences" ("Sinne" [I], 11).

## II. "JORDAN" (II) AND THE POLLUTING SELF

A revised sequence in *The Temple* also focuses on the "selfnesse" of "Affliction" (I). "Miserie," originally titled "The Publican," ends in both versions with a sudden recognition of the speaker's implication in the sins he is decrying: "My God, I mean myself" (78). But in the revised manuscript, "Miserie" is followed by a poem that gains a new title and a new, crucial line. Originally titled "Invention," "Jordan" (II) includes this revision: "So did I weave myself into the sense" (14). With these changes, Herbert creates an autobiographical story by linking the two Jordan poems, a connection nonexistent in the earlier manuscript.[23] The audience of *The Temple* can now consider a shift from the first poem's cocky disdain for the elaborate fictions of secular love poets to the reformed humility of the second poem, which acknowledges that a religious poet can be just as implicated in self-display as the sonneteers he derides. Sacred parody does not shield one from human craft, and the "Jordan" references warn us that the dangers of that craft are now located in a polluting "self," tainted because constructed as a commodity and marketed for profit.

"Jordan" (II) parodies Sidney in its account of writer's block, but, like "The Posie," it avoids the competitiveness of "Jordan" (I) and the aggression associated with the answer poem. "Jordan" (II) does rebuke the first poem of *Astrophil and Stella* to some extent, not only because religious love replaces secular love, but because "Invention Nature's child" (Sidney, 10) becomes the problem rather than the solution. Nevertheless, it is the religious poet who revels in his own clever devices:

> When first my lines of heav'nly joyes made mention,
> Such was their lustre, they did so excell,
> That I sought out quaint words, and trim invention;
> My thoughts began to burnish, sprout, and swell,
> Curling with metaphors a plain intention,
> Decking the sense, as if it were to sell.
>
> (1–6)

Sidney's solution, to "look in the heart and write" (14) is, for Herbert, to allow one's thoughts to "burnish, sprout, and swell" (4). This birth process engenders not a natural relation between words and matter, but "curling" (5) and "decking" (6). Thoughts and words spontaneously generated "in my brain" (7) curl, bend, or twist a "plain intention" (5) into something indirect, subtle, and crooked. The speaker-poet mistakes the inventive "lustre" (2) of his lines for the radiance of "heav'nly joyes" (1), just as we are encouraged to do in the first two lines of the poem.

The poem suggests that the process of rhetorical invention engages the poet in a whirl of industrious mental effort that is finally disruptive to his project. Like the thousands of notions which "runne" (7) in order to speed the progress of the poet, he is continually blotting and revising in order to discover an invention that is "quick enough" (10). This bustling itself seems to be part of the problem:

> As flames do work and winde, when they ascend,
> So did I weave my self into the sense.
> But while I bustled, I might heare a friend
>
> . . .
>
> (13–15)

The holy whispering of the divine truth becomes audible, not because of, but in spite of, the speaker's excessive efforts. The imagery of the flames is a significant one, not only because they sinuously wind upwards, like "Jordan" (I)'s "winding stair" (3) and therefore provide a model for the ornate aesthetic that the poem rejects; these flames also "work" (13), fervently burning, progressively climbing, actively engaged in enlarging themselves. This intertwining radiance turns into the weaving of a tapestry in which are threaded the strands of self, a voice and talent elegant, refined, and continually developing through the exercise of its own aesthetic powers. Elaborate aesthetics are associated with elaborate self-fashioning, and both are directly linked with too much labor, which the friend attempts to quiet:[24]

> How wide is all this long pretence!
> There is in love a sweetnesse readie penn'd:
> Copie out onely that, and save expense.
> (16–18)

These last lines imitate the last lines of Sidney's poem, directing the speaker to look to the heart rather than the brain. But Herbert alone seems to be emphasizing the release from energetic effort rather than the use of *energia*.[25] The "expense" of spirit (18), which is here mental and ambitious rather than sexual, is nevertheless also a waste of shame, which embarrasses the poet and makes him look a bit foolish.

If we assume that the poem is self-reflexive, that is, that it refers to the imitation of Sidney while performing it, then the poem suggests that imitative poetics, the project of sacred parody, was both an important labor and a religious problem for Herbert. His correction of love poetry in the family debate was too fully implicated in the process of announcing his own verbal power. This announcement included the presentation of a self that was woven into the sense because the trim, burnished, and quick style advertised a polished, "brave" speaker, and because that bravery was artificial, constructed by the poet's labors and his engagement in the process of debate. Whereas the plain style in "Jordan" (I) is a riddling and witty rebuke to the excessive artifice of others, "Jordan" (II) defines this riddling wit as its own form of artifice, since it claims to praise God but actually produces images of the poet.[26]

In the Herbert family, poetry and patronage were closely intertwined. "Jordan" (II) reflects the poet's uneasiness with the necessity of pleasing his primary patron, William Herbert, through the imitation of a poem by his uncle, Sidney. Shakespeare, who may have been writing for the same man, perhaps felt the same pressure:

> O, let me true in love but truly write,
> And then believe me, my love is as fair
> As any mother's child, though not so bright
> As those gold candles fixed in heaven's air:
>   Let them say more that like of hearsay well;
>   I will not praise that purpose not to sell.[27]

Shakespeare bows to Sidney in the formulation of his own plain style but does not follow him in all things: he will not be a "star-lover," an Astrophil, since the "gold candles fixed in heaven's air" are inappropriate metaphors for his lover, who is "as fair / As any mother's child." Shakespeare refers to Sidney's image for invention, "Nature's child," and also insists that no "Stella" modeled on the stars could exemplify the aesthetic ideal of authenticity.[28] If William Herbert is an important reader of the sonnets, then we can speculate that Shakespeare here wittily but significantly resists the force of his client position, which might require flattering his patron's ancestor: "I will not praise that purpose not to sell." For both Shakespeare and George Herbert, employing the plain style is contrasted to the use of elaborate invention to flatter or attract attention: "Curling with metaphors a plain intention, / Decking the sense as if it were to sell" (5–6). Both the professional playwright composing sonnets and the younger son of a gentry family writing religious lyrics express their anxiety about being associated with the tainted labor of having to earn one's living. For Herbert, "sacred parody" verged on a commercial project, since it was his way of announcing his name and gaining the patronage he needed. The stilling of the poet's labors by the whispering friend urges a kind of religious *sprezzatura*; grace here frees one from religious "works" in the same way that a courtier hides the effort involved in appearing as a gentleman.[29] The poem voices the anxiety of one caught between status categories—neither manual laborer nor established gentleman. A fixed nobility would free one entirely from the need for pleasing others:

> Let others Muses fayn;
> Myne never sought to set to sale her wryting;
> In part her friends, in all her selfe delighting
> She cannot beg applause of vulgar sort,
> Free born and bred, more free for noble sport.
> (John Harington, "Epigram 424")[30]

In "Jordan" (II), the "stigma of print" is used to shame the poet-speaker out of his industrious bustling.

The difficulty of Herbert's status position implicit within "Jordan" (II) is clarified by a comment by George's elder brother Edward, who also identified verbal competition as a commercial project:

111

> I do not approve for older brothers that course of study which
> is ordinary [sic] used in the University, which is, if their par-
> ents perchance intend they shall stay there four or five years
> to employ the said time as if they meant to proceed masters
> of art and doctors of some science; for which purpose, their
> tutors commonly spend much time in teaching them sub-
> tleties of logic, which as it is usually practiced, enables them
> for little more than to be excellent wranglers, which art,
> though it may be tolerable in a mercenary lawyer, I can by no
> means commend in a sober and well-governed gentleman.[31]

Edward Herbert links the determined effort to win a debate with a
crass profit-seeking, acceptable for those who have to earn their
living but nevertheless marking them as "mercenary" and therefore
inherently non-genteel. He also acknowledges that only "older
brothers," expecting the family legacy, have the option to ignore
learning the verbal skills of logic and debate, since the younger
brother may have to depend on them for his income. But Edward
Herbert avoids the awkward questions arising from his comments:
Where is the place of the younger son within the seemingly irrec-
oncilable difference between the mercenary wrangler and sober
gentleman? How can one work industriously to take on a status
that excludes industrious labor?

George Herbert's plain style, like the truth-telling of Sidney and
Shakespeare, is to some extent a means of disavowing or hiding
the fervent efforts to develop a genteel style and the status that
such a style could earn. The "sweetness readie penned" becomes
the unforced, natural result of truth-telling, rather than writing that
gives the appearance of studiously acquired charm—the traditional
definition of the sweet or beautiful style.[32] Therefore, the poem,
like the Courtier, makes "whatever is done or said appear to be
without effort and almost without any thought about it."[33]

Both "Invention" and "Jordan" (II) distinguish themselves from
"the victims of an inflated and unnatural style."[34] But, in the earlier
W manuscript, the poem that follows "Invention" suggests that the
proper writing of poetry can contribute toward a "Perfection" that
hovers between the social and the spiritual:

> Lord teach mee to referr
> All things I doe to thee
> That I not onely may not erre
> But allso pleasing bee
> . . .
>
> All may of thee partake:
> Nothing can be so low
> Which with his tincture (for thy sake)
> Will not to Heaven grow
> . . .
>
> (1–4, 13–15 in *W*)

"Perfection" seems honestly to follow the lead of "Invention" by asserting that God must be put first in all the speaker's actions, including the writing of poetry. But we might speculate about the meaning of the word "pleasing" in line 4: Who is the speaker hoping to please, God or those before whom he performs? I suggest that the revising Herbert began to be concerned about these very matters when he so drastically changed "Perfection" into "The Elixir." He might also have worried about the ambiguities in the growth toward heaven predicted by the poem, especially given the original ending of "Employment" (I): "Lord that I may the Sunns perfection gaine / Give mee his speed" (23–24 in *W*).[35]

The revisions that created "Jordan" (II) and "The Elixir" allow for no such ambiguities. "Invention" is lifted out of its original position preceding "Perfection" and placed within the context of self-reproach: "My God, I mean myself" ("Miserie," 78). "Jordan" (II) turns the cunning literary indirection in "Invention" into the more serious religious problem of self-display, a fictional self forged in the process of coterie poetry, polluting pure expression through competitive imitation. "The Elixir" shifts its ideal from "high perfections" ("Perfection," 21) to that which is "bright and clean" ("Elixir," 16). Both poems aim at a new standard of freedom from pollution.

That pollution is connected in "Jordan" (II) with a self that aims at gentility through its "curling" artifice (5) and yet displays its vulgarity though the profit-motive, "as if it were to sell" (6). Both of

113

these class associations meld together in the image of weaving, which evokes the rich arras and tapestries of upper-class households as well as the manual labor of the craftsman: "So did I weave myself into the sense" (14). When Herbert chose to bring "Invention" into the Jordan complex of poems, he seems to have been intent on identifying the craft of gentility and the pursuit of promotion as a personal flaw from which he wished to be cleansed. But his words also display his anomalous position within the structure of status from the beginning of his career: neither sober gentleman nor mercenary lawyer, neither an established member of the upper classes nor tradesman. The Jordan allusions, as well as the character of holiness, provided a sense of purity in the midst of contradictory status obligations.[36]

### III. HERBERT'S REVISED ANSWER

The later *B* manuscript includes poems that respond specifically to the context of coterie poetry, but from a new perspective. "The Answer," "The Rose," and "The Quip" depend on the ritual of repartee for their effect, but they all refuse to comply with the requirements of that ritual. "The Answer" evokes the milieu of the answer-poem, only to explicitly not deliver the anticipated witblow or competitive proof of mastery:

> My comforts drop and melt away like snow:
> I shake my head, and all the thoughts and ends,
> Which my fierce youth did bandie, fall and flow
> Like leaves about me: or like summer friends,
> Flyes of estates and sunne-shine. But to all,     5
> Who think me eager, hot, and undertaking,
> But in my prosecutions slack and small;
> As a young exhalation, newly waking,
> Scorns his first bed of dirt, and means the sky;
> But cooling by the way, grows pursie and slow,     10
> And setling to a cloud, doth live and die
> In that dark state of tears: to all, that so
>     Show me, and set me, I have one reply,
>     Which they that know the rest, know more then I.

The poem locates a moment in the career of the speaker associated with loss—a loss of purpose, of success, of "fierce youth" (3), of "summer friends" (4). "My fierce youth" (3) recalls the "youth and fierceness" (18) that drives the speaker in "Affliction" (I). Like that poem, the efforts that were at first "eager, hot, and undertaking" (6) become "slack and small" (7). Here again is the "selfnesse" in Herbert's poetry that seems both erotic and ambitious and is finally curtailed by an unsatisfying turn of events or a disciplining God. "The Answer" differs from "Affliction" (I) because "The Answer" includes a powerful sense of audience—a group that wants to measure the outcome of the speaker's life, what it will amount to, what the speaker makes of himself. One wonders if "The Answer" was sung within the Herbert family homes: it seems rather unlikely since, in the poem, the relations between the speaker and his audience are rather strained. If it was not sung in public, then the dialogue of the answer poem nevertheless continued into the privacy of Herbert's study: the poem is modeled on a number of sonnets by Sidney. These poems admit Astrophil's lack of success in the public world and compare that world to his more private, rather debilitating, but finally more significant love for Stella:

> Your words my friend (right healthfull caustiks) blame
> My young mind marde, whom *Love* doth windlas so,
> That mine owne writings like bad servants show
> My wits, quicke in vaine thoughts, in vertue lame:
> That *Plato* I read for nought, but if he tame      5
> Such coltish gyres, that to my birth I owe
> Nobler desires, least else that friendly foe,
> Great expectation, weare a traine of shame.
> For since mad March great promise made of me,
> If now the May of my yeares much decline,      10
> What can be hoped my harvest time will be?
> Sure you say well, your wisdome's golden mine,
> Dig deepe with learning's spade, now tell me this,
> Hath this world ought so faire as *Stella* is?[37]

Astrophil silences his friend with an epigrammatic "answer," a last line that sums up the power of love and overcomes his friend's challenge. Herbert's poem is just as witty but far less satisfying. Conflating the expectations that his acquaintances have about his life with the expectations of friendly competition implicit in the "answer" poem, the speaker does not satisfy either, but declares the speaker's own ignorance about "the rest" (14): the rest of his life, of his poem, and perhaps the everlasting rest of final salvation, which the poem may imply is the only vantage point from which one can truly understand the course of one's life. Astrophil represents his friend's argument in order to "answer" it; Herbert's speaker lists his acquaintance's explanations for his life in order not to. The resonance of the poem is increased by the status of Sidney, who provided the model of achievement for all lyric writers during this period; the poet of "The Answer" imitates Sidney in order to highlight ruefully the unfulfilled "great expectations" associated with doing so. The poem may offer a religious life as an alternative to public success, just as Astrophil refers to the power of love, but in "The Answer," even this possibility is so thoroughly understated that the final impression of the poem remains one of enigma.

"The Rose" provides the most ascetic "answer" of this group of poems:

> Presse me not to take more pleasure
> In this world of sugred lies,
> And to use a larger measure
> Then my strict, yet welcome size
>     . . .
>
> But I will not much oppose
> Unto what you now advise:
> Onely take this gentle rose,
> And therein my answer lies
>     . . .
>
> So this flower doth judge and sentence
> Worldly joyes to be a scourge:
> For they all produce repentance,
> And repentance is a purge
>     . . .
>
> (1–4, 13–16, 25–28)

The speaker presents the rose as a symbol for both beautiful, earthly pleasure and bodily purge in order to "answer" an opponent who is tempting the speaker into an engagement with worldly ritual. The "strict, yet welcome size" (4) refers to temperance in general but perhaps also to a refusal to imagine any increase in one's social rank.[38] In "The Answer," the surrounding audience waits to discover what the speaker can make out of his status; answering seems to be either a process by which one can increase one's status or the act of informing one's social milieu that such an increase has occurred. In "The Answer," the speaker refrains from answering, as if waiting for possible developments in the future. In "The Rose," the speaker makes a clear choice: "But I health, not physic choose . . . / Say that fairly I refuse, / For my answer is a rose" (29, 31–32).

The title of "The Quip" leads us to expect an urbane, courtly wit as a speaker, but the poem provides one who is unable or chooses not to speak at all. He is confronted by a set of temptations quite similar to those listed in "Frailtie" and in "The Thanksgiving." "Beautie," "Money," and "Glorie" restate the triad in "Frailtie"—"*honour, riches, or fair eyes*"(3)—as well as the "three maine Idols among us; Vaine pleasure, vaine Honour, and Riches" of Adams's sermon *The Temple*.[39] Herbert's *Temple*, from the outset, meant to purify these upper-class idols from the heart, but this poem admits that Herbert wasn't entirely successful:

> The merrie world did on a day
> With his train-bands and mates agree
> To meet together, where I lay,
> And all in sport to geere at me
>      . . .
>
> Then came quick Wit and Conversation,
> And he would needs a comfort be,
> And, to be short, make an oration.
> *But thou shalt answer, Lord, for me.*
>        (1–4, 17–20)

In the fifth stanza (lines 17–20), the most autobiographical moment in the poem, the speaker presents a portrait of the artist as a young

man. "The Church-porch" lists the rules for using wit and conversation to best effect: "In thy discourse, if thou desire to please / All
such is courteous, useful, new, or witty" (289–90). "The Church-
porch" promises that, when all is said and done, religion is the
heart of the matter, and yet it also implies that pleasing one's acquaintances is not a bad idea either:

> Be usefull where thou livest, that they may
> Both want and wish thy pleasing presence still.
> Kindnesse, good parts, great places are the way
> To compasse this. Finde out mens wants and will,
>     And meet them there. All worldly joyes go lesse
>     To the one joy of doing kindnesses.
>
> (325–30)

"Doing kindnesses" (330) seems unquestionably charitable, and
yet the first lines of the stanza reveal the self-interest at stake: this
man needs a place to live. "The Quip" unmasks the desire of "Wit
and Conversation" (17) to be "a comfort" (18), as an opportunity
for self-display. This quick wit fails both to be a comfort or to
please; he commits the *faux pas* of talking too much: "And, to be
short, make an oration" (19). This line refers almost directly to Herbert's career as Public Orator at Cambridge. The stanza suggests
that that career was marked by the same mixed motives of "Wit
and Conversation," that is, devotion and ambition.

The last stanza attempts to construct an answer free from the
worldly motives that the speaker tries to avoid through his silence:

> Yet when the houre of thy designe
> To answer these fine things shall come;
> Speak not at large, say, I am thine:
> And then they have their answer home.
>
> (21–24)

The poem attributes to God the voice that the speaker has renounced and imagines a defense that is purely divine. This sacred
quip is both witty and potent. "I am thine" (23) is direct and indirect discourse, a clasping of hands that confers ownership on both
parties, a sign of devotion that restores to the speaker the identity,

stature, and community lost through his separation from his secular role and milieu.[40] One wonders what this "quip" represents exactly: God's conferral of salvation? Is it a series of events that would publish the speaker's favored position with God, like receiving employment? The source for the poem's refrain, Psalm 38 in the Book of Common Prayer, suggests that the audience here includes the speaker's "enemies" and his "kinsmen":

> My lovers and my neighbors did stand looking upon my trouble: and my kinsmen stood afar off. . . . For in thee, O Lord, have I put my trust: thou shalt answer for me, O Lord my God. I have required that they, even mine enemies, should not triumph over me. (Psalms 38:11–16)

The audience of "The Quip" turns out to be not unlike that of "The Answer": both include close and distant acquaintances who judge the speaker's social success. It is therefore significant that "I am thine" (23) reproduces in a new form the pair "mine" and "thine" used in William Herbert's poetry as well as in "The Altar" and other poems by George Herbert.[41] "I am thine" is an answer aimed at the Herbert family coterie but delivered by a God who can overcome all skeptics. It is also directed at certain aspects of a former self, which did not so effectively resist the temptations the poem describes.

### IV. MONEY AND POLLUTION

"The Quip" suggests that attaining the lifestyle of a gentleman was not only a religious problem for Herbert, tempting him with false gods, but also a class dilemma, since it required producing the image of gentility through an energetic effort that was both necessary and corrupting. Upper-class ritual is in fact represented by the poem as mixing the aristocratic and the common: the figure of "Glory" is in "silks" and thrives on the recognition of high status, yet he is part of a group comprised of "the merry world . . . / With his trainbands and mates" (2, 13–14). "Train-bands" refers to the citizen armies of London; "mates" suggests vigorous but lower-class companions.[42] The speaker both lacks and fears the strength to compete, as if failure would mean impotence and success debasement:

> Then Money came, and chinking still,
> What tune is this, poore man? said he:
> I heard in Musick you had skill,
> *But thou shalt answer, Lord, for me.*
>
> (9–12)

The stanza contrasts the vulgar "chinking" (9) of financial cleverness with the refinement of musical talent. The speaker's opponent implies that this "poore man" (10) can become rich only by turning that musical skill to more practical ends. The reference to "Musick" (11) is no doubt autobiographical, since it evokes Herbert's ability on the lute, viol, and as a singer.[43] It may also refer to the performance of his songs and sonnets within his family circle. If so, then the somewhat curious link between money and music becomes quite literal: the speaker is taunted for his failure to acquire lucrative patronage through the use of his lyric powers. When the speaker does not produce the conventional answer, or answer-poem, he opts out of a ritual that is polluting because "worldly," but also because it would turn refined lyricism into a form of "chinking."

The revisions and added poems in the *B* manuscript imply that Herbert reacted against *The Temple*'s original linking of spiritual development with a social success that included financial accumulation. The revisions often change poems that originally suggested that the reception of God's grace would lead to an improvement in the poet's social estate. This issue becomes explicit in the contrast between "Praise" (I) and "Praise" (III). The first "Praise" was included in the earlier Williams manuscript; "Praise" (III) was written later, but both are shaped around the compositional strategy of ending each stanza with the word "more." Both poems aim at an increase in praise for God, but only "Praise" (I) suggests that such praise could result from an increase in the speaker's income:

> To write a verse or two is all the praise,
> That I can raise:
> Mend my estate in any wayes,
> Thou shalt have more
> . . .

> O raise me then! Poore bees, that work all day,
> Sting my delay,
> Who have a work, as well as they,
> And much, much more.[44]
>
> (1–4, 17–20)

Such a "work," which wavers in the poem between devotional praise and an occupation, becomes in "Praise" (III) exclusively religious. The comparative force of the word "more" changes in "Praise" (III), ruling out financial gain:

> Lord, I will mean and speak thy praise,
> Thy praise alone.
> My busie heart shall spin it all my dayes:
> And when it stops for want of store,
> Then will I wring it with a sigh or grone,
> That thou mayst yet have more
>
> . . .
>
> Wherefore I sing. Yet since my heart,
> Though press'd, runnes thin;
> O that I might some other hearts convert,
> And so take up at use good store:
> That to thy chest there might be coming in
> Both all my praise, and more!
>
> (1–6, 37–42)

"More" describes the supply of repentant tears, the grace that makes the tears possible, and the new means by which the speaker imagines himself in terms of others: "O that I might some other hearts convert" (39). The poem consciously presents a version of abundance that has little to do with material fortune. Loss and gain, poverty and good store exclusively measure contrition and gratitude. What is quantified here is not the speaker's "estate," but his willingness to repent.

"Business" echoes "Praise" (III) by using the language of worldly employment and gain for exclusively religious purposes:

> Canst be idle? canst thou play,
> Foolish soul who sinn'd to day?

> Rivers run, and springs each one
> Know their home, and get them gone:
> Hast thou tears, or hast thou none?
>
> . . .
>
> But if yet thou idle be,
> Foolish soul, Who di'd for thee?
>
> . . .
>
> He that loseth gold, though drosse,
> Tells to all he meets, his crosse,
> He that sinnes, hath he no losse?
>
> He that findes a silver vein,
> Thinks on it, and thinks again:
> Brings thy Saviours death no gain?
>
> . . .
>
> (1–5, 15–16, 31–36)

In this later poem, Herbert is much more careful than in "Praise" (I) to draw a distinction between material and spiritual poverty and riches. "Drosse" (31) and "vein" (34), with its pun on "vain," inform the reader that economic well-being is relatively insignificant, at the same time that the poem appropriates the energy and diligence necessary to the success of a commercial endeavor for the purposes of repentance.

Money was the sticking point in the doctrine of vocation because Protestants provided a new sanctification for commerce, but they were also threatened by the worldliness that such commercialism could provoke.[45] Herbert's *Country Parson* includes both justifications for the acquisition of wealth and warnings against the evil that could result from it. In "The Parson Surveys," the chapter most thoroughly devoted to vocation, Herbert comments:

> Every gift or ability is a talent to be accounted for, and to be improved to our Masters Advantage. . . . Riches are the blessing of God, and the great Instrument of doing admirable good; therfore all are to procure them honestly, and seasonably, when they are not better imployed. (274)

The "talent" in this passage, as in the Bible, refers both to abilities and to a kind of coin invested for the good of Christ and the commonwealth. Yet this defense for procuring riches also includes its own limits: "honestly and seasonably" suggests that diligence can too easily become greed. Elsewhere in the manual, the Parson urges his parishioners to find that delicate balance between avarice and idleness so crucial to the Protestant ethic:

> Those that he finds busie in the works of their calling, he commendeth them also: for it is a good and just thing for every one to do their own busines. But then he admonisheth them of two things; first, that they dive not too deep into worldly affairs, plunging themselves over head and eares into carking, and caring; but that they so labour, as neither to labour anxiously, nor distrustfully, nor profanely. . . . *Then they labour profanely, when they set themselves to work like brute beasts, never raising their thoughts to God, nor sanctifying their labour with daily prayer.* (247–48)

Here, labor is both holy and corrupt, a blessing and a temptation. Sacred labor fulfils one's debt to God and country, but work can also be "profane," polluted by worldliness and self-interest. Herbert echoes the warnings of Perkins and other writers on vocation, but the image of the "brute beasts" reveals his class origins: it surprisingly links energetic effort with a lack of civility and follows tradition by suggesting that manual labor and commerce are forms of defilement.[46] Herbert feared the energy needed to acquire money through labor because both were associated with the common classes.

In "Avarice," money is an allegorical figure representing not just the misguided greed of human beings but the very mixture of class positions within courtiership that Herbert found polluting:

> Money, thou bane of blisse, & sourse of wo,
>     Whence com'st thou, that art so fresh and fine?
>     I know thy parentage is base and low:
> Man found thee poore and dirtie in a mine.
> Surely thou didst so little contribute           5
>     To this great kingdome, which thou now hast got,
>     That he was fain, when thou wert destitute,
> To digge thee out of thy dark cave and grot:
> Then forcing thee by fire he made thee bright:

> Nay, thou hast got the face of man; for we         10
> Have with our stamp and seal transferr'd our right:
> Thou art the man, and man but drosse to thee.
> Man calleth thee his wealth, who made thee rich;
> And while he digs out thee, falls in the ditch.

The poem argues that the practice of measuring human beings through money obscures the fact that this system of value is humanly constructed and so neither natural nor divine. Insignificant metals have been made significant through mining and coinage. Yet the poem's standard of quality is itself neither natural nor divine but reproduces the system of status. Bright, valuable coins are like commoners who pose as gentlemen. "Man" commits this crime against propriety by winning for "Money" the status of a courtier without high birth or land. The image of fineness is produced through the use of craft and artifice: "Whence com'st thou, that thou art so fresh and fine?" (2). The true origins of this pretender reveal his baseness; only man's craft could obscure money's vulgar beginnings in a pit. The poem associates mining, digging, and metalwork with forgery. In "Avarice," the poet is not offended solely by the upstart commoner, but also by the greedy aristocrat: "our stamp and seal" (11) refers indirectly to the face of the king on the coin of the realm, and implies that money, rather than justice or wisdom, governs "this great kingdome" (6). The poem dreams of a social and political system untouched by the power of money or the power of man to create counterfeit authority. Here is the "false hair" and "winding stair" of "Jordan" (I), the capacity of spectacle, expense, and language to forge the illusion of excellence. Here is the disturbing mixture of fiction and fineness, which hints that the system of status is human, not divine, and at the same time indicts those who manipulate that system as "base and low" (3) and "poore and dirtie" (4). The poem suggests that there is no way to use the arts of craftsmanship and keep one's hands clean.

For Herbert, pollution was located in work because labor was both his social salvation and his curse. It marked him as outside the ranks of established gentlemen but gave him, first, the means of achieving that rank, and, later, a limited but significant financial independence and a sense of personal value. According to Nicholas Ferrar's preface to *The Temple*, on his deathbed Herbert said, "*It is a good work, if it be sprinkled with the bloud of Christ*" (4). Whether or not this is an accurate account, the answer sums up Herbert's attitude not just toward good works but toward work in general: it was polluted and needed purification. The comment includes a use of the typology of the temple characteristic of Herbert: the grace obtained through the blood-sacrifice of Christ purifies Herbert's labors, just as the blood of the sin-offering purified the Hebrew temple and "the uncleanness of the children of Israel" (*Leviticus* 16:15–16).[47] For Herbert, each work had to be purified by the blood of Christ because it was unclean, a mixture of status positions, a combination of ascribed value and achievement, the "weaving" of an anomalous social status.

# Five

## The Character of Holiness
## in *The Temple*

The character of holiness in the revised *Temple* creates a model of selfhood in which the social role becomes a clear expression of the devotion within. This transparency lights up the darkness made possible by the original contrast between inside spirituality and outside gentility and dispels the possibility of private, hidden motives. Like *The Country Parson*, the revised *Temple* insists on a coordination between being and seeming; the holiness of the general calling must now appear explicitly in the social behavior of the particular calling. In this chapter, I will continue to examine the revisions to *The Temple*, in this case, for evidence of Herbert's developing sense of this holy "character."

One major difference between the two manuscripts is that the revised version subordinates sacred parody to self-examination. For the original *Temple*, sacred parody was at the heart of things, since it represented Herbert's commitment to a purely religious subjective experience and his identification with such devotionalism within his family's coterie. In the first manuscript, "Love" (I) and (II) immediately follow the opening sequence on entering the church. These sonnets announce Herbert's intention to write only sacred love poetry, a purpose linked by both poems with the "true desires" that motivate the sanctified heart ("Love" [II], 4). The *W* manuscript also places poems on sacred parody immediately before the ending sequence, since "Invention" and "Perfection" precede the poetic series on preparation for death. Although "The Thanksgiving" makes clear from the outset that writing sacred parody is not enough for redemption (39–50), nevertheless the earlier manuscript suggests that such poetry could become evidence of the appearance of the new life.

As described in Chapter 3, the first version of "Easter" voices an expectation of the appearance of the "new man" similar to the autobiographical poem "On the concurrence of a birthday and Good Friday" and is linked to Herbert's personal experience of this annual church holiday: "A hart can never come too late. / Teach it to sing thy praise, this day, / And then this day, my life shall date" (9–12 in *W*). This new life would mark the beginning of sanctification, a process in which the speaker would not simply be justified by grace, but able to enact the holiness obtained through it.

The revised manuscript, however, makes sacred parody secondary to the need for contrition. In the later manuscript, "Easter" focuses throughout on Christ, not the new man. The opening sequence is followed by the group of poems on sin and repentance, including "Affliction" (I), discussed in Chapter 4.[1] The announcement of Herbert's commitment to sacred poetry in "Love" (I) and (II) is now placed after this group. The revised cluster of poems on sacred parody at the end of the work, "The Posie," "A Parodie," and "The Elixir," are now followed by "A Wreath," which warns the speaker against his "crooked winding ways" (4), even though it follows "The Elixir," the poem that most surely manifests the new goal of "simplicitie" ("A Wreath," 4, 9). Certainly, it is significant that Herbert's original confession of faith, his dedication to sacred love poetry, is now hedged about by poems emphasizing self-examination.

A poem added to the opening sequence, "The Agonie," reinforces this emphasis. Like the revised "Easter," it meditates throughout on the experience of Christ, not on the inner soul. It alludes to Augustine's *Confessions*, but excludes Augustine's delight at discovering the spiritual self within. Both versions of *The Temple* use Augustine's *Confessions* as a source. But the revised manuscript develops these references in order to emphasize the need for continuing watchfulness over sin and to mute the work's original attention to an emerging sanctified subjectivity. Such attention to the potential for the new man perhaps came to seem like an obstacle veiling the state of the heart, including the "cunning bosome-sinne" ("Sinne [I]," 14). In the revised manuscript, transparency is not a matter of exploring the inner realm, but one of ensuring that the heart is visible enough to be disciplined.

Both manuscripts use Augustine to mark the shift in the opening sequence from the attempted imitation of Christ to the need for confession, a shift announced by "The Reprisall": "Yet by confession will I come / Into thy conquest" (13–14). This emphasis on confession is also present in the earlier manuscript in "The Sinner," which refers to the use of memory in chapter 10 of Augustine's *Confessions*: "Lord, how am I all ague, when I seek / What I have treasur'd in my memorie!" (1–2). In the revised manuscript, however, Herbert consolidates these references to Augustine by placing "The Reprisall," "The Agonie," and "The Sinner" in succession. The naming of the first two poems also calls attention to the difference between the competitive imitation first attempted by the speaker and the full recognition of Christ's passion that such reprisals, both aggressive and lyric, could obscure. The title "Agonie" brings these issues together by evoking and contrasting meanings of struggle, or agon, and suffering.

But unlike *The Confessions* and the original *Temple*, "The Agonie" excludes any wonder at the mystery of the newly visible inner self. What for Augustine is the infinity of the inner landscape becomes in the revised manuscript a stark vision of Christ's suffering:

> Philosophers have measur'd mountains,
> Fathom'd the depths of seas, of states, and kings,
> Walk'd with a staffe to heav'n, and traced fountains:
> But there are two vast, spacious things,
> The which to measure it doth more behove:
> Yet few there are that sound them; Sinne and Love.

> Who would know Sinne, let him repair
> Unto Mount Olivet; there shall he see
> A man so wrung with pains, that all his hair,
>   His skinne, his garments bloudie be.
> Sinne is that presse and vice, which forceth pain
> To hunt his cruell food through ev'ry vein
>   . . .

(1–12)

"The Agonie" alludes to a passage from the exploration of human memory in the tenth chapter of *The Confessions*: "Men go out and gaze in astonishment at high mountains, the huge waves of the sea, the broad reaches of rivers, the ocean that encircles the world, or the stars in their courses. But they pay no attention to themselves."[2] To Augustine's external world of mountains and seas, Herbert adds "states, and kings" (2) in order to refer to his own conversion away from court-promotion. For Augustine, this external world is replaced by an internal world of greater dimension; he refers to "vast cloisters of my memory," and its "vast, immeasurable sanctuary."[3] Augustine celebrates this realm because "in it I meet myself as well."[4] Such a meeting evokes an awe at its measureless significance: "What, then, am I, my God? What is my nature? A life that is ever varying, full of change, and of immense power. The wide plains of my memory and its innumerable caverns and hollows are full beyond compute of countless things of all kinds."[5] This sense of infinite space becomes in "The Agonie" not the "vast, immeasurable sanctuary" of the memory, but the "vast, spacious things, / . . . Sinne and Love" (4, 6). These qualities are metaphysical but not explicitly personal, and they seem less to dwell inside the soul than in a meditative, Biblical landscape filled with the passion of Christ. The "high mountains" in Augustine are internalized as the extensive inner spaces of the soul; for Herbert, the mountains become Mount Olivet appearing in meditative vision.[6] The poem looks in the heart and writes under the aegis of Augustine rather than Sidney, but both forms of poetic introspection seem equally disturbing. The poem confronts the speaker with an image of the Crucifixion as torture and indicts him as the cause and beneficiary of such torture. This is the wrenching vision of the suffering Christ that the speaker of "The Thanksgiving" seems to have avoided, despite his protestations of devotion. This confrontation is terribly painful and yet strangely muted because the figure of Christ blocks out the autobiographical landscape within. If human interiority is represented at all, it is through the very general category of "Sinne," here only represented in its effect on Christ, who is the source of all "Love." The revised *Temple* seems to be far less interested in tracing out and celebrating the development of the new man, as if such celebration were another version of a competition with Christ. The revising Herbert is much less willing to imagine a sanctified self or the possibility of any sort of religious perfection.

A poem in the later manuscript, "Confession," stresses the importance of self-examination for the purposes of cleansing from sin, not self-exploration:

> O what a cunning guest
> Is this same grief! within my heart I made
> Closets; and in them many a chest;
> And, like a master in my trade,
> In those chests, boxes; in each box, a till:
> Yet grief knows all, and enters when he will.
>
> No scrue, no piercer can
> Into a piece of timber work and winde,
> As God's afflictions into man
> . . .
>
> Onely an open breast
> Doth shut them out, so that they cannot enter;
> Or, if they enter, cannot rest,
> But quickly seek some new adventure.
> Smooth open hearts no fastning have; but fiction
> Doth give a hold and handle to affliction
> . . .
>
> (1–9, 19–24)

The word that stands out in this poem is "fiction" (23); it refers to the self-deceit that prevents the acknowledgment of sin, and that results in the visitation of God's griefs or afflictions. But it also means something made, and recalls the closets, chests, boxes, and tills described in the first stanza and fabricated by the speaker. As in the Jordan poems, skill at a craft turns into craftiness.[7] The speaker here does not begin with a recognition that his works are schemes to avoid divine perusal of his heart. The interior carpentry of the speaker, of which he is a master, seems rather an act of self-protectiveness, even privacy, an elaborate effort to defend himself against what seems unambiguously negative—grief and a well-intentioned effort to preserve what is valuable about himself from a harsh outside world. But the sequence of the poem reveals that this grief is a divinely decreed affliction, and the spiritual building going on within the heart is actually a clever attempt to preserve a private fiction, his own belief about his life and its value, carefully stowed away from penetrating, skeptical eyes. This self-protective story, delicately shaped, turns out to be a form of cunning, defeated only by a more cunning God: "They [afflictions] are too subtill for the subt'llest hearts" (11). Both the master craftsman and God's afflictions work and winde imperceptibly and secretly, but the elaborate structures of the cunning workman must fall away when they are revealed to be fictions, made up because made by human hands. The "cunning guest" (1) of affliction is not trespassing on a private area, but bringing the light of truth into a private delusion. Like the original *Temple*, which devised a clever contrast between outside and inside in order to protect what was spiritually valuable about the self, this personal fabrication falls away before careful self-examination and the result is a transparent heart:

> Wherefore my faults and sinnes,
> Lord, I acknowledge; take thy plagues away:
> For since confession pardon winnes,
> I challenge here the brightest day,
> The clearest diamond: let them do their best,
> They shall be thick and cloudie to my breast.
>
> (25–30)

As in *The Country Parson*, the "cunning workman" is replaced by the power of "smooth open hearts" (23). As in "The Elixir," the new ideal in the poem is to be "bright and clean" (16). The contrast between gentility without and holiness within is banished as a device that generated "thick and cloudie" (30) fictions, personal devices inimical to spiritual truth. As in so many poems, fiction is associated with human labor and truth with the razing of that labor. In this poem, as in the original *Temple*, the work demolished is the self-protective, self-deluding difference between inside and outside. Requiring that what is inside flow outside defeats a subjectivity associated with self-fabrication.

The important poetic sequence on the church, including "Church-monuments" and "The Windows," reformulates the *Temple*'s original model of religious subjectivity, from the "true substance" hidden behind upper-class status to a holiness within that must be published without. This autobiographical sequence not only reproduces Herbert's move from young gentleman to rural cleric, it revisits the issue of the temple, fundamental to the lyric work but now expanded to include Herbert's vocation as minister. The sequence moves from meditation in a church ("Church-monuments," "Church-musick") to a fully internalized communion ("Church-lock and key," "Church-floore"), and back into a church ("The Windows"), but in this last poem the minister conducts the service in a temple made with hands, as he radiates out from within himself the temple made without hands. The cunning works of fashioned gentility described by "The Church-porch" are replaced by the character of holiness presented in *The Country Parson*.

In this new version of the intersection between inside and out, the "Jordan" allusions reappear indirectly, as the sequence suggests that both the general and the particular calling must be constructed with the unhewn stones unpolluted by any "workmans tool" ("The Altar," 4). This spiritualized self is intended to purify all that is fictional about subjectivity and social experience, whether the private stories of the inner life, the bombastic displays of the upper-classes, or the profit-seeking schemes of those below them. The series solves the problem of Herbert's anomalous social status by grounding identity in divine making and, unlike *The Country Parson*, by wiping out any trace of human labor, even in the production of social performance. In "Windows," the effort of creating an impression is entirely projected onto the divine "Architect," whose technical expertise alone shapes the minister's expressed character.

"Church-monuments" meditates on the kind of upper-class family memorials placed in European Christian churches, and uses them as *memento mori* to teach that family names and genealogies are just as transitory and frail as the bodies they "point out," whether in life or in tombs.[8] The tombs are another version of genteel fabrication, satirized in "Jordan" (I) and (II), because they give an appearance of substantial value, like "fictions and false hair" ("Jordan" [I], 1), but they actually celebrate nothing but ashes. As "Charms and Knots" puts it, "When th'hair is sweet through pride or lust, / The powder doth forget the dust" (13–14). Like the enjambments of "Church-monuments," which collapse one stanza into the next, the solid, prestigious monuments are imagined as dissolving into a "heap of dust":

> While that my soul repairs to her devotion,
> Here I intombe my flesh, that it betimes
> May take acquaintance of this heap of dust;
> To which the blast of deaths incessant motion,
> Fed with the exhalation of our crimes,
> Drives all at last. Therefore I gladly trust
>
> My bodie to this school, that it may learn
> To spell his elements, and finde his birth
> Written in dustie heraldrie and lines;
> Which dissolution sure doth best discern,
> Comparing dust with dust, and earth with earth.
> These laugh at Jeat and Marble put for signes,
>
> To sever the good fellowship of dust,
> And spoil the meeting
>      . . .
>
> (1–14)

The "heraldrie and lines" (9) engraved in "Jeat and Marble" (12) pretend to commemorate and praise the deceased through the publication of their family pedigree, but this wry, ascetic meditator insists that the only lineage at issue is that which links dust to dust, earth to earth. The body learns its lessons best when it can "discern" (10) the dissolution inevitable to "dustie heraldrie and lines" (9). Or, since "discern" also means separate, the speaker urges the body to recognize that the force of dissolution most effectively breaks those family "lines" that men conceive as tying them to others and to immortality. A family name and the connections with which it resonates, as well as the yearning to build monuments to that name, are ridiculed in line 12 as empty misguided pretensions that can never acquire the eternal life for which they yearn.

The poem blackly puts its description of the eventual dissolution of these monuments into the terms of a "meeting" of family relations:

> These [earth and dust] laugh at Jeat and Marble put for signes,
>
> To sever the good fellowship of dust,
> And spoil the meeting. What shall point out them,
> When they shall bow, and kneel, and fall down flat
> To kisse those heaps, which now they have in trust?
> Deare flesh, while I do pray, learn here thy stemme
> And true descent; that when thou shalt grow fat,
>
> And wanton in thy cravings, thou mayst know,
> That flesh is but the glasse, which holds the dust
> That measures all our time; which also shall
> Be crumbled into dust
>
>        . . .                 (12–22)

When the monuments collapse, they will "bow" (15) and "kneel" (15), and "kisse" (16) in their final "good fellowship of dust" (13), a gruesome parody of the homecoming. Family customs, and the concern for naming one's ancestry, become for the speaker an analogy for the way in which "the flesh" (18) ignores its materiality and inevitable ruin. He teaches the body the foolishness of pride in one's flesh through the foolishness of pride in one's origins, because both flesh and family are subject to the same force of death and dissolution that renders them inconsequential.

In the original *Temple*, this poem stood on its own, reproducing the work's definition of gentility in "The Church-porch," as an external appearance like the jet and marble signs, and finding real substance in the spirituality of "The Church." But the revised manuscript sets up a series of poems that develop and transform the first poem's black satire of genteel pretensions into what it claims is a value system determined entirely by the Church. Each poem considers an aspect of church architecture, as well as the art that constructs it, and responds in different ways to this issue. The underlying concern is always the extent to which this art can express the unhewn and unpolluted stones of God's spiritual building. The derision that "Church-monuments" expresses about the tombs and "Jeat and Marble put for signes" (12) is surprisingly followed by a celebration of the aesthetic beauty of the poem "Church-musick," which seems genuinely to contribute to spirituality. "Church-lock and key," "The Church-floore," and "The Windows" use their examples of architecture only as a means of considering their spiritual counterparts. The poems answer and try to resolve Puritan dilemmas about the externals of religion by suggesting that these forms are primarily occasions for the development of a spiritual interiority. But firmly linked with this doctrinal issue is the autobiographical concern about "cunning works"; delicate and subtle craftsmanship of the self in fact turns out to be the ideal to aim at, but only when God does the fashioning.

"Church-lock and key" and "The Church-floore" consider not the physical church but the spiritual state of the heart, which either locks one out of the presence of God or builds a trustworthy foundation for entertaining that presence. In both, the "stones" of the "Jordan" allusions reappear. In Deuteronomy 27:5, Moses calls on the Israelites to use uncut stones to make an altar when they have crossed over the Jordan: "And there shalt thou build . . . an altar of stones: thou shalt not lift up any iron tool upon them." "Church-lock and key" characterizes sin as a kind of stone that excludes man from holiness and yet makes his prayers ardent: "For though sinnes plead too, yet like stones they make / His bloods sweet current much more loud to be" (11–12). "The Church-floore" transforms the hardness yet persuasive power of sin in the preceding poem into the strength of a regenerated heart:

Mark you the floore? that square & speckled stone,
    Which looks so firm and strong,
        Is *Patience*:

And th'other black and grave, wherewith each one
    Is checker'd all along,
        *Humilitie*
        . . .

                          (1–6)

The repetition of the word "stone" in both "Church-lock and key" and "The Church-floore" suggests that one stone can become another; sin can be the material for spiritual strength when mercy is properly sought. "The Church-floore" develops this idea throughout the poem, because the variegated beauty of its stones results from the mixture of good and evil, sin and reformation, which makes the floor "speckled" (1) or "checker'd" (5) with contrasting colors, and which makes the marble's veins "neat and curious":

Hither sometimes Sinne steals, and stains
The marbles neat and curious veins:
But all is cleansed when the marble weeps
     . . .
Blest be the *Architect*, whose art
Could build so strong in a weak heart.
        (13–15, 19–20)

The divine art that lays out this checkered marble floor provides the spiritual alternative to the upper-class "Jeat and Marble put for signes" ("Church-monuments," 12) in the first poem of the sequence. The ostentation of those signs contrasts to the profound inner experience by which sin is transformed into repentance. The "neat and curious veins" (14) in the reformed heart are not the work of human cleverness or a display of wealth, but the precision and skill of a divine process. It is interesting that "neat" means both clean and cleverly contrived; such an unusual combination in Herbert's poetry seems only possible because this beautifully wrought object is God's work, not man's. Therefore, it is logical that this neatness is stained by human sin (see lines 13–15); the unpolluted self is elegantly shaped, but always vulnerable to human tampering.

That unpolluted self reappears in the next poem as a brilliant stained-glass window, again wrought by divine craftsmanship. Like the "curious" marble floor, this version of subjectivity and style differs considerably from the unhewn stones and the plain style usually appearing in the context of the Jordan allusions, as well as in the version of the internalized temple in "Sion." That poem considers God's spiritual "Architecture" and concludes: "All Solomons sea of brasse and world of stone / Is not so deare to thee as one good grone" (17–18). In "Sion," the rough but heartfelt repentance felt within has more value than any precious object; in both "The Church-floore" and "The Windows," that heartfelt repentance turns into a precious object.

The terms of "The Windows" are curious and not too neat. The contrast in the poem is between "man" (1) as "brittle crazie glasse" (2) or as stained-glass window, letting the light of divine truth into the church so that it either "shows watrish, bleak, & thin" (10) or brilliant in "light and glorie" (8). But the metaphor of the light of "thy eternall word" (1) changes rather drastically from full brilliance (see line 7) to "a flaring thing" (14).[9] Although man at the beginning of the poem allows the light of truth in simply by virtue of his office, by the end he is emitting "speech alone" (13):

> Lord, how can man preach thy eternall word?
> He is a brittle crazie glasse:
> Yet in thy temple thou dost him afford
> This glorious and transcendent place,
> To be a window, through thy grace.                    5
>
> But when thou dost anneal in glasse thy storie,
> Making thy life to shine within
> The holy Preachers; then the light and glorie
> More rev'rend grows, & more doth win:
> Which else shows watrish, bleak, & thin.              10
>
> Doctrine and life, colours and light, in one
> When they combine and mingle, bring
> A strong regard and aw: but speech alone
> Doth vanish like a flaring thing,
> And in the eare, not conscience ring.                 15

The formulation of the minister as a weak, flawed pane of glass contrasts strikingly to other parts of *The Temple*, where the heart is characterized as a hard rock, a closet, or a harborer of "bosome-sinne" ("Sinne" [I], 1) that shuts out the power of divine influence. The first stanza of "The Windows" suggests that, through the grace conferred by ordination, the minister becomes a form of transparency, and has only to read from the Bible or the state-prescribed homilies and the divine light will enter the temple, at least to some extent. The poem delays the expected contrast between "thy eternall word" (1) and human speech and focuses on the linking of doctrine and life because it wants to avoid the issue of humanly crafted verbal representation altogether. This is, however, the fundamental issue of the poem: How can man preach thy eternal word? But the poem does not want to dwell on language, because it is seeking a kind of sign beyond language, one that is, surprisingly enough, "within" (7).

The annealing of the glass, which suggests suffering through fire, strengthening, and the eventual embodiment of doctrine, creates a window that tells "thy storie" (6) but yet dwells within the preacher. In medieval allegory, stories are the lively "outside" within which the nugget of truth resides. So the "colors" of rhetoric, the tropes and schemes that embellish the meaning, are used to move and persuade the reader.[10] In this way, the colors and stories of the literal stained-glass window bring to life the doctrines of the Bible. But in this poem, inside and outside are reversed: colors, stories, and rhetorical power are defined as an inner reality that breaks out into public view: "But when thou dost anneal in glasse thy storie, / Making thy life to shine within / The holy Preachers" (6–8). This formulation is rather illogical: the colors of a stained-glass window are not "within" the original glass, nor is it easy to understand how "thy storie" and "thy life" are "within" the life of the minister.[11] Is the annealed glass the holy preacher, or within him? "Within" is like a magical talisman, breaking the terms of the metaphor, but re-evoking the issue of the internalized temple. Herbert wants this part of church architecture to be both an outward sign and an inward spiritual state.

As many have pointed out, this poem reproduces the chapter in

*The Country Parson* on "The Parson Preaching." However, there is a significant difference between the two. "The Windows" has no place for the human effort and craft prominently considered in the handbook: "When he preacheth, he procures attention by all possible art. . . . By these and other means the Parson procures attention. . . . Such discourses shew very Holy" (232–34). These careful labors disappear in the poem as "thy storie" (6) shines out through the Preacher and rings in the conscience without the arts of rhetoric. The stories the parson tells in Bemerton are quite different:

> Sometimes he tells them stories, and sayings of others, according as his text invites him; for them also men heed, and remember better then exhortations; which though earnest, yet often dy with the Sermon, especially Countrey people; which are thick, and heavy, and hard to raise to a poynt of Zeal, and fervency, and need a mountaine of fire to kindle them; but stories and sayings they will well remember. (233)

Stories here operate in the conventional way, as embodiments of the chosen Biblical text. The passage also refers to an actual rhetorical situation, in which a cleric from an upper-class family strains with some impatience to engage the farm-owners and laborers that make up his parish. It is useful to compare the Parson's "mountaine of fire" to the poem's "flaring thing" (14) of "speech alone" (13). In practice, Herbert did not hesitate to use a few verbal sparks to light up his audience. The poem, however, turns this difficult situation and the rhetorical colors used by Herbert to control it into a divine crafted display that is the minister himself.

There is a direct link between this poem and "The Parson Preaching" in the account of the character of holiness:

> By these and other means the Parson procures attention; but the character of his Sermon is Holiness; he is not witty, or learned, or eloquent, but Holy. A Character, that *Hermogenes* never dream'd of, and therefore he could give no precepts thereof. But it is gained, first, by choosing texts. (233)

Herbert's very precise rules on developing his new style of speech surround a formulation that works like "The Windows": just as the poem projects inward into the Preacher what is normally considered an outward sign, the stained-glass window, so the prose projects outward into a rhetorical style what is normally considered an inward spiritual condition, holiness. Both work to obliterate the difference between inward and outward and to demand an unmediated interchange between speaker and audience.

The chapter, "The Parsons Library," works in the same way. The first sentence, "The Countrey Parson's Library is a holy Life," also surprises by collapsing words into experience and by discounting the necessary role played by language even in the next sentence: "For the temptations with which a good man is beset, and the ways which he used to overcome them, being told to another, whether in private conference, or in the Church, are a Sermon." This minister can preach "much more feelingly, and judiciously, then [if] he writes his rule of temperance out of bookes," but only "if he tell this to another" (278). These comments contrast the academic forms of book and sermon to the vibrancy of lived experience, but they also assume that this liveliness can be communicated without academic methods like rhetoric. What the minister actually tells belies the divine architecture that builds the minister as beautiful object in the church sequence. Reformation and regeneration turn out to be a lot of hard work: "So that the Parson having studied, and mastered all his lusts and affections within, and the whole Army of Temptations without, hath ever so many sermons ready penn'd, as he hath victories" (278). What *The Country Parson* describes as the minister's arduous mastery and victory becomes, in "The Church-floore" and "The Windows," the unpolluted beauty wrought by the divine Architect.

What is the significance of the "magical extraction of . . . labor" from the church sequence in *The Temple*?[12] Many critics would insist that Herbert bows here to the Protestant doctrine of salvation by grace alone, not by works, and demonstrates that the preacher thereby loses any claim to the sense of accomplishment possible through these works. Some critics might identify this process as a loss of self.[13] On the other hand, we can speculate that other critics, especially those who use the methods of Raymond Williams, might argue that the erasure of labor is an elaborate effort on Herbert's part to reclaim his upper-class heritage, to sustain what was for him the crucial difference between cleric and people.[14] In this view, the beautiful marble floor and the rare stained-glass window would become spiritual reproductions of the genteel status criticized in "Church-monuments" but nevertheless associated with rich and ornamental artwork, the "Jeat and Marble." This quality ensures that the minister is in his proper "glorious" place ("The Windows," 4) and that he will produce reverence, "a strong regard and aw" (13) in his audience.

But these two views identify as self what are actually two aspects of ideology: the dominant belief of innate quality in the noble or gentleman, and the emerging ideology of achievement and merit.[15] Herbert combines both. In "The Windows," high status and craftsmanship are projected onto the spiritual level. The elegance of marble floor and stained-glass window is not inherent within them, like gold or gem, but something built, a "cunning work." God as master craftsman preserves the mixture of labor and high status that were the elements of Herbert's original social performance. The stained-glass window is the religious, spiritualized version, not of the natural ease and fineness of the authentic aristocrat, but of the self that "Jordan" (II) weaves into the sense—the brilliant, manufactured, fiction-self built by the skillful, clever technician of social dynamics. The poem preserves what was anomalous about Herbert's social position by locating craftsmanship and fineness in God, who could keep such a combination "neat."[16]

It would be inaccurate to say that in this poem the minister is diminished.[17] The poem's conflation of inside and outside is problematic; nevertheless, the ideal is not: the holiness of spirituality radiates out in social performance and allows for little distinction between the devotional and the social. This model of transparency is not a loss of self but simply a different version of Herbert's original model. Instead of an upper-class surface based on a religious core, now the devotional calling expresses itself explicitly in the social role. "The Windows" differs from *The Country Parson* only because, in the poem,

the social calling collapses into the devotional calling, which, "breaking out" (228), shapes and determines all social appearances.[18]

The sequence on the church is followed by another important
group of poems, also fundamental to the organization and purpose
of *The Temple*. The revisions made to this sequence again display
the shift from an upper-class surface and religious core to a model
of transparency. The earlier *W* manuscript lays out a contrast between the "two regiments" in "Frailtie," "Content," and "Poetry,"
but the *B* manuscript develops a model of coordination through its
added poem, "Constancie."

Both sequences include the poem "Frailtie," which uses the
Protestant doctrine of "dual persons," or two regiments: the spiritual, in which Christ is Lord, and the temporal, in which each take
a place in the hierarchy of social roles. In the earlier *W* manuscript,
"Frailtie" follows immediately after "Church-monuments" and develops that poem's meditation on the ultimate irrelevance of the
temporal regiment, family or status, "this heap of dust" (3), in contrast to the crucial importance of spirituality:

> Lord, in my silence how do I despise
> What upon trust
> Is styled *honour, riches*, or *fair eyes*;
> But is *fair dust*!
> . . .
>
> But when I view abroad both Regiments;
> The worlds, and thine:
> Thine clad with simplenesse, and sad events;
> The other fine,
> Full of glorie and gay weeds,
> Brave language, braver deeds:
> That which was dust before, doth quickly rise,
> And prick mine eyes
> . . .
>
> (1–4, 11–16)

Given the doctrine of the two regiments, this poem in no way re-
nounces participation in the world, but rather requires that the spiritual regiment be uppermost in the desires of the heart. This em-

phasis continues in "Content" ("Give me the pliant minde, whose gentle measure / Complies and suits with all estates" [13–14]), and "Poetry" ("But it is that which while I use / I am with thee, and *most take all*" [11–12]). In its original position in the *W* manuscript, "Affliction" (I) followed "Poetry" and emphasized not an ambitious "selfnesse" but the difficulty of maintaining the primacy of the spiritual realm: "When first thou didst entice to thee my heart, / I thought the service brave" (1–2). According to "Frailtie," this speaker conflates spiritual and temporal realms, since he associates his relationship to God, "clad with simplenesse, and sad events" (11), with the ways of the world, "Full of glorie and gay weeds, / Brave language, braver deeds" (14–15). "Affliction" (I) in *W* demonstrates how difficult it is to keep the two realms apart in lived experience, and a solution is offered in the next poem, "Humilitie."

The *B* manuscript transforms this sequence almost completely, not only by offering a new model of the social self in "The Windows," but by creating a bridge between the spiritual and temporal realms in "Constancie." Sidney Gottlieb comments that if the first new sequence in *B* builds a church, then the second dismantles a court: the revised sequence is even more critical of the aristocratic ethos.[19] But it also dismantles the original division between temporal persona and one's relationship to God. Now, that spiritual relationship determines social behavior:

> Who is the honest man?
> He that doth still and strongly good pursue,
> To God, his neighbour, and himself most true:
> Whom neither force nor fawning can
> Unpinne, or wrench from giving all their due
> . . .
>
> Whom none can work or wooe
> To use in any thing a trick or sleight;
> For above all things he abhorres deceit:
> His words and works and fashion too
> All of a piece, and all are cleare and straight
> . . .
>
> (1–5, 16–20)

This model is quite different from the constructed "excellency" that Herbert urged his brother to develop "in knowledge, or in fashion, or in words" (366) in an early letter and in "The Church-porch." The temporal realm is not ignored; "giving all their due" (5) means acting properly according to social and status proprieties. But as Marion Singleton puts it, "the constant man is so composed of moral virtue that exterior and interior are joined in one continuous fabric."[20] The honest man abhors deceit not only because he doesn't lie, but because his external behavior is "cleare" (20), transparently communicating the internal realm within. "Constancie" rephrases a passage from "The Parson in reference":

> The Countrey Parson is sincere and upright in all his relations. And first, he is just to his Countrey. . . . To do otherwise, is deceit; and therefore not for him, who is hearty, and true in all his wayes, as being the servant of him, in whom there was no guile. (252–53)

"Constancie" and *The Country Parson* replace "the cunning works" of "The Church-porch" with an honesty that is "hearty," that is, it reports the heart within and breaks through the surfaces of social appearance. Like *The Country Parson*, the poem uses the character genre to bring together inside and outside, and to exclude the cunning "selfnesse" of performative gentility.

# $\mathcal{S}ix$

# Pastoral, Vocation, and "Private Benefit"

Chapters 4 and 5 considered how *The Temple* used religious purity to resolve the contradictions in Herbert's marginal social position. The next two chapters will argue that Herbert's pastoral imagery reformulates in a new way the dilemmas about labor implicit in the imagery of pollution and purity and reveals the economic implications of his struggles with status. Like the revisions that emphasize the imagery of purity, Herbert's use of the pastoral evolves over time by excluding references to ambitious desire. This pastoral puts the complex into the simple, to use William Empson's definition; that is, it puts the complex work of subject-formation in the early seventeenth century into a simpler agricultural world. Achievement becomes natural growth; self-fashioning becomes a form of cultivation that operates according to divine law. Herbert's poetry displays an attitude toward labor and the economy characteristic of the transitional period between feudalism and capitalism since, in his formulations, individual achievement is justified only when the "fruits" of such labor are dedicated to the "common good" rather than used to increase "private benefit." In this way, Herbert reproduces the conflicts in the sermons on vocation, which insist on hard work

but condemn as deviant both social mobility and the acquisition
of wealth for its own sake.[1]

❧

"The Flower" tells the story of individual growth that transgresses
as it ascends:

> How fresh, O Lord, how sweet and clean
> Are thy returns! ev'n as the flowers in spring;
>     To which, besides their own demean,
> The late-past frosts tributes of pleasure bring.
>         Grief melts away
>         Like snow in May,
>     As if there were no such cold thing
>         . . .
>
> O that I once past changing were,
> Fast in thy Paradise, where no flower can wither!
>     Many a spring I shoot up fair,
> Offring at heav'n, growing and groning thither:
>         Nor doth my flower
>         Want a spring-showre,
>     My sinnes and I joining together.
>
> But while I grow in a straight line,
> Still upwards bent, as if heav'n were mine own,
>     Thy anger comes, and I decline:
> What frost to that? what pole is not the zone,
>         Where all things burn,
>         When thou dost turn,
>     And the least frown of thine is shown?
>         . . .
>
> These are thy wonders, Lord of love,
> To make us see we are but flowers that glide:
>     Which when we once can finde and prove,
> Thou hast a garden for us, where to bide.
>         Who would be more,
>         Swelling through store,
>     Forfeit their Paradise by their pride.
>                         (1–5, 22–35, 43–49)

Ascent in this poem is both required and dangerous. To "shoot up
fair" (24) is to risk divine punishment: "Thy anger comes, and I de-

cline" (31). The poem reveals that such upward movement is in fact motivated by ambition and the desire to possess: the flower-soul grows "Still upwards bent, as if heav'n were mine own" (30). Ownership is an issue from the very beginning of the poem, when the rebirth of spiritual joy is expressed through the flower's renewed "demean" (3), a word that refers to both the demeanor, or stature, of the growing flower and to its domain, or demesne, that part of a lord's estate kept exclusively for his private purposes. We find that this estate-owning flower is imagined complete with vassals, the frosts, which deliver their tributes, or taxes, to their new master. The imagery of the speaker's ownership and status continues throughout the poem but is undermined by the developing awareness of God's definitive ownership, and the flower's domain is eventually replaced by God's ultimate estate, Paradise. As in so many Herbert poems, "we say amiss, / this or that is" (19–20) when we use possessive pronouns carelessly: "their own demean," "my flower," "as if heav'n were mine own." These possessive pronouns have to be revised: "Thou hast a Garden" (46). The poem concludes that he who claims to own himself and his life shall lose them: "Who would be more / Swelling through store, / Forfeit their Paradise by their pride" (47–49). The possessive pronouns in the last line contrast heavenly and earthly possession and suggest that all merely human versions of ownership are forms of vanity and self-glorification.

The image of the flower is used to both imagine a form of identity that would emerge as naturally as does a flower, and to measure the difference between this spontaneous growth and a willed self-cultivation that is both distinctly human and inevitably sinful. In stanza 5 (29–35), as many critics have noticed, the inadequacies of the metaphor of the flower become evident, as we find that this flower-soul does not die because it is winter but because of God's displeasure ("What frost to that?" [32]).[2] The metaphor of the flower cannot account for the work involved in religious growth, nor for the sin that results from it—the ambitious desire that haunts the process of religious self-cultivation, especially as it is described

147

in stanza 4: "Nor doth my flower / Want a spring-showre, / My sinnes and I joining together" (26–27). Here, the flower-soul claims to be able to produce its own "spring-showre."[3] The poem subsequently suggests that it is this very attempt to make the self that brings about God's anger. But the poem also cannot tell us just when and how the "sweet and clean" (1) renewal of spiritual hope and joy that opens the poem turns into the presumptuous self-interest that brings about the soul's demise. The image of ascending upward simultaneously represents the flower's growth and the soul's willful attempt to rise. "The Flower" depicts a form of growth that is both required and transgressive.

It is this very contradiction that plagues theologians and preachers during this period in their exposition of the Protestant doctrine of vocation. Luther's attack on the monastic life as a form of idleness had given a new sanctification to work in the world, but, as the critics of Weber have noted, Protestant exhortations to labor industriously were accompanied by admonitions against covetousness and self-interest.[4] William Perkins's *Treatise of the Vocations* was published in 1603 during a period when the labors of merchants and yeomen in England were sending them into the ranks of the upper classes in increasing numbers. Perkins tries to reconcile a doctrine that sanctifies labor with a social system that requires individuals to stay in their place:

> A vocation or calling, is a certain kind of life, ordained and imposed on man by God, for the common good. . . . He abuseth his calling whosoever he be that, against the end thereof, employs it for himself, seeking only his own and not the common good. And that common saying, Every man for himself and God for us all, is wicked and is directly against the end of every calling or honest life.[5]

Perkins quotes 1 Corinthians 7:20, "Let every man abide in the same calling wherein he was called," and comments:

> The practice of this duty is the stay and foundation of the good estate both of church and commonwealth, for it maketh every man to keep his own standing and to employ himself

> painfully within his calling: but when we begin to mislike the
> wise disposition of God and to think other men's callings bet-
> ter for us then our own, then follows confusion and disorder
> in society . . . hence come treacheries, treasons and sedi-
> tions, when men, not content with their own estate and hon-
> our, seek higher places: and being disappointed, grow to
> discontentments, and so forward to al mischeife. (733)

Perkins praises hard work but condemns upward mobility. He diagnoses the dilemma of his time as the clash of two ethical systems, one based on what he calls a concern for "the common
good," the other, "the respect of private benefit" (750), but he
imagines that the doctrine of vocation and the ethic of work can
be confined within the cultural model of a static hierarchical order and kept from contributing to the changes he fights against—
what we define as social mobility and the development of possessive individualism.[6]

Herbert accepts a humble position as rector of a tiny parish,
moves to the rural community of Bemerton, and edits out of his
poetry images of upward mobility.[7] The revised "Employment" (I)
substitutes the desire to gain "the Sunn's perfection" (23 in *W*) with
the prayer, "give one strain / To my poore reed" (23–24).[8] In "Employment" (II), an image of a busy and upwardly mobile honeybee
is revised into the firmly grounded but equally productive orange
plant. The first version reads:

> O that I had the wing and thigh
> Of laden Bees;
> Then would I mount up instantly
> And by degrees
> On men dropp blessings as I fly.
> (21–25 in *W*)

The phrase "by degrees" (23) refers both to the process of social el-
evation and to the charity that such honor and wealth will make
possible. Even in this earlier version, Herbert is quick to associate
"private benefit" with "the common good." But the revised version
edits out upward advancement completely:

O that I were an Orenge-tree,
            That busie plant!
Then should I ever laden be,
            And never want
Some fruit for him that dressed me.

(21–25)

The difference between this stanza and the original is not only the contrast between mounting up and remaining stationary; the second also introduces the figure of the powerful caretaker, the God who dresses—that is, the God who cultivates but also punishes and corrects. Although both the honeybee and the orange plant are images from nature, the revision evokes, like "The Flower," the ideal of a spontaneous vegetable growth that eludes the potential for ambition.[9] Herbert surrenders his ideal of "mounting up" as he settles in the Chalk country of South Wiltshire, an agrarian community where social ascent was relatively uncommon and the age-old traditions of the manor house and communal farming were still particularly strong.[10] He accepts a position offered him by the Earl of Pembroke, head of the Herbert family in England, to serve as chaplain in the manor house of Wilton and as parson for his kinsman's tenants in Bemerton. Herbert's shift from urban and courtly gentleman to country parson is analogous to his replacement of the image of the ascending bee with the productive orange plant. He does not give up his ideal of industrious labor, but it becomes a form of work that observes the boundaries of hierarchical limits and proceeds under the auspices of a benevolent but powerful lord.

The Earl of Pembroke himself may have provided Herbert with the model for coordinating the feudal system of a static hierarchy and the modern ethic of improvement and possessive individualism. Economic historian Eric Kerridge has argued that the Chalk country of Wilton was one of the few areas in England where manor-house institutions continued strong at the same time that capitalist systems of farming were introduced with great success. The Earl of Pembroke publicized and put into practice new methods of capitalist farming without injuring the customs of communal farming and the manor house.[11] George Herbert comments on these new methods in his prose manual, *The Country Parson*, in a discussion of the duties or vocation of a landowner:

> There are two branches of his affaires; first, the improvement of his family, by bringing them up in the fear and nurture of the Lord; and secondly, the improvement of his grounds, by drowning, or draining, or stocking, or fencing, and ordering his land to the best advantage both of himself, and his neighbours. The *Italian* says, None fouls his hands in his own businesse: and it is an honest, and just care, so it exceed not bounds, for everyone to imploy himselfe to the advancement of his affaires, that hee may have wherewithall to do good. (275)

Herbert sanctions the improvements that modern economic historians have associated with the agricultural revolution, but only if landowners "exceed not bounds," that is, that they make sure that industry never becomes greed, or ambition self-interest, that the common good is never disrupted by "respect for private benefit," as Perkins puts it. Herbert imagines, quite incorrectly for England as a whole, that enclosure and other agrarian improvements can take place to the best advantage of one's neighbor as well as the capitalist farmer.[12] Like Perkins, he assumes that the ideals of industry and diligence can be coordinated with the communal traditions of "good neighborhood."[13]

The passage in *The Country Parson* then comments on the relationship between the improvement of one's grounds and the religious cultivation of individuals:

> But his family is his best care, to labour Christian soules, and raise them to their height, even to heaven; to dresse and prune them, and take as much joy in a straight-growing childe, or servant, as a Gardiner doth in a choice tree. (275)

The "but" here in "But the family is his best care" is intended to contrast the material and "private benefit" of cultivating one's estate to the unselfishness of nurturing the family's "common good," but the gardening imagery used in reference to the family actually conflates religious instruction of children and servants with estate-management. This management is first put in terms of upward ascent: through their religious development, the members of the household rise to heaven, but only with the help of an authoritative father. Notice how the image of rising is replaced by the image of the tree, again grounded, again stable and dominated by the powerful and correcting patriarch. This passage reproduces the "Orenge-tree" revision from the poem "Employment" (II), as well as one of Herbert's poems, "Paradise," which represents the soul as a fruit tree growing within God's enclosure and subject to His dressing and pruning. The improving landowner becomes the model for Herbert's God. The problematic issue of labor, which can so easily shift from diligence to self-interest, is almost entirely removed from the soul and projected onto its divine caretaker. God performs the work involved in the development of the religious self, whereas the soul and its fruits appear naturally and spontaneously. The threat of an ascending independence that disrupts hierarchical norms is warded off through a structure of imagery that places the soul firmly within the protection and confines of a patriarchal superior.

The poem "The Flower" brings together the imagery of rising with the figure of the correcting patriarch. The poem describes a recurring pattern of upward growth that is punished as soon as it becomes a process of ambitious self-cultivation. Unlike the "Orenge-tree" stanza or the poem "Paradise," "The Flower" acknowledges that the spontaneous development natural to a flower is impossible for human beings, but the poem nevertheless preserves the ideal of natural growth by which it measures the trespasses of excessive human effort:

> And now in age I bud again,
> After so many deaths I live and write;
> I once more smell the dew and rain,
> And relish versing: o my onely light,
> It cannot be
> That I am he
> On whom thy tempests fell all night.
>
> (36–42)

When the flower-soul "buds again," the process of "versing" emerges as that form of artfulness and artificiality that defines the difference between plants and humans; yet it also puns on the Latin word for "turning," and so attempts to reproduce the movement of the flower toward its "onely light" (39). The poem therefore posits an ideal of the "natural" use of human skills in self-development and self-representation in which the traces of human creativity are minimized. The act of writing poetry becomes analogous to the development of one's "demean," one's spiritual estate, but the industry that the speaker pours into this development is both essential and suspicious. The goal may be to discover that "we are but flowers that glide" (40), but this dependence on grace also results in and requires the energy of works. That suspicious energy will accompany the soul's rise to heaven, but it will also evoke the censorious punishment of a disapproving God to the extent that its purpose is to make the speaker "more," as in line 47, that is, swelling any sense of autonomous selfhood. The process of writing, then, is the process both of attempting to grow and accepting the limits on that growth.

The limits are enforced by a patriarchal "Lord of power" (15) in a struggle that has Oedipal overtones. God the Father disrupts not only the upward ascent of the soul, in line 30, but also the rather idyllic communion between the flower and its mother-root, in stanza 2 (lines 8–14). In an article on *As You Like It*, Louis Montrose has argued that the process of "establishing or authenticating a self in a rigorously hierarchical and patriarchal society" could take on an Oedipal character for any adult male, and especially for younger sons, who had to struggle with the obstructions created by a father's will and an elder brother's status as heir. In "The Flower," the speaker's divine Father wrests away any independent form of personal estate and requires that this son accept his lowly position on the spiritual chain of being. Such a position demands that the speaker believe that his God is both a "Lord of power" and a "Lord of love" (43), that is, that the declines the speaker suffers are legitimate and moral. It is in this coordination of power and love that we find the ideology of the poem. By imagining power as love, Herbert accepts his subordination to those wealthier than he, and quite specifically, he accepts his role as a member of the service classes, which, according to social historian David Cressy, enforced the hegemony of the ruling minority. Herbert's ethic of improvement, preached to himself and to the tenants of the Earl of Pembroke's manor in Wiltshire, taught simultaneously the duty to work and the duty to obey one's hierarchical lord. Such teaching coordinated the medieval ideology of service with the modern ideology of improvement and sustained the position of aristocratic agrarian capitalists.[14]

ᕬᕬ

Herbert's agrarian poems also represent God as a possessive but benevolent landlord. "Love unknown" best exemplifies this uncovering of power as love, but "Redemption" and "Love" (III) also weld together the conflicting ideals of improvement and hierarchical submission through an aristocratic lord whose process of cultivation requires both growth and obedience. "Redemption" is particularly interesting in this regard, since it is itself built on the question of whether or not the divine "Lord" can be imagined as an estate-owning great man. The poem continually wavers between the use of the landlord-tenant relationship as an ironic distortion of and an appropriate analogy for the relationship between God and human. The status inversions of the poem undermine such an analogy and seem to level all social distinctions into one estate, that of unregenerate, sinful mankind. Yet the poem also resurrects such distinctions through the relationship between its speaker and his God and its implicit claim that, in religious terms, each individual is the "servant" of Christ. We will find that this conflict between the inadequacy and the appropriateness of hierarchy to define religious experience characterizes sermons on vocation as well. Protestant preachers struggle to overcome the power of status categories to determine human value, yet cannot escape using these categories to describe the sacred relationship. This problem is not simply the result of the inability of seventeenth-century language to describe the Christian equality of souls or "the priesthood of all believers"; these preachers feel compelled to control the implications of such equality with exhortations to stay in one's place and obey one's master. Like "Redemption," Protestant theories of vocation both destroy and re-create the hierarchical order.

In "Redemption," the speaker's mistaken sense of human value and divine benevolence are revealed though his use of hierarchical distinctions. His reference to God as a "rich Lord" (1) clarifies that his sense of wealth and status blinds him to the precise way in which his God has "dearly" (7) paid for this redemption. Yet such priceless love also establishes God's absolute ownership over his property, the souls within his domain:

> Having been tenant long to a rich Lord,
>   Not thriving, I resolved to be bold,
>   And make a suit unto him, to afford
> A new small-rented lease, and cancell th'old.
> In heaven at his manour I him sought:                    5
>   They told me there, that he was lately gone
>   About some land, which he had dearly bought
> Long since on earth, to take possession.
> I straight return'd, and knowing his great birth,
>   Sought him accordingly in great resorts;               10
>   In cities, theatres, gardens, parks, and courts:
> At length I heard a ragged noise and mirth
>   Of theeves and murderers: there I him espied,
>   Who straight, *Your suit is granted*, said, & died.

The status inversions of the poem, in which the Lord of the manor resides and dies indecorously with thieves and murderers, reproduce those of the Crucifixion, in which God becomes man and is taken for a "malefactor" or "transgressor" and hung on the cross between two thieves.[15] The placement of God with the thieves not only demonstrates the dimensions of the human failure to recognize divine worth, it also reveals the divine neglect for human social categories, since Christ promises redemption to one of the thieves, as well as to the "publicans and sinners" with whom he has dined before. The tenant's surprise at and perhaps contempt for his Lord's companions is rebuked by the effect of his suit, which reduces him to the level of the thieves and murderers, not only because his suit murders his Lord, but because his request, unbeknownst to him, is essentially the same as the thief's: to be redeemed through divine restitution rather than through any human merit or social accomplishment.

In many ways, the poem's challenge to the principles of hierarchy logically undermines the ability of the landlord-tenant relationship to describe the bond between God and human. Yet the poem also depends on this analogy, since the difference between the Old and New Testament, or old and new covenant, is put in terms of "th'old" and "a new small-rented lease" (4).[16] A demanding high rent rather than a more compassionate low rent represents the difference between salvation through works rather than grace. We find in the second quatrain that the Lord intends to "take possession" (8) of this land, which implies that he will establish close supervision or exclusive control over his property. Of course, the terms used by the tenant in the second stanza are to some extent as misguided as those in the first: he may be imagining his lord as a profit-seeking aristocrat, ready to extinguish the tenant's "customary rights" and completely destroy the terms of the lease in order to improve his property. The ironies of the word "dearly" (7) again suggest the tenant's inability to understand his lord's motives. As such, the poem questions both the feudal lord and the capitalist aristocrat as models for the Christian deity. Yet the poem cannot fully escape its metaphor of the soul as a kind of land over which the individual's "works" have more or less influence. That the lord will "take possession" (8) may be an act of divine benevolence; nevertheless, the poem characterizes God as a property-owner whose "gracious" efforts cultivate the territory of the human soul in order to make it thrive (see line 2).

The same disruption of and dependence on the terms of the status hierarchy impel Protestant theorists on vocation. The accounts of the relationship between spiritual and social estate differ from those of Catholic theologians, who, like St. Thomas Aquinas, taught for the most part that social degree accurately reflected religious and moral difference.[17] Protestants, however, urged the equality of all occupations and the equal value of all religious souls. Protestant ministers agreed with William Tyndale that "in Christ we are all of one degree, without respect of persons." This led to an insistent attack on the power of the hierarchical social order to determine human value. Tyndale argued that an apostle and a shoemaker could serve God equally; whether you preached the word of God or "washest thy master's dishes," sanctification came from working "with a true heart." Hugh Latimer provocatively defined a preacher as God's ploughman, and William Perkins announced that the role of a shepherd was as significant as that of judge, magistrate, or minister.

Nevertheless, these ministers quickly moved to counteract the egalitarianism of their remarks.[18] According to Perkins, "persons are distinguished by order, whereby God hath appointed, not making all equal, as though the body should be all head and nothing else." One major purpose for the minister's use of hierarchical inversion was in fact to urge those in "base" callings to value their work and stay in their place. Tyndale praises the dishwasher, but not at the risk of disturbing the master-servant relationship: "Now thou that ministerest in the kitchen, and art but a kitchen-page, receivest all things of the hand of God: knowest that God hath put thee in that office; submittest thyself to his will; and servest thy master not as a man, but as Christ himself." Again and again in these sermons, Christ becomes the master to whom laborers owe their allegiance and from whom they will receive their reward, no matter how badly their human masters treat them or how humiliating their work seems to be: "Let them consider, that in serving of men, by performance of poore and base duties they serve God: and therefore that their service is not base in his sight."[19]

Hugh Latimer's sermon on the Christmas story reveals the anxiety that status inversions could cause in those very ministers who made the most of them.[20] Latimer's account of the shepherds who came to Bethlehem to see the Saviour recalls the tenant's surprise in "Redemption" at the indecorous company kept by his lord: "They thought they should have found him keeping a state after his name, that is, like a Saviour; but they found a poor child, which, after man's reason, was not able to help himself" (91). By this we should learn "not to be offended with the poor kingdom that our Saviour kept in this world: for we see, most commonly, that the rich and wealthy of this world despise and contemn the word of God" (91). Like "Redemption," Latimer contrasts the "poor kingdom" that Christ kept in this world to the high style of the rich and wealthy who frequent "cities, theatres, gardens, parks, and courts" (11). But such an attack on the socially powerful results not in a skepticism about the value of obeying those highly placed but irreligious authorities. The inversions of the Christ story seem to spur Latimer on to harp excessively and continually on the need for servants to obey these masters: "Here therefore learn, O ye servants, and consider that God no less regardeth you than the greatest lords of the world if you live after his commandments; which is, that you shall serve your masters truly and uprightly, and not with a feigned heart" (87). The equality that Latimer gives with one hand he takes away with the other, by insisting not that servants can display God's favor by becoming masters but by bowing to those they serve. The pressure Latimer feels to protect the feudal bond from his own critique becomes clearest when he discusses the shepherds' haste to leave their flocks in order to find the Christ child: to Latimer, this reveals their devotion to God, since the shepherds "were but servants, and were bound to make amends for all that should happen to be lost" (89). But such an event does not prove that at times obedience to one's religious lord requires disobedience to one's social lord: the haste with which the shepherds travel to Bethlehem becomes instead a moral tale about industrious activity in one's daily service: "Let every man learn quickly to go about his business to which God hath appointed him; especially servants may learn here to do their business truly and speedily; not spending the time in vain going up and down, when their masters are absent; but rather to be diligent, knowing that they serve not only their bodily masters, but Christ himself" (90). The disjuncture between religious commitment and social duty that Latimer himself points out must be repaired quickly through invoking the notion of Christ as master, a title that attempts to launch a religious assault on the social order, but that nevertheless preserves its fundamental distinction.

In Nicholas Ferrar's short biography of Herbert, in his introduction to *The Temple*, Ferrar points out that the work is dedicated to no great man but to God himself (3–5). He also insists on the free choice that moved the "nobly born" Herbert to "serve at God's Altar" rather than to "seek the honour of State-employments" (3). Ferrar implies that no aristocratic patron or condition of poverty forced Herbert into the decision. Herbert would affirm this freedom of action in his daily conversation, according to Ferrar: "To testify his independencie upon all others, and to quicken his diligence in this kinde, he used in his ordinarie speech, when he made mention of the blessed name of our Lord and Saviour Jesus Christ, to adde, *My Master*" (4). Like the use of the term in sermons on vocation, Herbert's phrase wavers between an attempt to free himself from the determinate power of the status system and a desire to fit himself back in. His appetite for independence seems to include both a religious contempt for worldly relations and a class-based anxiety about the appearance of dependency expressed by his rather lowly ecclesiastical position. Vocation may have freed Herbert from the pressures of the status system, but it also allowed him to preserve the sense of independence and honor associated with the "nobly born." Ferrar himself seems intent on reassociating Herbert with his original high estate, as if readers might mistakenly identify him with a lower rank. Notice that the phrase "Jesus Christ . . . *My Master*," above, includes both an assertion of freedom and a confession of obligation. Believing in his own religious independence from the patronage network, Herbert nevertheless evokes the obedience and reverence that such a relationship required, and that his gentility may have made difficult, through his allegiance to Christ. Herbert's attempt to "quicken his diligence in this kind" seems to replace social obligation with religious commitment, but it also results in a spirited dedication to his public duties.[21]

Herbert's service at "God's Altar" included his chaplaincy at Wilton House, where the Earls of Pembroke acted the part of great estate-owners and dispensers of patronage. During the period of Herbert's ministry at Bemerton and chaplaincy at Wilton, the Earl of Pembroke was raising rather than lowering the rents of his tenants. He was engaged in a series of enclosures that occurred outside the local area but not far from home, many of which resulted in armed revolt. Pembroke took "possession" in several places, as had his great-grandfather, who turned the village of Washern Grange just behind the Wilton manor house into one of those gardens and parks that decorously but inadequately characterize the lord's "great birth" in "Redemption."[22]

Herbert's poem attacks the figure of the idle or power-hungry great man while preserving the feudal ideal of aristocratic benevolence. Christ's unselfishness demonstrates the charity that was to lie behind all industrious activities; his role as "landlord" mirrors the aristocrat's ability to labor for others through the ownership of a large estate. This very feudal form of unselfishness was preserved in the literature on vocation through the distinction made between the works of the body and the brain, or the hand and the mind, which, in the case of the estate-owner, validated his feudal role:

> It may be a sufficient Calling, and enough to take up his whole time, even to keep Hospitality, and to order and overlook his family, and to dispose of his Lands and Rents, and to make Peace, and preserve Love and Neighborhood among them that live near or under him.[23]

Such aristocratic "Love" included the willingness to give up private profit for the good of the whole: according to William Tyndale, "this term, myself, is not in the gospel."[24] But Herbert's poem, like his society, applies this ideal of the "commonwealth" with a difference: aristocrats retain their property and their ability to cultivate it if they act for the common good; the disenfranchised classes learn that possessiveness is sin. The poem attributes to its Lord the entire responsibility for the improvement of His estate: the analogy between a "new small-rented lease" and New Testament grace tends to elide the very significant role that the labor of a tenant farmer plays in his efforts at thriving, especially under a less demanding rent.[25] The poem paradoxically preserves the role of the upper-class estate owner as it attacks his sins.

The same process occurs in the following passage from a sermon by Dod and Cleaver. The sermon attacks

> wicked worldlings, that thinke to advantage and advance themselves by sinnefull and naughty courses. . . . They think . . . they shall make themselves and theirs, by joyning house to house and land to land; by oppressing the poore and needie . . . they have right to nothing, but are meere thieves and usurpers, and shall answer for laying hold of those things, that are in truth none of their owne. . . . They are intruders into other mens possessions, and the great Landlord of the world may thrust them foorth when it seemeth best unto himselfe.[26]

This passage attacks the rich for greed and oppression, but it shapes its model of possession and property according to the feudal norm. "The great Landlord of the world" both punishes profit-seeking property-owners and validates their social estate. Like "master," the word "landlord" as a description for God mediates between a Protestantism that promises the individual religious equality and a social system constructed in terms of hierarchy and feudal models of property. That the self becomes God's private property in "Redemption" welds together two conflicting social ethos: that of the religious self, whose value and significance is derived exclusively from God apart from social differences, and that of the hierarchical community, in which all individual interests become negligible before those of the common good. This is the social significance of Herbert's "Redemption": it defuses the potential threat to the community posed by the Protestant religious self whose membership in the "priesthood of all believers" destroys the social fabric of the feudal hierarchy. Such a threat is overcome through the figure of a Protestant God who as "master" and "landlord" brings back into being on a spiritual level the model of a hierarchical commonwealth and reconfirms the reverence and obedience that Protestant equality erodes.

"Love unknown" asserts, like "Redemption," that one's spiritual estate is more like leased land than a rich inheritance, and that the willingness to accept God's power as "Love unknown" is like the willingness of a tenant to accept the terms and the supervision of his landlord. The agrarian context of the poem operates in two ways: to "spiritualize" the speaker's expectations of the rewards he can expect from his God by reminding him of the difference between religious regeneration and social success, and to "socialize" these expectations as well by incorporating the religious relationship within the social nexus. The result is a poem that both depends on and fractures its structural analogy, as if intent on proving that the religious lord is both like and unlike the social lord. The soul is described as both a tenant farmer and his rented land "which may improve" (4); God is described as an estate owner who acts unexpectedly and painfully in order to bypass the tenant's inefficacious self-management and to enforce His own autocratic but nevertheless terribly successful methods of cultivation. On the other hand, the country landscape keeps turning into an allegorical landscape, the manor house into a church and the first "fruits" of the tenant into a "heart":

> Deare Friend, sit down, the tale is long and sad:
> And in my faintings I presume your love
> Will more complie then help. A Lord I had,
> And have, of whom some grounds, which may improve,
> I hold for two lives, and both lives in me.     5
> To him I brought a dish of fruit one day,
> And in the middle plac'd my heart. But he
>           (I sigh to say)
> Lookt on a servant, who did know his eye
> Better then you know me, or (which is one)     10
> Then I my self. The servant instantly
> Quitting the fruit, seiz'd on my heart alone,

> And threw it in a font, wherein did fall
> A stream of bloud, which issu'd from the side
> Of a great rock: I well remember all, 15
> And have good cause: there it was dipt and dy'd,
> And washt, and wrung: the very wringing yet
> Enforceth tears. *Your heart was foul, I fear.*
> Indeed 'tis true. I did and do commit
> Many a fault more then my lease will bear; 20
> Yet still askt pardon, and was not deni'd.

Like the farmer and the clown who bring their gifts into the manor house to "salute / Thy lord and lady" in "To Penshurst," the tenant proffers himself and his work as a sign of dedication to his landlord.[27] But such an offer is rejected as an empty gesture, or as motivated more by a desire for favor than "heartfelt" dedication. We find that the terms of the lease require a much deeper commitment than usually required of a rural laborer. The tenant holds his grounds for "two lives, and both lives in me" (5); in seventeenth-century farming, this lease would remain in force during the longest life of two people, perhaps father and son. Here, the lease extends beyond the speaker's death into the afterlife. He rents his soul from the Lord, and, it seems, it must be returned to its owner on Judgment Day; until that time he must cultivate it, but his methods are unsuccessful. They are replaced by the seemingly cruel but ultimately productive acts of his Lord. Again, the necessity of grace to the renewal of the heart is put in terms of the bounty and mercy that a landlord extends to his tenants: "I did and do commit / Many a fault more then my lease will bear; / Yet still askt pardon, and was not deni'd" (19–21). The poem turns patriarchal power into love known by translating a complaint about the injustices of the master into a confession of the frailties of the servant. Nevertheless, the limits of the analogy and the interruption of the rituals of the manor house by the allegory of baptism remind us that the "service" dramatized here is far more religious than social.

Within these conflicting structures of imagery, the secular and the sacred, the soul is cultivated, groomed, developed:

> *Truly, Friend,*
> *For ought I heare, your Master shows to you*
> *More favour then you wot of. Mark the end.*
> *The Font did onely, what was old, renew:*
> *The Caldron suppled, what was grown too hard:*
> *The Thorns did quicken, what was grown too dull:*
> *All did but strive to mend, what you had marr'd.*
> *Wherefore be cheer'd, and praise him to the full*
> *Each day, each houre, each moment of the week,*
> *Who fain would have you be new, tender, quick.*
>
> (61–70)

This reanimation of the heart bears an unclear relationship to the acts of service initiated by the tenant. His offer of his heart, as well as of "a sacrifice out of my fold" (30), signifies internal and external allegiance, yet without the radically complete dedication required and with too much attention to the profits to be gained from such devotion: "which I did thus present / To warm his love, which I did fear grew cold" (31–33). The clean, new, tender, and lively heart replaces superficial acts of worship; religious regeneration replaces social ritual; yet the process also seems to simply increase and deepen the very readiness of the tenant to do his Lord's bidding. His ambitious efforts to improve himself may be exposed as weak and ineffectual, yet the poem's regeneration of the heart simply reproduces this energy in a different and more fully internalized form: "*Wherefore be cheer'd, and praise him to the full / Each day, each houre, each moment of the week*" (68–69).

When worldly and spiritual "imployment" are compared by seventeenth-century ministers, the two shift uneasily between contrast and coordination. Dod and Cleaver use agrarian metaphors in terms of the regeneration of the heart both to evoke the industry of secular effort and to modify an emphasis on the "profit" that may ensue:

> But what is that good and honest heart which they are commended for? it is a heart, that doth fullie purpose to doe well, though it faile much in that which it performeth. . . . Now wheresoever there is such a ready inclination unto goodnesse, there will be a bringing foorth of fruit; though not in all alike, yet everyone will doe somewhat: and God will ac-

> knowledge them for good ground, and honest-hearted Christians, that yeeld him but thirtie fold, as well as them that yeeld him sixtie fold, or an hundred fold: for a lesse measure of fruitfulness is an argument of truth, as well as a greater measure, and therefore shall bee respected and rewarded.[28]
> (Dod and Cleaver, p. 119)

Worldly standards of success do not apply to the devotional process, but a heart brings forth its fruit when it can "fullie purpose to doe well" in as diligent a way as a husbandman cultivates his crops. Spiritual energies must recognize their differences from secular ambition, since in religion what matters is the intent not the success of the act, yet that "ready inclination unto goodnesse" seems to need the same degree of concentration, commitment, and diligence. As Thomas Adams put it: "There is no usury tolerable, but of two things; *Grace* and *Time*! and it is onely blessed wealth, that is gotten by improving them to the best."[29]

Such a paradoxical use of the imagery of secular success to prove the superiority of spiritual endeavors exemplifies the ambiguous link that these preachers constructed between spirituality and worldly engagement. Religious regeneration was of course the first consideration, yet regeneration could not take place separate from society, as it would for a monk, but required social involvement. In addition, the direct relationship between God and the individual that Protestantism provided could not be used as an excuse for insubordination or neglect of one's social duties. Much of the preaching on vocation seems motivated by the need to overcome the implication that a theology of grace and God's law of election frees the chosen from doing their social duties or observing the dictates of the interdependent hierarchy. "The Christian Calling," according to Sanderson, does not "*prejudice*, much less *overthrow*, it rather establisheth and strengthenth those interests that arise from *natural relations*, or from voluntary *contracts*."[30] Doing well, in the passage by Dod and Cleaver previously quoted, is quite literally to "doe the good duties that shall bee commanded." Luther had been forced from nearly the beginning of the Reformation to control the politically disruptive implications of his theology, whose emphasis on

Christian liberty played an influential role in the Peasants' Revolt.[31] Not only Anglicans, but the Puritans Dod and Cleaver respond to this threat when they chastise servants who have "a little knowledge of religion" and who think this knowledge gives them "a dispensation to be idle and slothfull: headstrong and masterfull, testie and impatient" with their masters. The priesthood of all believers has to be controlled by stories like that of Jacob, who served Laban, "though a covetous, deceitful and hard master," and by a religious ethic that hammered out a coordination and sometimes an identification between religious faith and social faithfulness:

> Therefore those servants are much to be blamed, that make religion an occasion of their unfaithfulnesse, which by how much it is more thorowly and deeply rooted and setled in the hearts of any, should, and will make them more true and trustie; more conscionable and faithfull to their rulers and governours. (Dod and Cleaver, p. 81)

As they urge masters to pray for the spiritual growth of their servants, Dod and Cleaver try to direct such growth into the channels of social obedience instead of the testiness or religious self-confidence that could very well be the result of their theology: masters should "become suitors to the Lord for [servants], that he would frame their hearts to doe as they are taught" (Dod and Cleaver, p. 116). It is here that the religious image of the broken and regenerate heart gains social resonance for Dod and Cleaver: God is asked to "take away the stonie, and unbeleeving, and carnall hearts out of [servants'] bodies" in order that they might no longer be "willfull, and heady, froward, and rebellious" (Dod and Cleaver, p. 117). In these passages, spiritual regeneration becomes identical with secular pliability.

The suppling of the tenant's hard heart in "Love unknown" is both a religious and a social event. The agrarian context of the poem and the power and love of the divine landlord ensure that such improvement will proceed within the confines of a hierarchical social system that depends more on the fidelity of its servants than the election of their souls. The "knowledge of religion" (p. 81) which Dod and Cleaver fear will disrupt social norms of behavior is given to the tenant through a "Friend" who stands outside of the agrarian order, but who teaches his student the promises of Christianity in such a way as to strengthen the link between master and servant. In John 15:15, Jesus offers his disciples a relationship that disrupts hierarchical expectations; in "Love unknown" this potential fissure is minimized through the agrarian analogy:

> Henceforth I call you not servants; for the servant knoweth not what his lord doeth; but I have called you friends; for all things that I have heard of my Father I have made known unto you.

The knowledge that the tenant receives in "Love unknown" is to some extent Biblical, since it explains the dynamics of regeneration and sanctification; in fact, this religious transformation depends on mystical relationships difficult to assimilate to the social hierarchy: the Lord "lookt on a servant, who did know his eye / Better then you know me, or (which is one) / Then I my self" (9–11). This series of identifications implies that the "Friend" is as close to the speaker as the speaker is to himself, and that the "servant" is even closer to the Lord. Unlike the Biblical passage, in which "the servant knoweth not what the lord doeth," the servant in the poem seems almost to be at one with the Lord, or to actually be His Son, who not only does his Father's will, but makes it known unto his "friends." But the mysteries of the incarnation and individual regeneration become socially weighted in this poem, since the "Friend" teaches the speaker that his hard heart not only prevents his religious rebirth but makes him "willfull, and heady, froward, and rebellious" (Dod and Cleaver, p. 117). The result is a reverent obedience to one's master that reaches into the very heart of the soul.

The poem is fundamentally interested in the internality of this reverence. The first two allegorical events, in which the heart is cleansed and softened, refer to the liturgical sacraments of baptism and the Eucharist. The third, however, is intensely personal and occurs through the invasion of the Lord into the tenant's private house:

> soon I fled
> Unto my house, where to repair the strength
> Which I had lost, I hasted to my bed.
> But when I thought to sleep out all these faults
>                    (I sigh to speak)
> I found that some had stuff'd the bed with thoughts,
> I would say *thorns*. Deare, could my heart not break,
> When with my pleasures ev'n my rest was gone?
> Full well I understood, who had been there:
> For I had giv'n the key to none, but one:
> It must be he. *Your heart was dull, I fear.*
> Indeed a slack and sleepie state of mind
> Did oft possesse me, so that when I pray'd,
> Though my lips went, my heart did stay behinde.
>                              (46–59)

The tenant is denied any rest or protection from the power of his master, whose presence penetrates into the depths of experience and consciousness. That his thoughts punish him for "these faults" (49) and his heart breaks in response to such punishment reveals that the drama of regeneration is complete, since he has internalized the loving cruelty of his master. In this religion, "heart" must match "lips" (59) not in order to produce an identity based on personal integrity, but in order to bring into being a form of obedience that is heartfelt, dedicated to a master "who fain would have you be new, tender, quick" (70). The agrarian analogy of the poem channels the alert spiritual energy evoked by the theology of grace and the doctrine of vocation into willing and active service.

The ethic of vocation developed by Protestant ministers and the pastoral and agrarian imagery in *The Temple* call into question the evaluation of personal value through the system of status, but also place the self back into a static, organic community in order to overcome the threat of privacy, either in religious devotion or social self-interest. Internality is produced in close association with external ceremony and secular duty, and results in a form of devotional energy that can be poured into social activity without disturbing the hierarchical boundaries and structures of church and commonwealth. In poetry and sermon, the distinctions between inside and out, "general" and "particular" callings, attempt to create a difference and a fusion between the religious and the social "master." In this structure of identity, the religious does not determine the social, despite Herbert's claims to be free from any other master than Christ. But neither does the social determine the religious. Rather, the two depend on each other for definition, and the difference between the two is the source of their unhappy but symbiotic relationship. In attempting to overcome the development of privacy in religion and society, the Protestant emphasis on the inner and outer callings provided a model of identity that actually sped its progress.

This process of distinguishing and incorporating occurs in Herbert's "The Elixir," which uses the imagery of alchemy to make secular action sacred and safe by what Perkins calls "the holy use of our callings":

> Teach me, my God and King,
> In all things thee to see,
> And what I do in any thing,
> To do it as for thee:
>
> Not rudely, as a beast,                              5
> To runne into an action,
> But still to make thee prepossest,
> And give it his perfection.
>
> A man that looks on glasse,
> On it may stay his eye;                              10
> Or if he pleaseth, through it passe,
> And then the heav'n espie.
>
> All may of thee partake:
> Nothing can be so mean,
> Which with his tincture (for thy sake)               15
> Will not grow bright and clean.
>
> A servant with this clause
> Makes drudgerie divine:
> Who sweeps a room, as for thy laws,
> Makes that and th'action fine.                       20

> This is the famous stone
> That turneth all to gold:
> For that which God doth touch and own
> Cannot for lesse be told.

The tincture in Herbert's poem, "for thy sake" (15), is the means by which religious feeling is united with social action, as well as the way in which holiness counteracts personal self-interest; the speaker serves Christ, his master, rather than himself or a specific human patron in his particular calling. This structure of identity claims to free one from hierarchical evaluations of worth: the lowly acts of the servant in the fifth stanza become as valuable as gold when performed for Christ. But such a reference echoes the double-edged preaching of the sermons on vocation, which celebrate religious freedom from the social hierarchy as they assure those in base callings that they can be content with their lot. According to Richard Sibbes, if actions are performed "with an eye to God," they are all "good, and religious actions. For the Grace of God is a blessed Alcumist, where it toucheth it makes good, and religious." William Perkins agreed: "And thus may we reap marvailous contentation in any kind of calling, though it be but to sweep the house, or keep sheepe, if we can thus in practice unite our callings."[32] In these comments and Herbert's poem, the coordination of holy motive and sanctified action promises that the drudgery needed for the maintenance of the traditional order will get done. The second stanza of Herbert's poem rebukes the precipitant aggression of a "beast" (5), whose forceful energy might damage the link between religious feeling and social duty. Such a link controls excessive energy and contains labor and identity within the traditional order. Not so with Herbert's first version of the poem, called "Perfection," which prizes not purity but mounting up to socioreligious heights:

> Lord teach mee to referr
> All things I doe to thee
> That I not only may not err
> But allso pleasing bee.

A man that looks on glasse,
On it may stay his eye:
Or if he pleaseth, through it passe
And then the heav'n espy
. . .

All may of thee partake:
Nothing can be so low
Which with his tincture (for thy sake)
Will not to Heaven grow.

A servant with this clause,
Makes drudgerie divine.
Who sweeps a chamber for thy Laws,
Makes that and th'action fine.

But these are high perfections:
Happy are they that dare
Lett in the Light to all their actions
And show them as they are.

(1–8, 13–24 in W)

The servant in this poem is a far more troublesome figure than in
the final revision, since his or her "knowledge of religion" results in
actions that verge on "high perfections" (21) in the divine scale of
value. The stanza on the servant explicitly and consistently upsets
the hierarchical social norm, since the word "chamber" (19) emphasizes the difference between the housecleaner and those he or
she serves. The word "fine" (20) also intentionally challenges the
upper-class notion of elegance and cultivation associated with the
word and suggests much more pointedly than in the revision that
individuals first measured as "low" (14) can overturn upper-class expectations as they "grow" (16) upwards on earth, as it is in heaven.
The "high perfections" (21) that the poem itself makes possible to
servants becomes too threatening, and the last stanza warns its
reader and its author to beware of the motives that lie behind their
desire for such an ascent.

This last stanza provides the new model for labor and identity,
which in "The Elixir" will exclude ambition and protect the social
order. Letting in "the Light" (23) uses the image of the window in-

cluded in both poems to evoke a sense of the darkness within, the private motives of the heart that drive one to work in ways antagonistic to the commonwealth. In both poems, the glass that can stop one's view or reveal heaven refers to actions that are either simply secular or purified by sacred feeling. In the first version, however, seeing heaven through "the glasse" (10) seems to promise getting there; in the second, the transparency of the window represents the new ideal, not "high perfections" but the "bright and clean" actions (16) that now determine personal worth. The fineness of the servant's acts, as well as the "room" (19) that he or she sweeps, is now measured by its cleanness, its freedom from the dust of sin or the dirt of self-interest that threatened the religious purity of the first version. The revised poem continues to measure identity and labor according to a standard separate from the social hierarchy, but it is one that makes one and one's works valuable to the extent that the darkness of "private" interests has been replaced by God's possession of the soul: "For that which God doth touch and own / Cannot for lesse be told" (23–24).

In this process of cleansing, which includes the revision of the poem itself, the ideal of high achievement through a potential socioreligious ascent is refined into an ideal of purity that links holy intentions with holy acts, unites the "inward" and "outward" callings, and stays in its place. Herbert chooses the word "room" (19) for the second version of his poem, not only because it softens the hierarchical inversions of the stanza, but because the word can refer to social estate itself, one's "place" in the community. Therefore, the poem again emphasizes not the rewards to be gained by acting "for thy sake" (15) but the purifying spirituality that can transform any secular office into something "bright and clean" (16).

For Herbert, the plain style demanded holy motives and sanctified work, a model of transparency both within and without that demonstrated all was done "for thy sake." Language itself was considered one of these social actions, and "The Elixir," like "Redemption" and "Love unknown," upsets the evaluative power of high and low style in order to offer a new ideal of linguistic plainness that aims at transparency in motive and word. This plain style claims to unite Christian intentions with sanctified language and to free rhetoric from its social ambitions.

Such a model of language and identity, in which an upper-class poet can identify with a servant, should not be mistaken for egalitarianism. We find here the behavioral plain style that nevertheless preserves its difference from those regarded as common. In a chapter in *The Country Parson* that describes the parson's visits to his parishioners during their daily labors, Herbert uses the imagery of pollution to suggest not only that cleanliness is next to godliness, but that cleanliness was his mental defense against the disruption of class distinctions brought about by his very belief in the doctrine of vocation and his diligent efforts in his rural community. This suggests that the character of holiness was a protection not only against the contempt of those who judged from above, but from the "taint" of those who threatened him with pollution from below.

The virtues and vices of the plain style become apparent in the following passage from *The Country Parson*:

> Wherfore neither disdaineth he to enter into the poorest Cottage, though he even creep into it, and though it smell never so lothsomly. For both God is there also, and those for whom God dyed: and so much the rather doth he so, as his accesse to the poor is more comfortable, than to the rich; and in regard of himselfe, it is more humiliation. (249)

In this passage the genteel, sophisticated parson actually confronts the laborer whose poverty he likes to affect in his poetry, and his intense reaction against entering the cottage testifies to his acute consciousness of breaking the rules of social decorum by doing so and his deep fear of the polluting effects of this transgression.[33] To "creep" into the cottage is to risk contracting its commonness, which here threatens like a contagious disease. The Parson's anxiety over this encounter is measured by his inability to describe the people themselves in this cottage, whom he can only grasp as "those for whom God dyed." Herbert attempts to counteract this powerful class reaction by invoking Christian inversions of hierarchy; the passage recalls the explosion of social decorum in "Redemption," when the husbandman confronts Christ amidst the thieves and murderers. But the Parson's "humiliation" here is deeply ambiguous, since it both lowers him to the level of the poor laborers he visits and identifies him with the redeeming Christ who brought comfort to the poor rather than to the rich. In this passage and the experience it describes, Herbert may have honestly and decently tried to step outside the definitive power of the status system; certainly, we can see here that his "plain style" was no utopian pastoral aesthetic, but a model of Christian identity used to control his class responses and govern his everyday behavior in his rural community. Nevertheless, the brightness and cleanness that characterizes this plain style, and that he so desperately misses in this cottage, is centuries away from egalitarianism. If sweeping a "room" in "The Elixir" refers to sanctifying and purifying any worldly office or action, then we can see that such holiness was in part a method of protecting Herbert from the "mean" activities he describes in this passage.

The poet himself plays the role of unclean laborer confronted by aristocratic host in "Love" (III). Unlike "Redemption" and "Love unknown," the speaker of *The Temple* adopts the role of common husbandman with what is imagined as a full and painful knowledge of his unregenerate status, "guiltie of dust and sinne" (2). The process of humility staged by *The Temple* and culminating in this poem may spring from a religious attempt to throw off the blinders created by the speaker's original status pretensions, but it also reproduces the hierarchical assumptions inherent in Herbert's description of the holy Parson's confrontation with those in the poor cottages of his parish.

The poem places the redemptive communion service in the context of the traditional manor house feast to which the lord welcomes his tenants, no matter what their estate.[34] The poem juxtaposes incorporation into the holy religious community with incorporation into the social agrarian community:

Love bade me welcome: yet my soul drew back,
　　Guiltie of dust and sinne.
But quick-ey'd Love, observing me grow slack
　　From my first entrance in,
Drew nearer to me, sweetly questioning,　　　　5
　　If I lack'd anything.

A guest, I answer'd, worthy to be here:
　　Love said, You shall be he.
I the unkinde, ungrateful? Ah my deare,
　　I cannot look on thee.　　　　　　　　　10
Love took my hand, and smiling did reply,
　　Who made the eyes but I?

Truth Lord, but I have marr'd them: let my shame
　　Go where it doth deserve.
And know you not, sayes Love, who bore the blame?　　15
　　My deare, then I will serve.
You must sit down, sayes Love, and taste my meat:
　　So I did sit and eat.

In this poem, the means by which the guest becomes "worthy" (6) to enter mirrors the aristocratic largesse of a feudal lord who condescends to receive the tenants of his estate for holiday festivities. As in "Redemption" and "Love unknown," the tenant is included in this community as he is "improved," that is, as he receives the grace that will lead to the development of his sanctified identity. Like Herbert's other pastoral and agrarian poems, such an improvement of the self comes about through no labor of his own, but through the cultivating and renewing power of his Lord. This power, exercised according to feudal principles, comes to be known as love, which benevolently enfolds the soul within the traditional order.

Nevertheless, the elaborate social and religious ritual that surrounds this encounter mediates but cannot erase the problematic privacy of the "I-thou" relationship, a secret and internal communion that constituted the priesthood of all believers without a priest. The Church of England's homily on the Eucharist insists on this intimacy, as it requires communicants to understand the difference between the Catholic mass and the direct reception of grace in Protestantism: "so that thou acknowledge no other Saviour, Redeemer, Mediator, Advocate, Intercessor, but Christ onely. . . . Herein thou needest no other man's helpe, no other Sacrifice, or oblation, no Sacrificing Priest, no Masse, no means established by mans invention."[35] Such a "knowledge of religion" begins to undo the social fabric, since it denies that the hierarchical authority invested in a priest can be in any way redemptive and suggests, however slightly, that the framework of church and commonwealth may be the work of "mans invention." But the homily and other treatises on the Lord's Supper quickly counteract such suggestions by coordinating the power of minister and God. Dod and Cleaver insist that the communicant will meet at the Lord's table both the minister and "God himself in his own person," and that God's power will reproduce and deepen the power of the priest: "When men begin to make profession, God useth a more diligent search and examination than his ministers can doe: for they can but judge men by their actions, but the lord dealeth immediately with their hearts and consciences" (Dod and Cleaver, p. 158). In this formulation, God has more power than the minister, but that power simply extends more thoroughly inward the clerical function of examination and judgment.

In "Love" (III), the meeting between the speaker and his deity is both organized by the social nexus and deeply personal. The host meets the guest alone and requires an individual exchange. Though the speaker "drew back" (1), his host "drew nearer" (5) and "took my hand" (11). Love's personal questions and responses in this dialogue combine the religious power of the priest and the social power of the aristocratic lord, but they also turn the explosive confrontation between tenant and lord in "Redemption," and the tenant's ensuing guilt, into mutual affection: "Ah my deare, / I cannot look on thee / Love took my hand, and smiling did reply, / Who made the eyes but I?" (9–12). The poem enacts the intimate communion between "mine" and "thine" desired throughout *The Temple*. The experience seems to take place both within society and deep within the heart and conscience.

"Love" (III) is coordinated with but does not mirror the communion service over which Herbert himself presided. In that public ceremony, communicant met minister and God in a kneeling rather than a sitting position:

> For the manner of receiving, as the Parson useth all reverence himself, so he administers to none but the reverent. The Feast indeed requires sitting, because it is a Feast; but man's unpreparednesse asks kneeling. Hee that comes to the Sacrament, hath the confidence of a Guest, and hee that kneels, confesseth himself an unworthy one, and therefore differs from other Feasters: but hee that sits, or lies, puts up to an Apostle. (259)

Herbert struggles here with the image of the Eucharist as feast, which to the Puritans represented the community of Saints, but to the Anglicans required the ritual of kneeling, thereby reproducing the chain of "reverence" necessary to the hierarchical order. The sitting or the reclining position, which signified the freedom of those participating in the Jewish Passover service, could not be accommodated within the traditional liturgical ceremony. When the speaker in "Love" (III) sits and eats, he experiences individually and poetically what the Anglican service could never express publicly: the priesthood of all believers. That Love insists that the speaker sit rather than serve in this poem represents the conferral of grace as aristocratic largesse; nevertheless, it marks the disruptive moment when the individual no longer serves Jesus Christ as *"My Master,"* but takes on the role of disciple, or, as John 15:15 puts it, as friend. The relationship between this devotional poem and the actual communion service is doubly important, because the poem seems to represent both the speaker's entrance into heaven and the deep internal "truth" of the ecclesiastical ritual experienced throughout the religious life. Herbert's poem is both coordinated with and different from the communion service he celebrated at Bemerton, just as it is coordinated with but different from "The Altar," the poem that begins *The Temple* with the most ceremonious and "high church" of religious images, but which points toward the actual intimacy of religious communion and the full sanctification of identity experienced only at the "low church" table of "Love" (III).

Clearly, "Love" (III) is no unmediated image of the speaker's inward regenerated identity: at the moment that *The Temple* is most radical about religious identity, it is most conservative about social identity. Like the deeply personal improvement of the heart in "Love unknown," which nevertheless ensures that the tenant's obedience to his Lord will be "new, tender, quick" (70), so "Love" (III) constitutes religious sanctification according to the dictates of the hierarchical order. Herbert himself urges "Parents and Masters" to hasten the entrance of their "children and servants" into the communion of the church, because these authorities would thereafter be better "served and obeyed" (259). Like the master who prays for God to remove "the stonie, and unbeleeving, and carnal hearts" (Dod and Cleaver, p. 117) out of the hearts of his servant, "Love" (III) and the Anglican service turn potential apostleship into reverence for those in authority. The speaker's role in "Love" (III) as unclean agrarian laborer sitting at his master's table mediates his entrance into full-fledged religious apostleship and encloses Protestant models of religious and social improvement within the confines of the traditional order.

# Seven

## Religion and Enterprise in the Gardens of the Herbert Family

The last chapter considered pastoral and agrarian imagery in *The Temple* as a coordination of feudal and post-feudal ideologies. This chapter will extend that reading into an account of the gardens of the extended Herbert family. Gardening in the seventeenth century was an enterprise central to a new national project of commercial and technological "improvement," and a number of Herbert's relatives and patrons were important innovators in this project. Their gardening activities were in fact closely connected with their other, more commercial enterprises. As members of the extended Herbert family invested in colonization of the New World, joint-stock trading companies, and new agricultural techniques, they represented these commercial developments to themselves as the religious and patriotic cultivation of "nature" by "art," rather than as the pursuit of private profit, and their gardens brought to life this powerful myth of benevolent cultivation.

In this chapter I will argue that George Herbert's "Paradise" and the gardens of his relatives and patrons coordinate, however uneasily, the new ideal of improvement with the principles of a static hierarchical order by dedicating growth and productivity to communal rather than individual purposes. The gardens use the dichotomy of nature and art to achieve this coordination, since the concept of art is used to suggest not only the incorporation of the individual into the social fabric by controlling his or her unruly nature, but also the improvement of an uncultivated nature in order to increase productivity. The aesthetic shaping of the garden proclaims moral, religious, and political reformation but obscures the development of private property, whether that of the land or of the self. The cultivation of land in the gardens of the Herbert family becomes an aesthetic activity rather than a profitable enterprise; cultivation in Herbert's poem is defined as divinely generated rather than as a problematic form of self-interested performance.[1]

### I. HERBERT'S GARDEN

"Paradise" coordinates the principles of patriarchy with the ideals of improvement. In the poem, this coordination is achieved through the figure of the divine gardener whose power appears as art. The imagery of gardening links this use of power with an aesthetically pleasing and ultimately benevolent purpose, but nevertheless such aesthetics include the use of force. Although the first two stanzas of the poem promise that the poet will share in this aesthetic power, we later find that he is actually its victim. The result of the exercise of such power is to subordinate the poet to the principles of hierarchy by requiring that he stay in his place and yet be "more fruitfull" (12).[2]

The first stanza of "Paradise" lays out the divine order as an orchard or Renaissance formal garden with its attention to geometrical shapes and orderly patterns:

> I blesse thee God because I GROW
> Among thy trees which in a ROW
> To thee both fruit and order OW.
>
> (1–3)

The rhymed lines reproduce parallel rows of trees in an orchard, which, as Gervase Markham's *English Husbandman* clarifies, could

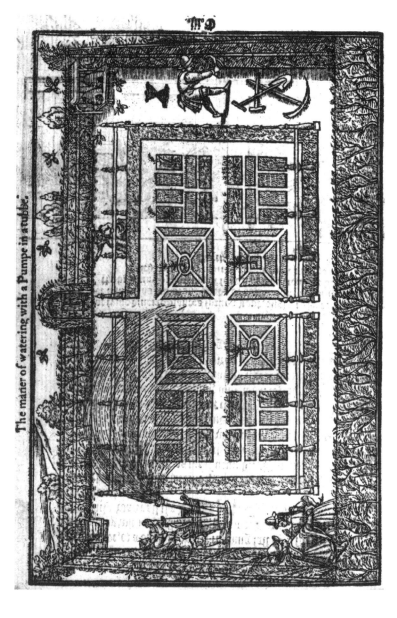

FIGURE 2. Corresponding plots in a Renaissance formal garden, from an illustration in Thomas Hill, *The Gardener's Labyrinth* (London, 1577), 453.a.3, page opposite 52. By permission of the British Library.

be structured quite artfully: "Which way soever a man shall cast his eyes yet he shall see the trees every way stand in rows, making squares, alleys, and divisions according to a man's imagination."[3] The rhymed lines in Herbert's poem suggest as well the rectangular beds of a formal garden, which were often laid out in corresponding pairs. Pope comments unfavorably on such a garden in "Epistle to Burlington":

> Grove nods at Grove, each Ally has a brother,
> And half the Platform just reflects the other.[4]

Both Pope and Herbert use rhyme to represent the aesthetics of this horticultural order, but Herbert foregrounds artfulness approvingly, not only to suggest the intelligent structuring of God's garden, but to claim that the poem itself and its clever rhyme pattern are examples of that "fruit and order" (3) that the poet owes to his creator. The poem argues implicitly that the shaping power of divine grace engenders human artfulness.[5] Pope may condemn Timon's villa,

> His Gardens next your Admiration call,
> On ev'ry Side you look, behold the Wall!
>
> (113–14)

But the assertion of the value of structure inherent in the enclosed garden represents for Herbert the orderly plan of salvation and the inclusion of the soul within it:

> What open force, or hidden CHARM
> Can blast my fruit, or bring me HARM,
> While the inclosure is thine ARM?
>
> Inclose me still for fear I START.
> Be to me rather sharp and TART,
> Then let me want thy hand and ART.
>
> (4–9)

The wall surrounding the formal garden not only announced the difference of the area from the uncultivated nature outside it, it also sheltered the trees and plants from livestock and a potentially destructive wind (the "open force" of line 4). But the phrase "hidden CHARM" (4) reminds us that this poem typologically evokes a specific garden, Paradise, and one which, despite divine protection, was invaded by the deceiving serpent.[6] Stanza 2, seemingly a rhetorical question, shocks the speaker into recognition of his own complicity in the Fall and a realization that harm comes not from outside the enclosure but from within the soul. "Nature" emerges in the latter half of the poem not as the sanctified growth of stanza 1, spontaneously appearing as the soul's "fruit" (3), but as human "nature," which is definitively fallen and fundamentally threatening to the divine order, and which appears in the poem as a form of growth that is wild and transgressive.[7] In the first stanza, fruit and order, nature and art cooperate, as the trees produce and the gardener lays them out in rows; in stanzas 4 and 5, we find that art carves its structure into nature through the use of excision. To shape is to amputate:

> When thou dost greater judgements SPARE,
> And with thy knife but prune and PARE,
> Ev'n fruitful trees more fruitfull ARE.
>
> Such sharpness shows the sweetest FREND,
> Such cuttings rather heal than REND,
> And such beginnings touch their END.
>
> (10–15)

In the poem, being pruned is preferable to being excluded from the garden through extirpation, or damnation, like the branch that "beareth not fruit" and is "withered" and "cast . . . into the fire" in John 15. The clever pattern of the rhyme scheme comes to represent not the spontaneous engendering of human art through divine inspiration, but the painful, repressive conflict between divine grace and forms of human disorder. If the "fruit" referred to in line 3 includes poetry, then stanza 3 changes this ingenious riddle in which inspired art "grows" as easily as nature to a much darker claim that human art can be as transgressive as uncultivated nature and human sin. We can imagine that several poems, the unwanted, disruptive "fruits" of the poet's soul, have been pruned away because they were deemed sinful or generated by the imagination of the poet alone, rather than being reproductions of the divine order suggested by the outlines of the garden. The formulation suggests, bizarrely, that the speaker, as tree and as Adam, will produce the very fruit that will bring about his own fall.

The issue comes to the fore in line 7: "Inclose me still for fear I START." In the seventeenth century, "start" could mean to shoot up suddenly, like a plant, or to be pulled loose from one's place, but it could also refer to animal or human movement, as in to move suddenly, to be startled by something, to get out of line, to go astray, to escape.[8] The word expresses the speaker's anxiety or "fear" about his weakness in the face of temptation. But the word also suggests that to move, in the poem, is to sin; moving implies the development of actions and creations that are self-initiated and that would destroy the careful regularity of the garden. "Starting" disrupts the analogy of the poem (God as gardener and soul as fruit tree) since it acknowledges the motive power of human will. It introduces the possibility of a quick shooting up, an upward ascension, a rise that would actually be a "fall," since it would threaten the divine powers. "Inclose me still" (7) suggests that motionlessness is identical with obedience and that such stillness demands an individual enclosure, as was used for frail plants, beyond that of the wall surrounding the garden. The poem modulates between the disruptive reference to movement back to the analogy of the garden through the image of father and child: "Be to me rather sharp and TART / Then let me want thy hand and ART" (8–9). But, as a result, the poem suggests that such vegetable imagery is one of the enclosures used by the poet to control the problem of an ambitious will, or of a poetic creativity that can too easily "start," or escape, from divinely instituted boundaries. The proper growth of the garden is made possible only when one stays in one's place.

The contrast between human action and vegetable stillness in "Paradise" mirrors an important revision made in "Employment" (II), which tries to limit its original expression of ambitious desire through the image of a productive but motionless "Orenge-tree":

He that is weary, let him sit.
    My soul would stirre
And trade in courtesies and wit,
    Quitting the furre
To cold complexions needing it
     . . .

When th'elements did for place contest
    With him, whose will
Ordain'd the highest to be best;
    The earth sat still,
And by others is opprest
     . . .

Oh that I were an Orenge-tree,
    That busie plant!
Then should I ever laden be,
    And never want
Some fruit for him that dressed me
     . . .

      (1–5, 11–15, 21–25)

The activity described by lines 1–5 and 11–15 above stands in stark contrast to the flourishing but motionless "Orenge-tree" in lines 21–25, which were included in the later revision of the poem. This tree was thought to be "busie" (22) because it produced both flowers and fruit simultaneously (*Works*, p. 504). In the cosmos of the original poem, particularly in lines 11–15, God "ordain'd the highest to be best," and the lethargic earth is "opprest" because it "sat still." In the revised lines 21–25, and in "Paradise," productivity and religious legitimacy require sitting still and submitting to the oppressive if benevolent knife of the divine father-gardener. The stirring and trading of the first stanza of "Employment" (II) is exchanged for a business that is tremendously fruitful but painfully static.

## II. THE FATHER'S GARDEN

The significance of the figure of God as paternal gardener in Herbert's poem is complicated by the powerful role that gardening played in the extended Herbert family: Herbert's stepfather and two of his patrons and aristocratic relatives had fashioned their own extremely artful enclosed gardens, all of which Herbert would have known quite well. The simplicity of the language in Herbert's poem suggests that he may have composed a plain-style religious poem as a contrast to the high-style pleasure gardens going up around him; nevertheless, all of these gardens draw attention to a process of cultivation that "prunes" the individual in order to put his or her powers into the service of a larger authority. By considering Herbert's garden in the context of those of his patrons, we can explore the relationship between the divine father-gardener in "Paradise" and Herbert's various social fathers, as well as the extent to which the poem's religious pruning participates in other cultural modes of the civilizing process, including the family and the larger forces of socioeconomic change. In my analysis, I am indebted to Roy Strong's techniques of analyzing gardens and his interpretations of the gardens of Danvers and Pembroke in *The Renaissance Garden in England*. I try to show here, however, that his emphasis on the political significance of gardens obscures what is an equally important socioeconomic significance.

The most interesting garden for our purposes is the one laid out by Sir John Danvers, George Herbert's stepfather, who was one of the first to introduce Italian gardening techniques to England at the family's Chelsea house in 1622.[9] Herbert would have spent a great deal of time at this house and in these gardens, and he seems to refer to them rather directly in his poems in honor of his mother.[10] These gardens included statuary and a grotto, and they were laid out in coordination with the house. Like William Herbert's gardens, Danvers's gardens were described by Aubrey as "curious."[11] The description and analysis that follow will show that, whereas Danvers's garden differs radically from Herbert's poem, because Danvers takes on the role of gardener, nevertheless, both garden and poem share a dilemma about the difference between acceptable and unacceptable forms of productivity. Illegitimate activity is pruned away through the figure of the gardener, whose own labor is validated as "art" and exclusively associated with the establishment of a social and religious order, rather than with individual achievement or competitive performance (see Figure 3).

Danvers's garden moves from "disorder" to order, from natural wilderness to the complex human structures of pavilion, banqueting hall, and grotto. The movement from wilderness to bowling green is particularly interesting because it reproduces the problem of "nature" in Herbert's poem and associates the use of art with the establishment of order. Danvers's gardens were structured in roughly three parts: the first, nearest the house, was called a "wilderness," "thicket," or "boscage"; the second was a large, oval, closely mowed bowling green; and the third, a terrace walk beyond, included two pavilions at either end, a brick banqueting hall in the middle, and, below this, a grotto.[12] In the wilderness area, made up of fruit trees, shrubs, and flowers, were statues of a gardener and his wife, which were, according to Aubrey, "both accoutred according to their Callings."[13] At the south side of the wilderness area, in a large graveled walkway that extended to the terrace walk, was a statue of Hercules struggling with Antaeus; on the north side was a statue of Cain killing Abel.

Danvers's "boscage" and the statues within and alongside it evoke the Biblical story of the Fall and the task of Adam and Eve after their Edenic surroundings had turned into a wilderness. The "nature" they must control, however, is their own, and the figures of Cain and Antaeus represent those aspects of human nature that must be restrained or pruned away. The result of such pruning is expressed in the second area of the garden, the closely mowed bowling green, which is also surrounded by emblematic statues. The central entrance to the green is flanked by two sphinxes, figures that, like the statues of Hercules and Antaeus, remind the visitor of the importance of knowledge of the classical world, through their reference to the story of Oedipus, and warn also of the value of proper interpretation and the danger of error. At each of the other three entrances to the green stand pairs of shepherds and shepherdesses in positions of increasing repose, from sitting,

to sitting and "inclining to sleepe," to "incumbent."[14] These are also "accoutred according to their Callings," but the difference between the vocation of shepherd and gardener is crucial: the pastoral figures have reached the goal of the reformation process, and have re-entered an Edenic state of innocence: "Where you read rustick beauty mixt with antique innocent simplicitie: there you may behold the Faithful Shepherd, and the Faithful Shepherdesse: who have the honestest innocent countenances that can be imagined."[15] Such innocence signals the end of the need for industrious activity—for the labors of a Hercules, the intellectual efforts of an Oedipus, and the toil of Adam and Eve. Dan-

FIGURE 3 *(opposite).* John Danvers's garden; model by John Aubrey; MS Aubrey 2, folio 59 recto. Bodleian Library, Oxford.

Transcription of Aubrey's key to Danvers's garden (MS Aubrey 2, folio 58 verso. Bodleian Library, Oxford).

1.1. the two paire of staires, that lead downe from the hall. On each side whereof sitt on their hinde leges two huge Dogs, gapeing like Lyons.
  2. the dore of the Gardiners house.
  3. A noble figure of Hercules and Antaeus.
  4. Cain slaying Abel.
  5. The figure of the Gardiners wife.
  6. The figure of the Gardiner, both coloured.
  7. Two Sphinxes.
  8. a fatherly Shepherd sitting; with high shoes laced, etc.
  9. the shepherds wife sitting.
 10. a young shepherdesse incumbent with flowers, etc.
 11. a young shepherd incumbent.
 12. a young shepherdesse sitting.
 13. a young shepherd sitting, both inclining to sleepe, with their eyes (almost) closed.

The little circles in the two squares signifie the Trees. and shrubbes, which make the thicket.

The Borders of the long Walkes are adorned with three or four lines of Thyme of several sorts, and near the Wall are rare Plants. The Walles you may imagine are furnished with choice Vines.

vers's garden moves from the labor resulting from original sin to the recovery of leisure in Paradise, a stillness analogous to Herbert's unmoving tree.

Nevertheless, the statue of Cain killing Abel turns the garden into a moral tale about different kinds of work. In *Genesis*, Abel is murdered because God has "had respect" for the offering of Abel, "a keeper of sheep," but refuses the offering of Cain, "a tiller of the ground." Cain's labors and the murderous competitive spirit that accompanies them are contrasted in Danvers's garden to the virtuous endeavors of Hercules and the community-minded work of the gardener and his wife, who, we can imagine, are their family's keepers. The transition from wilderness to bowling green suggests that those virtuous endeavors of husband and wife carve out the religious, social, and political order by which Paradise can be regained, whereas the actions of Cain generate the very wilderness that must be controlled.

Danvers's garden differs from traditional pastoral by making visible the transition from work to leisure, and by including a mediating figure, the gardener, who works with the soil and the "fruits of the ground" but nevertheless manages to keep his hands clean, to avoid the baseness associated with manual labor. Cain as triumphant villain, on the other hand, is associated with Antaeus, the defeated villain: both are linked with the earth. Antaeus the giant was invulnerable as long as he stayed in touch with his mother, the Earth, and Hercules defeated him by lifting him in the air and choking him. Douglas Bush, in *Mythology and the Renaissance Tradition in English Poetry*, tells us that during this period Hercules was interpreted as "the soul (or prudence, reason) who must raise Antaeus, the sensual body, above the contagion of earthly things."[16] But Antaeus's earthiness also evokes the labors of Cain, who produced "the fruits of the ground," which were judged inferior to Abel's offering. A frequent visitor to Danvers's garden, Francis Bacon comments on the kind of work that is acceptable to God, both in Paradise before the Fall and in the world after the Fall, that is, "no other than the work of contemplation":

> In the first event or occurrence after the fall of man, we
> see . . . an image of the two estates, the contemplative state
> and the active state, figured in the two persons of Abel and
> Cain, and in the two simplest and most primitive trades of
> life, that of the shepherd (also, by reason of his leisure, rest in
> a place, and living in view of heaven, is a lively image of a
> contemplative life) and that of the husbandman, where we
> see again the favor and the election of God went to the shep-
> herd, and not to the tiller of the ground.[17]

Bacon's comments reveal the link in Danvers's garden between the
divinely approved work of Abel and the leisure of the shepherds
and shepherdesses surrounding the bowling green: these pastoral
figures participate in "the work of contemplation," which wipes out
the taint of Cain's association with the earth. As Louis Montrose argues about Bacon's comments, the distinction between shepherd
and farmer in Danvers's garden is "at once social and spiritual."[18]
Montrose demonstrates that the contrast between Cain and Abel
was used by sixteenth-century writers to justify the distinction between those who worked with their hands and those who did not,
between the status categories of baseness and nobility. To maintain
one's position in upper-class society required enormous effort, but
an English gentleman could obscure the work involved in social and
courtly performance by representing himself in his pastoral poetry
or his pastoral garden as a shepherd whose contemplative life sim-
ulated the leisure required of members of the gentry. The movement from active labor to contemplative rest in Danvers's garden
erases the curse of Adam and attributes to Danvers the "great leisure
to use liberty where the meaner sort must labor"; nevertheless, it
calls attention to the Herculean efforts required along the way.[19]

Like George Herbert, John Danvers was a younger son in an upper-class family whose inheritance and title went to the oldest living brother, Henry, Earl of Danby. The relationship between elder
and younger brother, widely acknowledged during this period as
vexed and potentially antagonistic, gives new meaning to the statue
of Cain killing Abel in Danvers's garden. Danvers abjured competition through the statue, but nevertheless kept up with his elder

brother and consolidated his position as a member of the gentry through his marriages, his financial investments, and his pursuit of favor at court.[20] This kind of industrious activity is erased by the resting shepherds in his gardens but nevertheless acknowledged by the figure of Hercules and the statues of the gardener and his wife. By these figures, Danvers's industrious efforts to establish himself and his family amongst English society are mystified and legitimized as acts of religious cultivation, of "moral gardening." His garden proclaims his family's ability to contribute to the progress of the nation. The "vocation" of an upper-class courtier and the diligence it required is acknowledged; personal profit is obscured.

John Danvers was engaged in a number of financial enterprises, one of which was the Virginia Company, which sought to establish the English Church on American shores and to realize a profit for its investors. A letter written by Danvers to the Duke of Buckingham proposing a method of assigning control over Virginia import taxes illuminates the importance of openly subjugating personal profit to public service:

> Whereuppon & against your Lordship pleaseth next to command my attendance I will frame my proposition for his Majesty's further profit and service about the Customs of Virginia, the farming or managing of them. Wherin if I be admitted an undertaker, I desire not more benefit to my perticular then I shall (with thankfull minde for your Noble favor) consecrate and spend to do your Lordship service.[21]

An undertaker was both a participant in a business enterprise and a collector, or farmer, of custom taxes, one who leased out the profits from import duties. Danvers petitions for this lucrative position, but is careful to subordinate, at least on paper, his self-interest (the "benefitt to my perticular") to his service to the Duke and to the state in general. Notice that even in proposals that benefit the King, "profit and service" must be coordinated. Like the figure of the gardener in Danvers's Chelsea estate, whose efforts "prune away" the competitive spirit of Cain, so Danvers in his letter controls the profit motive by dedicating his "undertakings" to the state.

### III. PEMBROKE'S GARDEN

William Herbert, third Earl of Pembroke, who named Herbert to his post at Bemerton, maintained an elaborate garden at Wilton House described by John Aubrey, a seventeenth-century historian of the Wiltshire area, and John Taylor, the Water Poet. According to Taylor, these gardens, in the 1620s, were made up of "all manner of most delicate fruit trees . . . in such admirable art-like fashions, resembling both divine and moral remembrances, as three arbours standing in a triangle, having each a recourse to a greater arbour in the midst, resemble three in one and one in three."[22] Roy Strong reminds us that Renaissance gardens were most often emblematic and required "the mental and physical cooperation of the visitor as he moved through them."[23] Such a visitor would be invited to recognize the trinity as the "divine remembrance" suggested by the structure of arbors at Wilton that Taylor describes. Wilton's gardener, a Mr. Adrian Gilbert, had developed "several . . . ingeniouse contrivances about the House," as Aubrey puts it, and Taylor comments that the garden was "every way curiously and chargeably conceited. . . . He hath there planted certain walks and arbours all with fruit trees, so pleasing and ravishing to the sense, that he calls it 'Paradise'"[24]

The Italian gardens that replaced this "Paradise" were included in the famous remodeling of Wilton undertaken under Philip Herbert's auspices by Inigo Jones and Isaac de Caus. The new gardens were laid out between 1631 and 1634, largely during George Herbert's stay at Bemerton and while he served as chaplain to his aristocratic relatives. These gardens were far more elaborate than those of William Herbert as described by Taylor and Aubrey; they included statuary representing classical and Biblical figures, ornamental fountains, and a grotto covered outside with imagery from the sea and set up inside with artificial bird songs and a rainbow, all operated by de Caus's waterworks.[25] Although the gardens of William and Philip Herbert are clearly different in style, their emphasis on art is the same: both are filled with "ingeniouse contrivances."

FIGURE 4. William Herbert, third Earl of Pembroke, by an unknown artist, with his garden in the background. By courtesy of the National Portrait Gallery, London.

In the following analysis of Philip Herbert's Wilton House gardens, I hope to show that gardening was fundamentally associated with the development of new technology and that the aristocratic garden became the means by which such developments could be contemplated as the benevolent cultivation of "nature" by "art." In his gardens, the upper-class landowner and "undertaker" could dedicate his entrepreneurial powers to the state by subordinating "private benefit" to "the common good." By doing so, the aristocratic investor redefined himself as a "moral gardener" of society, and his commercial projects as religious and cultural enterprises.

Philip Herbert's grotto creates a close relationship between "art" as technology and "art" as aesthetic spectacle (see Figure 5). Grottoes were traditionally associated with the sea, and this one was artistically brilliant, with its figures of sea-monsters on the outside, Venus and Cupid in the sea on the inner facade, and the extremely elaborate "water-works" inside, which could produce artificial bird-songs, a rainbow, and sudden sprays that would surprise the visitor. Although some grottoes were linked with meditation, Pembroke has chosen to emphasize spectacle. But it is a spectacle that precisely stresses artistic control over water, and over the specific river running outside, in the wilderness area. The image of Venus evokes the myth of her birth from the ocean and represents the fertility arising from the powers of the sea. The sea-monsters suggest the need to control that power and that fertility, and the "water-works" bring such control into being, but again, in aesthetic form.

De Caus's "water-works" hint at, but also obscure, Philip Herbert's investment in more economically profitable schemes for controlling water, whether on land or sea. The images of Venus and the sea-monsters suggest the riches available from the overseas trade in which Philip so consistently invested through his membership in the East India Company, the Virginia Company, and others. The artificial bird-song and rainbow, which assert the human power to manipulate water in order to reproduce the products of nature, represent, but also obscure, Philip's investment in a new method of floating water meadows, also called "water-works," which increased the yield of grass in the fields, the number of sheep able to graze, and the corn harvest at the end of the season.[26] This method multiplied the yield of the land from threefold to sixtyfold and had recently been put into use on the Pembroke estate.[27] Philip's symbols of civilization clearly announce his ability to control the forces of water and vegetable growth present and represented in the wilderness area, but such symbols safely enclose the manipulation of natural forces within the confines of an aesthetic spectacle and

FIGURE 5. The grotto at Wilton, from Isaac de Caus, *Wilton Garden* (London: Thomas Rowlett, c. 1645), 441.g.19, plate 23. By permission of the British Library.

so exclude the commercial gain and social turmoil that such new "arts" could bring.

Both Philip and, earlier, his brother William, were engaged in projects for improving the land in areas surrounding Wilton, and several of these projects resulted in active protest. The ironworks in the Forest of Dean in Gloucestershire that William leased in 1612 and 1627–28 required the enclosing of forest land and the felling of trees for fuel; this led to riots among the inhabitants, who depended on the spoil of the woods, and to the infringement of William's monopoly by those area miners who pleaded their customary right to dig for ore. The Herberts would have received several enclosed acres from the King's plan to enclose and drain the vast area of Sedgemoor in Somerset, except that local commissioners could not overcome opposition from local residents who would have lost their extensive commons and gained little in return. In October 1631, Philip Herbert was instructed to call out the trained bands in Warminster in order to quell an armed rebellion against the enclosure of Selwood Forest on the border of Wiltshire and Somerset. The people of Warminster refused to take arms against the rebels, and the dispute was not ended until much later. George Herbert's term of office in the area, between 1630 and 1633, was in fact filled with riots and armed resistance against enclosure and disafforestation in the forests surrounding Wilton: Chippenham (1630–31), Selwood (1631), Gillingham (1627 and after), Braydon (1631 and after).[28]

The area closest to Wilton House was comparatively peaceful, partially because the traditions of the manor house were much stronger than in the forest areas, and partially because the Earls of Pembroke introduced capitalist modes of farming with great care closer to home. They no doubt had heard of the rioters who threw down hedges around Salisbury in protest against the enclosing of Washern Grange for Wilton's Park after the estate has been granted by Henry VIII to their ancestor, Sir William, in 1542. William and Philip's own plans for the floating of water meadows were put into practice only after the mutual agreement of their tenants.[29] Elsewhere, enclosure drew protests from the lower classes. Enclosure was described by John Norden as having "depopulated the places and converted the soyle to such endes and uses as have bene neyther pleasinge to God, beneficiall to man nor fitt for a Commonweale."[30] Although the Earls of Pembroke were responsible for enclosures not far from Wilton, the only visible enclosing that took place on their home grounds was in their garden.[31]

When John Taylor wrote a treatise in 1623 urging the town of Salisbury to make its river navigable in order to improve the "profit and commodities of it," he recounted his visit to nearby Wilton House and implicitly linked his own project of improvement with the house's gardens, which display the power of the gardener's "art":

> For Nature brings but earth, and seeds and plants,
> Which Art, like Tailors, cuts and puts in fashion:
> As Nature rudely doth supply our wants,
> Art is deformed Nature's reformation.
> So Adryan Gilbert mendeth Nature's features
> By Art, that what she makes, doth seem his creatures.[32]

Gardens and gardeners provided seventeenth-century culture with the means by which "improvement" could be viewed and contemplated as wholly benevolent; therefore, the human capacity to change the environment could be imagined as "deformed Nature's reformation," not as the disruption of age-old social conventions. The figure of the gardener, like the statue in Danvers's garden, makes visible the upper-class estate owner's commitment to progressive cultivation, but frees that commitment from the dangers of self-interest or the curse of manual labor. Therefore, the dichotomy of art and nature that the garden so easily suggests acknowledged the power of human labor, but only labor of a particularly upper-class sort: it defined the ability of the landowner to shape his land through his gardener as "art," but the attendant concept of "nature" erased the work of his tenants and the customs that had surrounded that work.[33] The dichotomy of art and nature in the garden obscures the complex social problems that arose during this period by defining the garden within the enclosing wall as cultivated and the fields without as needing such cultivation; it implicitly defines the transition from older to newer modes of agriculture, what we now call the transition from feudalism to capitalism, as the reformation of a wilderness.

## IV. THE AMERICAN GARDEN

It is not a coincidence that the imagery of gardening, planting, and natural growth is used in the literature on Virginia to identify the enterprise as God's civilizing or reforming process rather than as a self-interested business enterprise. If Virginia is a garden to be laid out, rather than a commercial investment, and if God is the gardener, then colonization becomes a divinely sanctioned process of aesthetic shaping. The sermons and pamphlets written to defend the Virginia Company against its enemies insist that the company's purpose is to advance the English nation and to publish the Gospel: "No doubt the *sound of the Preachers will goe out* into that corner of the world, and make it as a well watered garden."[34] The colony, called a plantation, was considered to have been founded by God:

"The finger of God hath been the onely true worker heere."[35] To plant America was not to invade it, and if the planter was God rather than man, then such planting was not being done for private interests but for the common good: "When he is our planter, hee becomes our husbandman; *and if he plant us, who shall plucke us up*? . . . When he giveth quiet, who shall make trouble? If God be the Gardiner, who shall plucke up what hee sets down?"[36]

During its most active years as a private joint-stock company, between 1609 and 1624, the Virginia Company had to defend itself against Spanish competitors and an English court faction that attacked it for mismanagement caused by greed. The company's defenders stressed repeatedly that the principle end of the colony was "the advancement of the kingdom of Jesus Christ," not the success of individual investors.[37] They preached this ideal not only to the enemies of the company, but to their investors and colonists as well. Whatever problem the colony or company might face, whether famine, attack by Indians, or the lack of English investment, the fault was always too much "covetousness" and too little piety. But the solution was not to lay up for oneself treasures in heaven, but to remember that spiritual values were primary and then wait for God to provide the increase. The preachers tied themselves into paradoxical knots trying to prove that the goals of the company were fundamentally religious and yet that God would not fail to reward his investors with hard cash. Alexander Whitaker tries to attract investors in a 1613 sermon on the Biblical text, "Cast thy bread upon the waters: for thou shalt find it after many daies" (Ecclesiastes 11:1). He urges, "Aime not at your present private gaine, but let the glorie of God, whose Kingdome you now plant, and good of your Countrey, whose wealth you seeke, so farre prevail with you, that you respect not a present returne of gain for this year or two."[38] Whitaker argues that though the colony may suffer afflictions caused by the sin of covetousness, it will flourish in the future like a plant that is pruned; as usual, the imagery of growth hovers ambiguously between spiritual and financial increase:

Since, when this English Colony hath taken better root; and as a spreading herbe, whose top hath bin often cropped off, renewes her growth, and spreads herselfe more gloriously then before. So this Plantation, which the divell hath so often troden downe, is by the miraculous blessing of God revived, and daily groweth to more happy and more hopeful success. . . . The finger of God hath been the onely true worker heere."[39]

Like Herbert's "Paradise," the imagery of vegetable growth provides a model of success, advancement, and expansion that is "natural" and therefore excludes the pursuit of power and wealth. To define God as worker, gardener, and planter of the colony is to legitimize the colony's existence as rooted in unselfish, communal purposes and to validate its structure, or social order, as the work of divine arts. To imagine the colony as "pruned" by its afflictions is to legitimize the suffering that such affliction caused, whether to the colonists or to the Indians, and to define these afflictions not as the result of the social order of the colony, but as reinforcing the very need for social order.

The "moral gardening" implicit in Herbert's poem, Danvers's Chelsea estate, and the literature on the Virginia Company attempts to cut away "private profit" for the sake of "God's glorie," but shapes as well a cultural order that celebrates expansion, whether religious, economic, or political. Herbert's poem clarifies the contradictory nature of this ideal of growth, since, in his poem natural flourishing is both the product of grace and the source of disorder. The transgressive growth of Herbert's fruit trees, like the "covetousness" of the Virginia investors, or the competitive instincts of Cain in Danvers's garden, must be pruned away to insure the stability of the larger order, whose health nevertheless depends on the very development that challenges it. In Herbert's poem, this contradiction, and the problem of differentiating between transgressive and sanctified growth, is solved through submission to the discriminating knife of the divine gardener and through a willingness to be "inclosed" (7), to restrict one's expansion in order not to upset the clearly delineated structure of the garden. To be incorporated in this structure includes the requirement to produce (one must be fruitful or be extirpated), but the ideal of growth is accompanied by the necessity to accept certain limits on that growth, limits that are carved out into the identity and psyche of the individual. The pruning in the poem, "such cuttings" (14), suggests an Oedipal drama, and if we take seriously Danvers's self-representation of himself and his wife as moral gardeners of their family and their society, then we can assume that Herbert's sense of the gardening metaphor had powerful paternal overtones.[40] This assumption is confirmed by a passage from *The Country Parson* on the duties of the householder: "But his family is his best care, to labour Christian soules, and raise them to their height, even to heaven; to dresse and prune them, and to take as much joy in a straight-growing childe, or servant, as a Gardiner doth in a choice tree" (275). Here, Herbert uses the notion of "moral gardening" active in the Danvers's household to describe the father's role in the transmission of cultural law. Again, the "pruning" involved suggests that this transmission included an Oedipal element, but this element must be understood as both personal and social in a fully historical sense. Herbert's God prunes away the competitiveness that might have sprung up between Herbert and his stepfather, who was only five years older than Herbert when he married his mother. The Oedipal pruning that the poem records not only insures the health of the family, it also reproduces a social order that requires growth as well as the subordination of self-interest to the common good; it requires personal development as well as respect for the principles of hierarchy. The garden carved out by the divine gardener in Herbert's poem may be called a religious "Paradise," but it is also the shape of a social patriarchy in transition between feudalism and capitalism.

This point can be clarified through a sermon preached and published by John Donne, Dean of St. Paul's, in support of the Virginia Company in 1622. Donne firmly asserts the justice of the enterprise, but diagnoses the central obstruction to its success as a profit-seeking individualism:

Beloved in him, whose kingdome, and Ghospell you seeke to
advance, in this Plantation, our *Lord* and *Saviour Christ Iesus*,
if you seeke to establish a temporall kingdome there, you are
not rectified, if you seeke to bee *Kings* in either acceptation
of the word; To be a *King* signifies *Libertie* and *independency*,
and *Supremacie*, to bee under no man, and to be a *King* signifies *Abundance*, and *Omnisufficiencie*, to neede no man. If
those that governe there, would establish a government, as
should not depend upon this, or if those that goe hither, propose to themselves an exemption from Lawes, to live at their
libertie, this is to be *Kings*, to devest *Allegeance*, to bee under
no man; and if those that adventure thither, propose to themselves present benefit, and profit, a sodaine way to bee rich,
and an aboundance of all desirable commodities from
thence, this is to bee sufficient of themselves, and to need no
man; and to be under no man and to need no man, are the
two acceptations of being *Kings*. Whom liberty drawes to
goe, or present profit drawes to adventure, are not yet in the
right way. O, if you could once bring a *Catechisme* to bee as
good ware amongst them as a bugle, as a knife, as a hatchet:
O, if you would be as ready to hearken at the returne of a
*Ship*, how many *Indians* were converted to *Christ Iesus*, as
what Trees, or druggs, or Dyes that Ship had brought, then
you were in your right way, and not till then."[41]

There are intriguing references here to the potential democracy of
the colony or its desire to be independent from English rule, but
these political forms of liberty are linked with an equally threatening kind of commercial liberty. To seek one's own monetary advancement, unless it is secondary to seeking the advancement of
Christ, is an act of rebellion against the Commonwealth; it is to
"devest *Allegeance*," and to "bee under no man." The "common
good" in this passage requires subordinating monetary enterprises
to religious and accepting one's subservient position in an interdependent hierarchy. The unchecked pursuit of private profit is a
form of independence, "to bee under no man" and "to neede no
man," that threatens to disrupt the proper order of society.

The poem at the end of Herbert's *Temple*, "The Church Militant," praises the piety of those going to America and claims that

this area will be reformed by what he calls Empire, the Church, and the Arts (263–66).[42] Herbert's lines referring to the Protestant Reformation of Germany seem equally relevant to the plantation of America: "Strength levels grounds, Art makes a garden there; / Then showres Religion, and makes all to bear" (87–88). The distinction made between nature and art in this image of the garden, as well as the triad of powers intended to reform America, justify the appropriation of territory, a radical restructuring of that territory, and the use of force by an imperial power ("strength levels grounds") not only in improving the land but in improving its inhabitants as well. "The Church Militant" proclaims the holiness of this improvement as it attempts to draw a definitive distinction between profit and piety:

> Religion stands on tip-toe in our land,
> Readie to pass to the *American* strand
>            . . .
> My God, thou dost prepare for them a way
> By carrying first their gold from them away:
> For gold and grace did never yet agree:
> Religion alwaies sides with povertie.
> We think we rob them, but we think amisse:
> We are more poore, and they more rich by this.
>                    (235–36, 249–54)

Through the figure of "Religion" (235) on its way to America, Herbert authorizes the English colonizing project to the extent that it is piously motivated. He identifies this process as occurring through "Empire and the Arts" (263), and yet free in itself from profit-seeking. This is the same dilemma that haunts ecclesiastical exhortations in favor of the colony: they believe they can cleanse religious growth from the pollution of financial gain.

In Herbert's poem, "Paradise," the image of the enclosed garden would have evoked traditional associations with the Christian Church, and Herbert's involvement in the Virginia Company suggests that he imagined that the walls of this Church could extend into the New World. In Christian iconography, the enclosed garden could, in fact, represent the design of all Christian history: the paradise from which man had been excluded after the Fall; the redemption of man through the birth of Christ; and the walls of the invisible Church, which included within them those souls who had been received again into the state of grace through their redemption from the "wilderness" of human will.[43] For Herbert, the Church was still "militant" because it was establishing itself in every part of the world through the forces of "Empire and the Arts" ("The Church Militant," 263).[44] Such imperial "strength" could lead to the "moral gardening" of other societies, lost in the wilderness of paganism, but such enterprises were legitimate only if they were motivated by the desire to give Christianity and not to take gold. As Donne puts it, one should count how many Indians are converted, not how many commodities are acquired. Donne and Herbert imagine that religious colonization can be separated from economic and political imperialism.

The connections between Herbert's "Paradise" and his "Church Militant" are fundamental. Both describe a religious and social order that sanctifies the use of force for the purpose of reproducing this order, psychically in the individual, and physically in the New World: "Strength levels grounds, Art makes a garden there; / Then showres Religion, and makes all to bear" ("The Church Militant," 87–88). The image of the garden turns this violence into benevolence and justifies suffering as the cost of religious and social reformation: "Such sharpness shows the sweetest FREND, / Such cuttings rather heal than REND, / And such beginnings touch their END" ("Paradise," 13–15). The "end" of this religious and social order, which in "Paradise" and "The Church Militant" is understood as individual and universal salvation, included as well the acquisition of foreign territory and the development of a worldwide trade nexus.

# Conclusion

## Modern Criticism and the Ideology of Sincerity

"In fact, the notion of a coherent, autonomous self is
really in danger here."
—Barbara Leah Harman, *Costly Monuments*

In Harman's intelligent close reading of "The Collar," she voices
the fear that plagues Herbert's readers: that the traces of modern
subjectivity that draw us to him will disappear, especially through
the use of an historicism that increasingly suggests his foreignness.[1]
Helen Vendler solves this problem by making Herbert securely
one of us:

> Herbert thought of God as someone equipped with a touch-
> stone which could distinguish authentic gold, and over and
> over Herbert himself applies to his work the single indis-
> putable touchstone of undeceived and undeceiving experi-
> ence: Is that what I feel? Is that what I mean? Am I permitting
> illusions? Am I writing for my own applause for my elevating
> sentiments?[2]

Vendler's touchstone for sincerity is not Herbert's. What God
touches and owns in "The Elixir" are not feelings, or "undeceived
and undeceiving experience," but acts performed socially, "what I
do," which are done "for thy sake," an elixir that, according to the
poem, gives those acts the highest value despite their specifically
low status associations.[3] For Herbert, sincerity was registered not in
"fidelity to experience" but in vocational labor. Yet Vendler and

Harman are not simply anachronistic in their evaluations of Herbert. *The Temple* contributes to the birth of the criteria by which it has been judged by modern critics. *The Temple*'s principle that religious purity must dwell at the heart of a professional worker developed into the modern notion of sincere authenticity at the heart of the autonomous individual, a notion required for the "genuine" artist. This model of creativity has been projected backward onto Herbert, and modern criticism has obscured the role that *The Temple* has played in the history of subject-formation. It replaces vertically structured, status-oriented models of personal definition with a horizontal structure, what might be called the centrality of self.

This book has outlined the ways in which Herbert would be horrified by his contribution to "self-centered" bourgeois subjectivity. His interior world of "The Church" is meant to articulate not the autonomous individual, but the transformation of a mortal being into a sanctified soul, a process that requires the consistent disciplining of the individual. Nevertheless, the placing of a devotional "internality" within a socially engaged "exterior," both in *The Temple* and in the doctrine of vocation, foreshadows the middle-class ethos that locates the subject and the domestic world at the center of things, surrounded by the "public."

The search for a personal voice in *The Temple* tells us more about our own need to believe in the mythology of a layered subjectivity than it does about a "person" named George Herbert. This mythology has also obscured from view the social milieu out of which the lyrics were generated, the importance of Herbert's extended family to his biography, and the social and economic ramifications of that family's Protestantism.

Herbert's use of the general calling as the interior of an external social role was the earlier, religious version of a developing secularized notion of character, a notion that was culturally required because of contemporary social change: the rise of the city, the disruption of the feudal order, and the system of status.[4] Standards of credit and personal motive were created as methods by which aspects of appearance, which had become detached from rank, family, and location, could be judged in terms of an invisible, inner essence. The intangible inside became the ground for validating the physical and the social. In this way, history constructed the notion of character, and, later, concepts of personality and individuality.[5] Modern versions of authenticity privilege this essence within as the source of creativity, producing a voice pouring out "emotion recollected in tranquility," not generated through or for social performance.[6] This is the origin of the belief that Herbert's poetry was fundamentally private, the result of personal meditation, rather than poetry produced within a milieu of upper-class writers sharing their work or a family known for its Protestant activism. For Herbert, the unique personal voice speaking "the spontaneous overflow of powerful feelings" would be a threat to society and religion.[7] For him, the dangers of privacy and autonomy were represented by religious enthusiasm and economic self-interest. Sincerity, for Herbert, was religious and social. It required locating the traces of divine grace in the soul and acting with what was claimed to be a concern for the "common good" in social life. It did not require transcribing what was unique about the self.

*The Temple* creates a model of the centered individual both different from and foreshadowing our own. It is evidence of the unstable subject in the early modern period, when status distinctions of higher and lower and hierarchical differences between ruler and ruled no longer provided trustworthy guidelines.[8] The work was produced in the vacuum left by the failure of these systems of personal definition. Lacking stable gentility, Herbert used the doctrine of vocation and *The Temple* to balance his life, both as he moved up the status ladder and as he moved down. To use Althusser's term, Herbert was "interpellated" in his poetry as the sincere subject, the man with a character, the professional who could be trusted in his employment because he resisted the self-interest that undermined seventeenth-century notions of the common good.[9] The "I-thou" relationship in the general calling pictured in "The Church" is less significant for its links with a modern private voice than in its resistance against early modern forms of "private bene-

fit." The "selfnesse" that threatens, especially in the later manuscript of *The Temple*, is to some extent the product of the structure
of the work itself, which originally allowed piety as a protection
from and a justification for professional advantage-seeking. Herbert
recognized that the doctrine of vocation could both authorize acquisition for its own sake and also be used as a method of counter-
acting this impulse. We see it as the disciplining of ambition, but
this is to use a moral and religious word to define a widespread social process. At stake was the social need for self-interest, which
could drive lives beyond the traditional stabilities of feudalism. Herbert's poetry voices this self-interest and disciplines it into sincerity.

In his work, *Sincerity and Authenticity* (1971), Lionel Trilling
traces the cultural changes that produced sincerity as a moral ideal.
He tells again the now discredited Burckhardtian story of the rise of
individualism and also makes its claims for historical advance. Nevertheless, Trilling's explanation for the new importance for sincerity
in the sixteenth and seventeenth centuries is still useful and is surprisingly similar to current New Historicist versions of this period:

> It is a historical commonplace that, beginning in the sixteenth
> century, there was a decisive increase in the rate of social
> mobility, most especially in England but also in France. . . . A
> salient fact of French and English society up to a hundred
> years ago is the paucity of honourable professions which
> could serve the ambitious as avenues of social advancement.
> To a society thus restricted, the scheme, the plot do not seem
> alien; the forging or destroying of wills is a natural form of
> economic enterprise. The system of social deference was still
> of a kind to encourage flattery as a means of personal ingra-
> tiation and advancement. The original social meaning of the
> word "villain" bears decisively upon its later moral meaning.
> The opprobrious term referred to the man who stood lowest
> in the scale of feudal society; the villain of plays and novels is
> characteristically a person who seeks to rise above the station
> to which he was born. He is not what he is: this can be said
> of him both because by his intention he denies and violates
> his social identity and because he can achieve his unnatural
> purpose only by covert acts, by guile. In the nature of his
> case, he is a hypocrite, which is to say one who plays a part.[10]

Trilling cites social mobility as the reason why the word *sincerity*, which originally was used to refer to *things* as "clean," "sound," or "pure," came to refer to "the absence of dissimulation or feigning or pretence" in *people*.[11] Sincerity was produced as a moral ideal so that society could monitor performances set free from traditional feudal norms. Trilling defines sincerity as genuineness in relation to society: "The moral end in view implies a public end in view, with all that this suggests of the esteem and fair repute that follow upon the correct fulfillment of a public role."[12] Trilling then demonstrates how authenticity replaced sincerity as the mark of the moral person and the true artist. In contrast to sincerity, authenticity is associated with genuineness in relation to oneself:

> From Rousseau we learned that what destroys our authenticity is society. . . . The work of art is itself authentic by reason of its entire self-definition: it is understood to exist wholly by the laws of its own being, which include the right to embody painful, ignoble, or socially inacceptable subject-matters. Similarly the artist seeks his personal authenticity in his entire autonomousness—his goal is to be as self-defining as the art-object he creates.[13]

Modern accounts of Herbert's sincerity are usually claims for a mode of authenticity free from the "taint" of social influence and performance.[14] On the contrary, sincerity for Herbert required social performance; it was evoked by his desire for "the esteem and fair repute that follow upon the correct fulfillment of a public role," whether as country parson or participant in a poetic coterie. Herbert uses the word in a chapter called "The Parson in reference": "The Country Parson is sincere and upright in all his relations. And first, he is just to his Countrey." (252). Authentic transcriptions of experience do not constitute sincerity for Herbert but rather social actions that are free from "deceit," or "guile" (252–53).

Modern criticism is fascinated with the subject of selfhood in Herbert, no matter whether *The Temple* is claimed to be self-expressive or self-diminishing. In most cases, the self that is at stake is the "authentic," autonomous individual unknown to the seventeenth century. This issue has been debated before. William Empson argued with Rosemond Tuve over the generating principle of *The Temple*: church culture or the individual artist. Richard Strier refers to this debate as "the problem of defining the predominant 'voice' of *The Temple*."[15]

The best deflator of this modern search for the personal voice is still Rosemond Tuve. She exposes the delight during her day and now over the "mere conveyance of an individual's emotion at a given time, that thin subject with which modern readers have to be content." Her distaste for this "sincerity-is-enough sentimentality" may be excessive, and it is clear from the work currently being done on the formation of bourgeois interiority that it is no "thin subject." Tuve goes too far in asserting the monolithic and immutable nature of inherited and shared church culture. Nevertheless, she speaks with a working recognition that Herbert's writing occurred before the constitution of modern versions of self.[16]

Joseph Summers agrees with Tuve that "the self to Herbert was not the valuable thing which it became to a later age," and asserts that "the primary purpose of the poems was not what we understand by self-expression," yet he believes the poems were written privately and withheld from circulation.[17] In *George Herbert: His Religion and Art* (1968), he stated that Herbert's "English poetry had probably been known to a distinguished circle of friends before the posthumous publication of *The Temple* in 1633," but in an essay published in 1987, he concludes that Herbert and Sidney kept their love poetry private.[18] He seems to come to this conclusion because of his belief in the poets' concern for "sincerity":

> Both facts may be related to the conviction of each poet that an effect of sincerity was essential to the poems he wrote, and to an unusual consciousness of the difficulties in achieving such an effect. 'Sincerity' is likely to become a problem if one thinks of poems not primarily as constructions or social gestures but as true accounts of experience and as expressions of personal commitment, particularly when experience fails to conform to traditional or idealized theory. Publication may invite the suspicion that the love poet is more moved by notions of poetic fame than by his supposed love.[19]

Unlike other critics, Summers is less committed to a model of authentic feeling than to something we might call "the sincerity-effect." This is a useful approach because it holds together what some critics would like to keep apart, re-creating experience and communicating it to an audience. This is Trilling's point: a new need developed in the sixteenth and seventeenth centuries to communicate one's experience to an audience, so that one would be perceived as "sincere," free from dissimulation or pretense. According to Trilling, "the sincerity-effect" requires an audience in order for one's "public role" to be legitimized. However, Summers decides that "publication," like Rousseau's society, would render the expression of personal commitment suspicious. Summers contrasts expressions of sincerity and social gestures. To Trilling, expressions of sincerity *are* social gestures.

Despite their differences, both Helen Vendler and Richard Strier analyze Herbert's poetry in a way that presupposes the presence of bourgeois subjectivity. Both argue that the poetry is primarily self-expressive. Vendler has stated:

> An expressive theory of poetry suits *The Temple* best: no matter how exquisitely written a poem by Herbert is in its final form, it seems usually to have begun in experience, and aims at recreating or recalling that experience. To approach such private poetry as an exercise in public communication with an audience is to misconstrue its emphasis.[20]

This account imagines authentic "experience" as beginning and ending in privacy, apart from an intruding society that can only make it less genuine. Strier points out the problem with this:

> The conception of originality on which Vendler relies is the one which the Romantic poets inherited from the eighteenth-century theorists of "genius"; it is the one which we, as post-Romantics have inherited. . . . Her major criterion is fidelity to unique personal experience. . . . The individual sensibility is unique, and what expresses the uniqueness of the individual sensibility is "original". . . . Another set of dichotomies emerges: "expression" and "communication"; "private" versus public poetry. . . . Vendler equates Herbert directly with

the "I" of his poems. The poems are direct transcripts—instances—of actual mental processes.[21]

Yet Strier has his own theory of Herbert's individualism:

> To insist on the personal nature of the poetry of "The Church" does not have to be anachronistic. Certainly Herbert was not a Romantic individualist. He was, however, a Protestant one.[22]

Strier's argument that Herbert is Protestant and not Anglo-Catholic is definitive. Also, his account of a particularly Protestant version of individualism is helpful, especially in his last chapters, entitled "The Heart Alone: Inwardness and Individualism," "The Heart's Privileges: Emotion," and "The Limits of Experience." This final chapter considers the difference between seventeenth-century and modern versions of autonomy.[23] But although Strier historicizes his interest in emotion through reference to Reformation theology, Herbert's poetry is authentic for him to the extent that it voices the feelings of private devotion: "Despite his undoubted personal loyalty to the . . . British Church, Herbert's ultimate commitment was to the Spirit and to 'feeling.'"[24] Strier's emphasis on the need for real feeling in Reformation Protestantism is accurate; yet he too quickly assumes that feeling legitimizes personal experience. He quotes Herbert's description of public prayer and preaching: "In prayer, the parson is, above all, 'hearty'—that is, sincere—so that, 'being first affected himself, hee may affect also his people' . . . 'every word is hart-deep.'"[25] These passages suggest not personal emotion legitimized, but feeling cut to the shape of public words—here, from the Bible or church prayer.[26]

Strier's analysis of the role of emotion in Herbert's poetry needs to be augmented by a recognition, not just of the "limits of experience" for theologians of this period, but of their sense of positive antipathy toward what was purely individual. The general calling was meant to be balanced by social engagement; the doctrine of the two callings was in part a method of diffusing the dangers of "the heart alone." According to Strier, Herbert was akin to the radical Protestants because of his emphasis on interiority:

> One of the essential impulses of the "radical Reformation"
> was the internalization of religion, the replacement of exter-
> nal or institutional realities with internal or spiritual ones.
> Where the orthodox called for correlation, the radicals called
> for replacement.[27]

I do not find this statement convincing about Herbert because it ignores the pressure he felt to do exactly what Strier denies: to cor-
relate "being" to "seeming," devotional feeling and vocational labor, the spiritual and the temporal kingdoms.[28]

The work of Stanley Fish has influenced many modern critics of
Herbert, including some who intend to historicize his poetry. Fish
does not approach the poems as transcriptions of a sincerity within;
rather he sees sincerity as associated with public, rhetorical proce-
dures, including catechism.[29] Associated with Fish's recognition of
the public purposes of this poetry is the acknowledgment that Herbert's work is not the expression of a unified sensibility but a site of
conflict over subjectivity, including a "dialectic of the self."[30]

Nevertheless, Fish's analysis displays the modern investment in
personality through its search for a voice that is more or less autonomous. Fish argues that Herbert's poetry is self-consuming or
self-diminishing. This "self" is imagined ahistorically. Despite Fish's
claims, Herbert's poetry does not assert and then relinquish autonomous, independent authorship. Herbert's culture made such
autonomy a near impossibility.

Fish's dialectic is built on a conflict between the omnipresence
of the Christian God and the independence attributed to the modern self:

> The insight that God's word is all is *self*-destructive, since ac-
> quiring it involves abandoning the perceptual and conceptual
> categories within which the self moves and by means of
> which it separately exists. To stop saying amiss is not only to
> stop distinguishing "this" from "that," but to stop distinguish-
> ing oneself from God, and finally to stop, to cease to be.
> Learning to "spell" in these terms is a self-diminishing action
> in the course of which the individual lets go, one by one, of
> all the ways of thinking, seeing, and saying that sustain the il-

lusion of his independence. . . . There is nothing easy about the "letting go" this poetry requires of us. We are, after all, being asked to acquiesce in the discarding of those very habits of thought and mind that preserve our dignity by implying our independence.[31]

For Fish, human dignity consists in a will and mind independent from others and from external authority. The issue was imagined by most people in the seventeenth century in a very different way: human value consisted in a will and mind in relation to authority, whether in reference to God or other people, whether one was above or below, ruler or ruled. One did not exist through separation but through community or communion. It is true that Reformation Protestantism singled out the I-thou relationship in the general calling, but human autonomy or independence in this relationship was never imagined as a matter of dignity. This modern sense of dignity determines Fish's reading of the reception of the speaker into the experience of communion in "Love" (III) as a loss of selfhood:

> It has the effect of leaving the speaker with nothing to call his own. . . . His opponent demands unconditional surrender. . . . He loses the contest (he never had a chance) and with it his independent will. . . . What shrinks or is shrunk is the speaker's self. He has been killed with kindness.[32]

To be dependent is to be nothing in this account; identity inheres in autonomy. Independence is registered in the speaking voice that authors itself and its works; therefore Herbert's poetry displays

> the undoing of the self as an independent entity, a *"making of no thine and mine"* by making it all thine, a surrender not only of a way of seeing, but of initiative, will, and finally of being (to say "I am" is to say amiss). To the extent that this surrender is also the poet's, it requires the silencing of his voice and the relinquishing of the claims of authorship.[33]

This account affirms as lost what has not yet been historically produced—the author-function, as defined by Foucault: "The coming into being of the notion of 'author' constitutes the privileged mo-

ment of *individualization* in the history of ideas."[34] Jonathan Goldberg comments on this issue:

> As Foucault says, the author is always a function of the text,
> and, classically, a name applied to a body of texts to signify
> their unity and propriety; at a certain point, when property
> defines the nature of the self, when copyright safeguards the
> text as the author's property, the author emerges as one
> whose existence is the transcendental guarantee for his texts.
> It is that sovereign author whose death Barthes, and Foucault
> (and Derrida) proclaim. And that sovereign author *has yet to
> be born* in Herbert (or in Spenser or Shakespeare)—except in
> the hands of his twentieth-century critics.[35]

Leah Marcus uses an historically informed method of interpretation and so avoids much of the anachronism in Fish's approach.
She considers the role of social change in the production of subjectivity and seeks to identify Herbert's position in the transition
from feudalism to capitalism. Nevertheless, she identifies Herbert's
"self" with a bourgeois subject-position:

> By retreating to the role of a child and servant in his Master's
> house, Herbert was able to recover the lost ideal of a church
> whose language and forms of worship were part of a single
> hierarchy extending from the pettiest human concerns up
> to the dance of the heavens. . . . But though Herbert seems
> to have had little difficulty in whittling down the complex
> seventeenth-century universe to simpler traditional patterns
> of church and cosmos, he was able to do so only because he
> had accomplished the more difficult task of whittling down
> his own spirit.[36]

By using the seventeenth-century hierarchical relations of master
and servant, father and child, Marcus contextualizes Herbert's devotional verse, and so offers a more historically accurate account of
subjectivity. But her assumption and privileging of an adult "spirit"
from which Herbert's poetry retreats interferes with a precise description of the process of subject-formation occurring at the time.
She associates emerging modern ideologies not only with maturity,
but with the real, and so labels Herbert's discomfort with them a

loss of self. I have argued that, because of his interest in vocation, Herbert was not as "medieval" as Marcus claims.[37] I do agree with Marcus that Herbert resisted new patterns of thought and behavior, but she mistakenly identifies these new patterns with Herbert's "own spirit."

Michael Schoenfeldt offers the most nuanced account of the constitution of the subject within hierarchical structures, especially in terms of the linked submission and resisting aggression inherent to the position of the courtier in relation to his patron. Schoenfeldt demonstrates how frequently the language of courtiership and devotion coincide. Nevertheless, his singling out of aggression as the site of "the subject's self-affirmation," through "unsettling, restless insurgence," repeats in a new way the modern preoccupation with autonomy.[38] Fish claims that such self-affirmation has to be relinquished; Schoenfeldt finds it "lurking within the terms of the surrender the poet extends to God"; in either case, religion is opposed to "real" identity, and is continually threatening its sources of energy.[39] For Schoenfeldt, "Love" (III) does not dramatize the absorption of the speaker into the deity, but investigates "mortal resistance to an overpoweringly beneficent God."[40] Schoenfeldt avoids Fish's and Foucault's monolithic version of power through attention to "an impertinently recalcitrant self" and the belief that "individuals shape the culture that shapes them."[41] Nevertheless, his book, illuminating as it is, does not explore how Herbert shaped his culture or how *The Temple* formulated new models of subjectivity.

Like Fish, Barbara Harman also looks for and laments the loss of the authorial voice of modernity. Nevertheless, she clarifies through her analysis the points of conflict between different kinds of subjectivity. For her, the dialectic is between culture and self. Without intending it, she makes visible a struggle between different culturally produced subject-positions.

Like Fish, Harman's version of selfhood is modern: "To speak is to *will* one's birth (to have a 'second birth'). . . . Speech is an act of inauguration, and what it inaugurates is the self."[42] Again, authentic speech voices or creates an identity and a work of art separate from social constraints. Speech is independent authorship of one-self. Self-relinquishment occurs in Herbert's poetry when culture, tradition, or religion speaks instead. For Harman, Fish's "dialectic of self" is the struggle between the independent author and the voice of tradition. Harman's analysis of "Jordan" (II) is especially useful because it allows us to historicize this dialectic:

> To 'work,' 'winde,' and 'deck' is necessarily to 'weave [one's]-self' not out of but 'into the sense' because the man who works and winds mixes his labor with the world—in order to make, in this case, a complex, rich, elegant, and ingenious object out of an otherwise 'plain intention'. . . . But Christ really interrupts, substituting his words for the speaker's words and recommending that the speaker copy out a sweetness already written elsewhere, in order to suggest that the speaker weave himself back *out* of the sense. This unweaving would be accomplished by the recognition that Christ's voice had priority over all personal voices and that one's proper work was not the original work of self-construction, but rather that secondary or derivative work of reproducing an already written text.[43]

In this book, I have argued that the doctrine of vocation, social mobility, and the changing economic structure eventually made it possible to believe that "labor and expense are what weave the self . . . into the world," but only after a great deal of cultural resistance.[44] Indeed, the idea that labor and expense are constitutive of self is exactly what Herbert entertains rather fully, and finally cannot accept. What Harman identifies as relinquishing the self is actually the abandoning of a particular perspective associated with emerging bourgeois values and the social "new man," the belief that anything is possible with the proper use of "labor and expense." In his earlier manuscript, Herbert creates "a complex, rich, elegant, and ingenious object," himself, a combination of "Church-porch" and "Church," a witty courtier deserving patronage partly because of the religious piety at his heart. But this form of "self-construction" is eventually demolished. Herbert's revisions reveal not only that "So did I weave myself into the sense" (in "Jordan"

[II]) was a later addition, but also that the line summarized Herbert's rejection of the self-made, socially mobile version of social identity produced through "labor and expense" and authorized in the earlier *W* manuscript.

The search in modern criticism for the "authentic" Herbert, whether heard in the voice of sincere personal expression, self-renunciation, or resistance, has prevented modern criticism from fully historicizing the structure of selfhood posited by *The Temple*. In a way, criticism has followed Burckhardtian models, assuming that Herbert's individualism must stand in opposition to the corporate structures of family and church. Post-structuralism and New Historicism have taught us that individualism is itself culturally constructed and supports rather than undermines modern social institutions.[45] Therefore, it is useful to notice that the aristocratic model of individualism available to Herbert, social mobility through courtiership and patronage, was practiced by many members of his family. The other model of individualism available to him, the doctrine of vocation, was offered by his church.

Debora Shuger has reminded us that,

> if no unchanging human nature exists, and what 'man' is cannot be separated from his culture, then we cannot approach a given period or its texts by disregarding the self-interpretation of that period. . . . Religion during this period supplies the primary language of analysis. It is the cultural matrix for explorations of virtually every topic: kingship, selfhood, rationality, language, marriage, ethics, and so forth. Such subjects are, again, not masked by religious discourse but articulated in it.[46]

This passage appropriately gives priority to religion, but does not acknowledge that religious discourse also explored economic issues, and that this exploration did indeed mask from itself some of its more disturbing implications. The doctrine of vocation provides the religious discourse in which the relationship between devotional and social subjectivity was explored by seventeenth-century culture, especially in relation to changing social and economic structures. What we find in this discourse is not only the Protestant ethic but an ongoing effort to ward off the power of "private benefit" by linking the general calling, with its new "priesthood of all believers," to a careful deference to authority and hierarchical status in the particular calling. Theologians during this period meant to preserve what they saw as a necessary prerequisite for social order, but they did not recognize that they were also opening up the possibility for a defense for social mobility, the acceptance of trade and commerce, and a modern subjectivity built in terms of private and public worlds of being. *The Temple* does not reflect these possibilities, not yet fully emerged, but Herbert's poetry contributes to their production.

In vocation, the "private" does not refer to a meditative or domestic way of life, but to the threat of personal interests that would erode the delicate structure of hierarchical interdependence.[47] The members of the Herbert family pursued their economic goals with more or less energy and success, but they all accepted this limit on their efforts: accumulation and improvement could only be justified in the name of the "common good." Nevertheless, anything was possible if this justification could be formulated. Protestantism both provided them with this justification and policed its infringements, requiring submission to God's order, but also extending that order into the New World.

Similarly, the lyrics of the Herbert family cannot be considered private in a modern sense. Although they referred to the heart and to love, either secular or sacred, nevertheless they spoke within a network of shared issues, genres, and evening entertainments. To imitate Sidney was not a private literary process but a social gesture, signifying within the system of patronage in the family, as well as evoking, the family's Protestantism. *The Temple* and especially the lyrics in "The Church" were, to some extent, George Herbert's means of identifying himself as the descendant of the Protestant Sidney. Therefore, the Lutheran emphasis on grace rather than works in "The Church" also had a "public," even a political, meaning.

*Conclusion*

The account of Herbert's biography in this book is meant to demonstrate that his problems with employment brought him in contact with the political conflicts of his time, as well as the changing social and economic structures of his society. *The Temple* should be considered as one document in the history of this social and economic change because it is a form of spiritual autobiography that, like many others, represents the relationship between piety and business in the world. For Herbert, labor was problematic but required, a blessing and a curse. He began by trying to reconcile gentility and vocation; he ended with the "character" of holiness, which authorized the Protestant ethic but was far less "modern" than his original model. The lyrics display the same struggle between old and new ideologies. In the imagery of pollution and the imagery of pruning, something must be excluded so that a cultural, religious, and personal sense of order can be maintained. What is excluded is not simply the new ideology of the self-made man; Herbert's lyrics also reject the pleasures of high status. What is included is not simply the old ideology of submission to hierarchical authority; the poetry also posits human internality as the site of communion with the divine, a claim to a classless subject-position, one precursor to our belief in individuality. Like the gardens of the Herbert family, the lyrics display a social patriarchy in transition between feudalism and capitalism.

# Reference Matter

# Notes

## INTRODUCTION

1. Baxter, *Poetical Fragments*, "The Epistle to the Reader," sigs. A7–A7v. I have used Parsons's translation, published in 1958, of Weber's famous book. Weber refers to Baxter's *Saint's Everlasting Rest* and *Christian Directory* in his chapter, "Asceticism and the Spirit of Capitalism." I consider Weber's critics later in the Introduction.

2. Paul Alpers, Danielle Freedman, and Thomas Hayward helped me with this translation. They are responsible for all of its virtues, and none of its vices.

3. Subjectivity as inwardness was the main focus of the New Critical interest in Herbert; for a history of the relationship between subjectivity and society, and of the division between home and work, see Armstrong, *Desire and Domestic Fiction*, pp. 3–27. For the use of the term in modern critical theory, see Paul Smith, *Discerning the Subject*. Maus explores the multiple contexts in which the terms *inward* and *outward* are used in *Inwardness and Theater in the English Renaissance*. Targoff objects to the belief that inner and outer selves were consistently separated during this period (see "The Performance of Prayer"). Selleck argues intriguingly that subjectivity is a term that itself privileges an inner self and so projects backward onto the early period a modern conception of identity. I thank Professors Targoff and Selleck for sharing their work with me.

4. Scholars have questioned the usefulness and historical accuracy of the term *individualism* in accounts of social change, either because its characteristics have always been part of English society (Macfarlane, *The Origins of English Individualism*) or because it suggests that selfhood could be autonomous rather than socially constructed (Greenblatt, *Renaissance Self-Fashioning*). I continue to use the term because it represents precisely what Protestant preachers are most disturbed about during this period. A useful book on this issue is Heller, Sosna, and Wellbery, *Reconstructing Individualism*. For my comments on Macfarlane's thesis, see Chapter 6, n. 6.

5. The theatrical model and the notion of social improvisation are de-

veloped by Greenblatt in *Renaissance Self-Fashioning* and throughout his work, especially in "Psychoanalysis and Renaissance Culture." Agnew's work on the subject is invaluable; he uses the term *artificial persons* in *Worlds Apart*. Targoff argues against an over-reliance on the theatrical model, and her study, "The Performance of Prayer," reveals an alternative religious tradition of a coordination of inner and outer selves. However, she does not explicitly consider the social and economic changes that generated a division between the inward and outward as described by Agnew. I believe that the doctrine of vocation was a Protestant attempt to formulate a connection between the two, an attempt that eventually failed. Shuger applies the term *persona* to Anglican conceptions of self and Herbert's poetry in *Habits of Thought*, but she does not consider the effort in the doctrine of vocation to link social persona to devotion.

6. See Seaver, *Wallington's World: A Puritan Artisan in Seventeenth-Century London*.

7. Perkins, *Treatise*, p. 731; see also the discussion of the necessity to join the two callings (p. 734).

8. Latimer, "The Sermon Preached Upon Saint Andrew's Day, 1552," pp. 23, 26.

9. Perkins, *Treatise*, pp. 735, 744–45.

10. Sanderson, p. 230.

11. Thomas Adams, "The Two Sonnes," in *Works*, p. 422.

12. This is a historical problem for all Herbert critics. Walton claimed that "all Mr. *Herbert's* Court-hopes" died in 1624 and 1625 with the death of his patrons, the Duke of Richmond, the marquis of Hamilton, and King James; but this list leaves out his actual patrons, William Herbert, Philip Herbert, and John Williams, and it cannot explain why Herbert received no preferment between 1625 and 1630 when all of his major patrons were still alive, why the final offer was so minor, or why it was accepted (Saintsbury, pp. 251–339). Hutchinson agrees with Walton's view and adds that a sense of unworthiness must have prevented Herbert from seeking or accepting offers from other patrons (George Herbert, *Works*, pp. xxx–xxxii). Joseph Summers has the best understanding of Herbert's connections and concludes that his lack of preferment resulted from a combination of unpopularity with the court and Herbert's antipathy to it; his ordination "implied an abandonment of his hope that, for a person of his connections and convictions, a 'life based on divinity' and 'great place' in civil affairs were then compatible" (*George Herbert*, p. 44). Charles concludes that "in the last months of 1624 Herbert was turning his back on worldly preferment," and implies that Herbert was planning from the outset of his career to be a minister; she cannot explain his lack of preferment

between 1624 and 1630 (*A Life*, p. 112). Benet revises Charles's account and makes an effective case that Herbert may have sought ordination for "practical considerations alone." See her illuminating "Herbert's Experience of Politics and Patronage in 1624."

13. This argument is expanded and supporting documentation is provided later in this Introduction.

14. Critics who recognize the special import of vocation to Herbert consider it as a primarily theological matter and not in terms of its sociological implications (see Benet, *Secretary of Praise*, and Shaw. Joseph Summers does comment on Weber's thesis in *George Herbert*, pp. 46–47).

15. On the Reformation Protestantism of Herbert's devotional poems, see Halewood, Lewalski, Strier in *Love Known*, Veith, and Hodgkins.

16. Schoenfeldt; Strier, *Resistant Structures*, pp. 83–117, "Sanctifying the Aristocracy," and "George Herbert and the World," pp. 211–36; Shuger, *Habits of Thought*, pp. 91–119. I discuss the arguments of Strier and Shuger more thoroughly in Chapter 3 and of all three critics in the Conclusion. For other recent studies on the relationship between Herbert's poetry and society, see Gottlieb, "The Social and Political Backgrounds of George Herbert's Poetry"; Marcus, *Childhood and Cultural Despair*; Summers and Pebworth, "Herbert, Vaughan, and Public Concerns in Private Modes." I have benefited from all of these works. Nevertheless, these critics do not discuss the influence of the doctrine of vocation on Herbert.

17. I find Williams's work on the pastoral, especially *The Country and the City*, most compelling in its treatment of historical and economic issues. Nevertheless, as many have pointed out, his approach needs revision (see Montrose, "Of Gentlemen and Shepherds"; Trachtenberg; Wayne, *Penshurst*, pp. 16–17). For Williams, the contrast between country and city or between country and court is an ideological strategy, an instance of "false consciousness," which served the interests of the upper classes by concealing their complicity in the power structure of the court and the development of capitalism in the city:

> It was no moral case of "God made the country and man made the town." The English country, year by year, had been made and remade by men, and the English town was at once its image and its agent. . . . If what was seen in the town could not be approved, because it made evident and repellent the decisive relations in which men actually lived, the remedy was never a visitor's morality of plain living and high thinking, or a babble of green fields. It was a change of social relationships and of essential morality. And it was precisely at this

point that the "town and country" fiction served: to promote superficial comparisons and to prevent real ones. (p. 54)

Williams implies that if members of the upper classes had simply thought hard and honestly enough, if they had made real comparisons rather than fictional ones, they would have seen the process of social change as clearly as we do (see Parfitt, pp. 160–61). Williams's argument is powerful because he claims that appeals to "the country" as an ideal form of life register one's disturbance about social change without actually interfering with it. The problem with his argument is that he suggests that (1) references to the country are always self-interested and (2) such references could be free from all mythical content. For other versions of pastoral, see Alpers, who handles the issue from the perspective of genre, and Patterson, *Pastoral and Ideology*, who defines ideology primarily as conscious political attitudes expressed indirectly by the writer (pp. 130–32, 138–41).

18. Weber quotes Benjamin Franklin in his chapter, "The Spirit of Capitalism" (pp. 48–50). The recent articles on the Protestant ethic include O'Connell; Seaver, "The Puritan Work Ethic Revisited"; and Sommerville. The book by Charles and Katherine George is still excellent; see chapters 3 and 4 in *The Protestant Mind of the English Reformation*.

19. Williams discusses his terms *dominant*, *emergent*, and *residual* in *Problems in Materialism and Culture*, pp. 31–49, and in *Marxism and Literature*, pp. 121–28.

20. E. P. Thompson, "The Moral Economy of the English Crowd in the Eighteenth Century."

21. Williams, *Marxism and Literature*, p. 114.

22. In a chapter entitled "Power, Sexuality, and Inwardness in Wyatt's Poetry," Greenblatt argues that Wyatt's translations of the Psalms build the speaker's relationship to God in terms of subject and King (*Renaissance Self-Fashioning*). Marcus analyzes the subjectivity in *The Temple* as analogous to that of a child in a late-medieval household (*Childhood and Cultural Despair*). Schoenfeldt claims that the "manipulative tactics of supplication" practiced by an aspiring inferior on a social superior determines in large part Herbert's devotional discourse (p. 13).

23. On the differences between these critical methods, see Dollimore, "Introduction: Shakespeare, Cultural Materialism, and the New Historicism," pp. 2–17; and Cohen, "Political Criticism of Shakespeare."

24. George Herbert's biographers seem unaware of the leading role William Herbert played in the Protestant court alliances, and it is only recently that historians have understood the nature of these factions. Hutchinson, Joseph Summers, and Charles all mention Pembroke, but only as one among many influential patrons. Summers comes close to my

view when he says, "The Privy Council steered an uneasy course among the projected policies, and Herbert's potential patrons, Pembroke, Williams, and Hamilton, found themselves continually at odds with Buckingham" (*George Herbert*, p. 42). Benet concludes, as I do, that Herbert was part of William Herbert's "political machine," but she does not identify that faction as Protestant ("Herbert's Experience," p. 37).

25. William Herbert was described as the "head of the Puritans" by the Venetian ambassador in 1616 (Brennan, *Literary Patronage in the English Renaissance*, p. 234). Simon Adams lists the leaders of the "puritan party" at court (p. 143; see also Rowe). The most helpful work on this issue is an unpublished dissertation by O'Farrell. The role of factions in English political history during this period is discussed by Kevin Sharpe and by Peck (in *Northampton*). See also Lake, "Anti-Popery: The Structure of a Prejudice," and Fincham, "Prelacy and Politics: Archbishop Abbot's Defense of Protestant Orthodoxy."

26. Simon Adams, "Foreign Policy," pp. 142–44, 146. See Edward Herbert's poem, "Ad Serenissimum Regem Gustavem," and George Herbert's poem, "To the Queene of Bohemia." For an account of a nationalistic, Protestant poem by their brother Thomas, see Powers-Beck, "'Proudly Mounted on the Oceans Backe.'" In his fascinating and important book, Powers-Beck considers the works of George Herbert within the context of those of his family, including Magdalene, Edward, Henry, and Thomas. I thank Professor Powers-Beck for sharing his work with me.

27. *Dictionary of National Biography* [hereafter cited as *DNB*]. See also Arthur Woodnoth, *A Short Collection of the Most Remarkable Passages from the originall to the dissolution of the Virginia Company* (1651).

28. See n. 12, this chapter.

29. Simon Adams discusses the links between Pembroke and Hamilton as well as the Duke of Lennox (p. 144). On the Earl's nomination of Danvers and the Herbert brothers to Parliament, see O'Farrell, pp. 329–31. The naming of Henry Herbert as Master of the Revels is considered closely in Dutton, pp. 218–48. For Edward's engagement in Protestant affairs on the Continent, see the *DNB*, and Eugene Hill, pp. 10–13. Danvers's and Pembroke's involvement in the Virginia Company is described in the *DNB*, as is Thomas Herbert's profession as a naval captain. George's brother William is described by Charles, *A Life*, p. 86. On George Herbert's request for the position of Public Orator, see his *Works*, pp. 369–70. The third Earl named Herbert to Bemerton but died before Herbert took the position; Philip Herbert was the head of the family while Herbert served as chaplain to Wilton House (Charles, *A Life*, pp. 145–48).

30. See note 12, this chapter.

31. *DNB.* Edward Herbert refers to Thomas's discontent: "After all these proofs given of himself, he expected some great command; but finding himself, as he thought, undervalued, he retired to a private and melancholy life, being much discontented to find others preferred to him" (*Autobiography*, p. 19).

32. On Buckingham's rise and his disputes with Pembroke, see O'Farrell, pp. 89–117, especially p. 97; and Lockyer, pp. 176–77.

33. Lockyer, p. 39. I am not claiming that George Herbert or his relatives never sought patronage from Buckingham. As the Duke gained control over court positions, it became absolutely necessary to do so. I am claiming that Buckingham from the beginning sought full loyalty from his clients, and as his conflicts with Pembroke grew, it became less likely that Buckingham would see Pembroke's relatives as attractive clients.

34. O'Farrell, p. 97. See also Evans, p. 35.

35. *DNB.*

36. *Calendar of State Papers, Domestic, 1625–1626,* ed. John Bruce (London: Longman, 1859), p. 111; cited in Powers-Beck, "'Proudly Mounted on the Oceans Backe'," p. 27.

37. Thomas received nothing; George and Edward were awarded the manor of Ribbesford in 1627, described below. Edward received some recognition: Council of War in 1624, 1632, and 1637; a relatively insignificant Irish title in 1624; and in 1629 he became Lord Herbert of Cherbury as financial recompense for his spending as ambassador of France. But throughout this period he felt neglected and sought to improve his position with the King through his literary efforts. Buckingham asked Edward to write a vindication of the Duke's conduct at La Rochelle in 1627, and, after Buckingham's assassination, Edward presented it to the King in 1630, but it gained no royal recognition except the King's request that he write a history of Henry VIII (*DNB*; Eugene Hill, pp. 13–14).

38. O'Farrell, p. 109; Lockyer, p. 276.

39. O'Farrell, p. 109.

40. Lockyer, p. 179; O'Farrell, pp. 150–51; Dutton, pp. 230–31.

41. Lockyer, p. 276; O'Farrell, p. 160. In *The Forced Loan* (pp. 23–27), Cust describes Buckingham's vengeance, after 1625, against those who crossed him, and Pembroke's "eclipse" in patronage and political influence because of Buckingham. Archbishop Abbot wrote in 1627 that he had lost favor with Buckingham because he refused to be his "vassal" (quoted in Fincham, p. 53). Benet discusses Williams ("Herbert's Experience," pp. 41–42).

42. Joseph Summers, *George Herbert,* pp. 40–42; Charles, *A Life,* p. 100.

43. Powers-Beck, "Conquering Laurels." Powers-Beck believes the speech reflects Herbert's genuine anti-war sentiments as well as his support for James's pacific foreign policy (pp. 6–7). Herbert does speak out strongly against war in *Lucus* 32, "Triumphis Mortis." I am indebted to Powers-Beck for his admirable research on this issue, but I disagree that the oration primarily displays Herbert's own views, or that the earlier speech to the Spanish ambassadors in February 1623 demonstrates "firm support for a peaceful foreign policy" (p. 5). Herbert does praise the Spanish marriage in this earlier speech, a view contrary to Pembroke's. The 1624 Parliament may have been traumatic for Herbert because he was expected to vote with Pembroke against King James's Spanish treaties and against the King's plan to dissolve the Virginia Company.

44. Powers-Beck, "Conquering Laurels," p. 14. See also Lockyer, p. 168; and Ruigh, p. 19.

45. Although Pembroke did not explicitly vote against Buckingham (and by this time Charles) until January 1624, nevertheless his suspicion of and opposition to Buckingham's pro-war stance would have begun as soon as he had heard about the favorite's change of attitude, which was known by early October 1623.

46. Trans. Richard Wilton, in Grosart, pp. 406, 414.

47. Lockyer, pp. 176–77; O'Farrell, p. 151. Benet incorrectly concludes that Pembroke was "neutral" on the issue ("Herbert's Experience," p. 39).

48. O'Farrell, p. 143; Ruigh, pp. 129, 177–78.

49. Charles, *A Life*, pp. 112–17.

50. Lockyer, p. 307.

51. Scholars disagree on why Edward was dismissed in August 1624 when Buckingham started to seriously pursue negotiations for a French marriage for Charles. The *DNB* claims King James was offended; Eugene Hill states that the French wanted him out (p. 11). I believe that Edward's appointment was a means of pleasing the Protestant faction and Pembroke, and that Herbert's support for the Protestant cause made him untrustworthy in these negotiations. See Eugene Hill on the monarchy's two sets of English diplomats and foreign secretaries: "One dealt with those diplomats (including Herbert) who worked against the interests of the Hapsburg powers; the other set worked in favor of those interests" (p. 11).

52. Charles, *A Life*, pp. 107–11; Craven, pp. 250–336. Simon Adams lists a specific faction important in the 1621 and 1624 Parliaments led by the Earl of Southampton and including Sir Edwin Sandys and the Danvers brothers. After Southampton's death in 1624, these individuals became Pembroke's clients and spokesmen in Parliament (pp. 144–45). The *DNB*

claims that John Danvers had the records copied; biographers of the Ferrars claimed it was Nicholas Ferrar (see "Life of Nicholas Ferrar by Dr. Jebb," in Mayor, p. 214). That the members blamed the dissolution on the Spanish faction is clear from John Ferrar's account of his brother's life and from the biographer A. L. Maycock, quoted by Charles: "These three forces—the Crown, the Spanish interest and the Warwick faction—were united in an effort to destroy the Virginia Company" (*A Life*, p. 109). That Danvers believed this as well is evident from a pamphlet, published by his servant during the Civil War, which identifies the "Court and *Spanish Party*" as the enemy of the Virginia Company (Woodnoth, p. 5).

53. Dutton, p. 245. Dutton finally concludes that there is no evidence for a conspiracy between Pembroke and Henry, and that "it remains an unnecessary conjecture." But he adds, "The real point is that, with Pembroke behind [Henry], he felt confident in 'allowing' a *potentially* controversial play" (p. 246).

54. Dutton, pp. 244–46; Brennan, p. 175.

55. Charles, *A Life*, p. 113. The date of the prorogued Parliament is misprinted in *A Life* as November 3 (see Gardiner, p. 234).

56. Schoenfeldt suggests that Herbert never gave up seeking higher office; Schoenfeldt quotes Maycock: "'Many men, in the ordinary course, entered the diaconate without any intention of becoming priests.'" The rest of Schoenfeldt's discussion is also pertinent (pp. 36–37; Maycock, p. 120). Benet comments, "Regardless of his spiritual inclinations, Herbert's abandonment of court hopes could have been dictated by practical considerations alone" ("Herbert's Experience," p. 44).

57. Charles, *A Life*, pp. 112–17, 122–25. Charles does not mention the political significance of Herbert's ties with Williams, especially in 1626.

58. Ibid., p. 121; O'Farrell, p. 167; Lockyer, p. 332–33.

59. McCloskey and Murphy, #17, p. 153; #7, p. 139.

60. Charles, *A Life*, pp. 131–35.

61. After Buckingham's assassination in 1628, Pembroke received more favors from King Charles than before, but Pembroke's clients suffered from the divisions that remained between the Earl and the King on issues of religion, government, and foreign affairs. See O'Farrell, p. 114–15.

62. It has been argued that George Herbert's Protestantism was not attractive to the Arminians, including Laud, who had a great deal of power over church appointments after 1625. This seems quite possible to me, although I would argue that Herbert's political association would have preceded or been synonymous with his religious affiliations: Pembroke and Archbishop Abbot were the leaders of a major Protestant faction (see Cust and Hughes). In fact, the royal grant in 1627 suggests that George and Ed-

ward were not acceptable for royal promotion for the same reason: their links with Pembroke. On Herbert and the Arminians, see Hodgkins.

63. See the collection by Cust and Hughes, especially their introduction, as well as essays by Cogswell and Lake.

64. Simon Adams, p. 144; Woodnoth, p. 4.

65. Kingsbury, vol. 4, p. 478. See Maycock: "For these engagements and his too free speeches against the will of his prince, though exceedingly well meant, were so deep and so long a regret and shame to him afterwards, that he was heard to say, (stretching out his right hand), *I would I were assured of the pardon of that sin, though on that condition this right hand were cut off* (p. 23; italics in original).

66. Charles, *A Life*, p. 118.

67. Ferrar, "The Printers to the Reader," in George Herbert, *Works*, pp. 3–4. All subsequent citations to Herbert's works will refer to this volume through page numbers in the text.

CHAPTER 1, *'The Country Parson' and Social Identity*

This chapter was first published in *Studies in Philology* 85 (spring 1988).

1. In his 1671 edition, Barnabas Oley seems to have added *The Priest to the Temple* to Herbert's title, *The Country Parson: His Character and Rule of Holy Life*, as Joseph Summers points out in *George Herbert*, p. 13. This is confirmed by a letter from Sir Robert Cooke, the husband of Herbert's widow, to Sir Robert Harley in 1641: "Mr George Herbert . . . left a book stiled the Country Parson." The letter asks Harley's help in getting the book published (Cooke to Harley, 21 June 1641, Loan 29, 119, pt. 3, Duke of Portland Papers, British Museum, London). I am particularly indebted to Alan Bewell for helping me to interpret this material, and for his comments on the chapter as a whole.

2. The most valuable discussions of *The Country Parson* occur in Charles, *A Life*, p. 157; Hodgkins, pp. 103–26; Kollmeier; Strier, *Love Known*, pp. 198–201, and "George Herbert and the World"; and Joseph Summers, *George Herbert*, pp. 64–65 and 99–103.

3. My work on this issue has been greatly influenced by Greenblatt's *Renaissance Self-Fashioning* and *Sir Walter Ralegh*. For the self-fashioning required of younger sons, see Thirsk, as well as Stone, *An Open Elite?*, pp. 5–6 and 228–39. The following is especially applicable to Herbert: "His fortune in the main had to be of his own making, and his only status was that of a gentleman, although a gentleman with connections. His early experience would have habituated him to handling differences in status and made him particularly aware of them" (Stone, *An Open Elite?*, p. 229).

4. Walton, *Lives*, p. 31.

5. Oley, M3.

6. Zagorin, p. 25. See also Laslett.

7. Christopher Hill, *Economic Problems of the Church*, pp. 202–10.

8. The history of the word *character* reflects the increasing importance of individualism in the modern world: what originally meant mark or sign comes to refer to personal ethical makeup. The *OED* lists no meaning of the word associated with the aggregate of distinctive features or the sum of moral qualities until 1647, and most occur later than 1659. The seventeenth-century character books use the word to mean a distinctive mark impressed in wax, a letter of the alphabet, or a short prose description of a social stereotype. By the eighteenth century, Samuel Johnson's dictionary includes the older definitions, but also "personal qualities," or a "particular constitution of mind." In 1859, John Stuart Mill could write, "A person whose desires and impulses are his own—are the expression of his own nature, as it is developed and modified by his own culture—is said to have a character. One whose desires and impulses are not his own, has no character, no more than a steam engine has a character" (*On Liberty*, 108; *OED* II.12).

9. According to Aristotle, in *Nichomachean Ethics*: "The virtues . . . we acquire by first having actually practiced them, just as we do the arts. . . . In a word, our moral dispositions are formed as a result of the corresponding activities" (II.i.4, 7). E. N. S. Thompson (p. 9) discusses the emphasis on motive in English characters. Whereas Theophrastus's character of "Meanness" or "Stinginess" emphasizes the acts of the miser (in "Micrologia," p. 64–66), Joseph Hall highlights desire and idolatry in his portrait of "The Covetous Man" (pp. 125–31).

10. Quoted in Elias, pp. 78–79.

11. Brooks, *The Novel of Worldliness*. See especially Earle's character of St. Paul's Walk, Jonson's *Every Man Out of His Humour*, which includes "characters" of the *dramatis personae*, and of course *The Alchemist*.

12. See Overbury for "The Courtier" (p. 52), "A Fine Gentleman" (p. 65), "An Intruder Into Favor" (p. 116), "The Dissembler" (p. 52). See Earle for "A Gallant" (#19) and "An Upstart Country Knight" (#18).

13. Stone, "Social Mobility."

14. Harrison, pp. 113–14.

15. I am indebted to Whigham's chapters on "Courtesy Literature and Social Change" and "Rhetorical Semiotics and Court," pp. 1–62. For the original discussion of the Tudor "new men," see MacCaffrey.

16. See also Earle's "A High-Spirited Man," who would "sooner accept the Gallowes than a mean trade" (#34).

17. Overbury, p. 60. See "A Noble Spirit" (p. 61), which defines an

ideal aristocrat in terms of reason and experience. My thinking on the "ideology" of the character genre has been greatly influenced by Wayne's discussion of Ben Jonson's praise and criticism of his patrons (pp. 150–73). Especially useful are Wayne's comments on social change (p. 154).

18. Schoenfeldt sees rhetorical tactics as fundamental throughout *The Temple* as well as in *The Country Parson* (pp. 5, 97–99). Strier notes the predominance of these tactics in "The Church-porch" but sees them as absent in the lyrics of "The Church" and in *The Country Parson* ("Sanctifying the Aristocracy," p. 59). I am arguing that rhetoric gains a new definition in Herbert's manual through the "character" of holiness, resulting in what might be called the construction of sincerity, and that this sincerity marks *The Country Parson* as significantly different from "The Church-porch." See the Conclusion for further discussion of the construction of sincerity.

19. Herbert was also concerned with temperance for health reasons; see his translation of Cornaro's *A Treatise of Temperance and Sobrietie* (pp. 291–303). It should be noted, however, that such health concerns are not entirely separate from class issues; Herbert may have felt comfortable adopting Cornaro's rules because he so explicitly describes himself as an upper-class landowner.

20. In *Some Versions of Pastoral*, Empson develops his famous definition of "the pastoral process of putting the complex into the simple" (p. 22; see also p. 11). By defining himself as the "country" parson, Herbert associates himself with the myth of authenticity surrounding rural life, a myth that Empson would call "a half-magical idea" that is "the quickest way to the truth" (p. 16). Through this myth, Herbert develops for himself a more decent mode of life than that available in the court, given the excesses of the Stuarts. Nevertheless, he also "naturalizes" hierarchical government and the respect demanded from inferiors. For a strictly political examination of myth, see Barthes's discussion of naturalization (pp. 109–59).

21. Hooker, 5.77.2.

22. See Hodgkins: "While Herbert's emphasis on the pervasive 'edification' of his parish moves him at times toward the idea of a shared ministry, *The Countrey Parson* never fundamentally questions the distinction between clergy and laity" (p. 107). For the election of ministers, see William Travers, p. 440.

23. For Herbert's poetry on the priesthood, see "Aaron," "The Priesthood," and *Musae Responsoriae*. Laslett describes social ranking during this period (pp. 36 and 38). Herbert's family lived in London between 1601 and 1627, although, after Magdalene's second marriage, they probably spent most summers in Danvers's house in Chelsea, which is fairly close to London (Charles, *A Life*, p. 61).

24. Davies discusses Laud's high style (p. 72). Joseph Summers points out the difficulty of predicting Herbert's alliance during the Civil War in *George Herbert*, p. 54. The term "crisis of confidence" is used by Stone in *An Open Elite?* See also Stone, *Crisis of the Aristocracy*. In *An Open Elite?* Stone defines the crisis of confidence as "a threat to the principles of paternalism and deference" (p. 400).

25. Herbert's affirmation of autonomy is similar to the claims of seventeenth-century professional writers. One example is Ben Jonson, who was financially dependent on his aristocratic patrons, but who nevertheless asserted "his right to think and speak with relative freedom" despite "his subjection to others within the prevailing social order" (see Wayne, p. 148). I am grateful to Paul Alpers and Margaret Ferguson, who, independently, pointed out this similarity to me. See also Ferguson's essay on Sidney.

26. For others who have commented on Herbert and vocation, see the Introduction, n. 14.

27. Perkins, *Treatise*, pp. 733–34. For an account of the history of the terms *general* and *particular*, see the Introduction, pp. 3–5.

28. Quoted in Charles George and Katherine George, p. 46.

29. Christopher Hill, *Society and Puritanism*, p. 124.

30. Cf. arguments regarding causation in Weber's *The Protestant Ethic* and R. H. Tawney's *Religion and the Rise of Capitalism*. For a useful guide through this thorny but rewarding historical problem, see M. J. Kitch.

31. "Homily Against Idleness," in *The Second Tome of Homilies*, p. 252.

32. See the King James Bible, translated in 1611, Matthew 25:14–30. For references to the talent and the "reckoning" demanded, see Perkins, *Treatise*, p. 755; and George Herbert, *The Country Parson*, in *Works*, p. 274.

33. Milton, Sonnet 16.

34. Herbert was not a member of the incipient bourgeoisie, but his social position made him particularly open to values that would later consolidate into a "bourgeois ethos." His status as a younger son of the gentry resulted in a powerfully urgent desire to achieve, evident in his poetry ("Employment" [I] and [II]) and his letters (see his *Works*, p. 373), and the doctrine of vocation provided him with the means of understanding that work as sacred. That he became a priest was crucial to his sense of the sacredness of his own labor, but the doctrine of vocation led him to conceive of all social roles, including that of the aristocrat (*Works*, p. 275), in terms of the work and duties appropriate to them. Although Herbert did not praise merchants and tradesmen at the expense of the nobility and gentility, he espoused a work ethic that later resulted in a new social respect for those involved in commercial activities. Anthony Low, in *The*

*Georgic Revolution*, comes to quite a different conclusion in his discussion of Herbert: "The Protestant strain in his thinking was an important factor in turning him away from a possible interest in what is sometimes called 'the work ethic'" (p. 95). But Low makes attitudes towards husbandry the crux of such an interest and so underestimates the importance of the doctrine of vocation for Herbert's sense of himself and society. See, especially, George Herbert, "The Parson Surveys," in *Works*, pp. 274–78.

35. Tawney, p. 39.

36. Weber, p. 121.

37. According to the *OED*, this meaning of the word *rule* was current from 1225 onwards: "The code of discipline or body of regulations observed by a religious order or congregation" (I.2).

38. Greenblatt, *Renaissance Self-Fashioning*, pp. 41–42.

39. Ibid., p. 45.

40. I am paraphrasing from the Yale edition of Thomas More's *Utopia*, 4: 99.

41. Charles George and Katherine George, p. 160.

42. Patterson, *Hermogenes and the Renaissance*. Strier, in *Love Known*, uses this passage to support his claim that sincerity of feeling was far more important to Herbert than forms of art (pp. 188–217); I am arguing that the "character" of holiness was crucial to Herbert precisely because it was a form of art, a method of self-representation, a style of language.

43. Fish first identified such a process in "Letting Go: The Dialectic of the Self in Herbert's Poetry," in his *Self-Consuming Artifacts*, pp. 156–223.

44. See "Jordan" (I) and (II), "A True Hymn," and "The Quip."

45. Bouwsma, pp. 215–46.

46. Williams, *The Country and the City*, p. 35.

47. See Mohl, pp. 12–15.

48. See Wright, pp. 19–42 and 170–200. On the "magical extraction of labor" from the country-house poems, see Williams, *The Country and the City*, p. 32, and Wayne, pp. 126–27. For a different account of Herbert's relation to cultural change, see Marcus, *Childhood and Cultural Despair*, pp. 1–41 and 94–120, and "George Herbert and the Anglican Plain Style." In *Childhood and Cultural* Despair, Marcus argues that Herbert's "poetic retreat" and "rhetoric of simplicity" were largely efforts "to reconstitute for himself the traditional late-medieval image of the universe" (pp. 94–97). I am indebted to Marcus's analysis of Herbert's "interaction with social and cultural history" (*Childhood*, p. xi). We differ, however, on Herbert's allegiance to medieval values.

49. I owe this point to Joan Dayan, who generously reviewed this essay and discussed it with me.

CHAPTER 2, *Herbert and Coterie Verse*

This chapter was first published in Jonathan F. S. Post and Sidney Gottlieb, eds., *George Herbert in the Nineties: Reflections and Reassessments* (Fairfield, Conn.: George Herbert Journal, 1995).

1. The question-and-answer session at the conference "George Herbert in the Nineties: Reflections and Reassessments" was an invaluable help in formulating these issues, and I thank everyone involved. Marotti has made evident the "forms of competitive versifying" that made up "a system of transactions within polite or educated social circles," and I am indebted to his account, in *John Donne: Coterie Poet*, pp. 12–13 and throughout. My thoughts on Herbert and patronage have been significantly influenced by Schoenfeldt's work. However, he does not discuss William Herbert as a patron for George Herbert at any length. Sidney was William Herbert's uncle, and William Herbert was George Herbert's fourth cousin; therefore George Herbert was Sidney's fourth cousin once removed. For the unstable status of younger sons of the gentry, see Thirsk, "Younger Sons in the Seventeenth Century." Stone describes the extended family in *The Family, Sex and Marriage* (pp. 86–90). See also Joseph Summers: "As an adolescent and an adult, Herbert probably read the poetry of the Sidney–Herbert connection for politic as well as literary reasons" (*George Herbert*, p. 31). For Sidney's views on divine poetry, see the *Apology*, pp. 137–38.

2. Martz coined the illuminating term *sacred parody* in *The Poetry of Meditation*, pp. 186, 261, 271. The term *coterie poetry* is often used to refer primarily to the exchange and copying of manuscripts, but the coteries themselves included social gatherings in which poetry was recited or presented with musical accompaniment. See, especially, Hart. On upper-class poetic exchange, see Marotti, pp. 3–24; Saunders, *The Profession of English Letters*, pp. 31–48; Grierson; and Love.

3. Many recent studies have called into question the assumption that Herbert's poetry was private. But most of these studies have claimed that Herbert's poetry voices social or cultural issues either explicitly or implicitly. I am arguing that the verse is public because it was written as an entry into a debate within a limited and elite social circle, and that the convention of upper-class poetic debate determined Herbert's responses to poetry, both before and after he gave up a secular career. I do not think that all of Herbert's poems were circulated or sung before an audience; "The Answer" is an ironic and private response to the normally public answer-poem. For recent studies on the relationship between Herbert's poetry and society, see the Introduction, n. 16. I agree with Targoff's refutation of the assumption in much modern criticism that Herbert's devotional lyrics

are private meditations. However, in "The Poetics of Common Prayer," she claims that his poems have a public dimension because of their similarity to liturgical forms of worship, not because they were performed before an audience.

4. See Saunders, "The Stigma of Print," and *The Profession of English Letters*, pp. 31–48.

5. Tuve reconstructs the musical evenings in the Herbert family but discounts their "emulative" aspect in "'Sacred Parody'" (pp. 235–39).

6. Charles, *A Life*, pp. 78–89; Joseph Summers, "Sidney and Herbert," pp. 213–14.

7. Charles, *A Life*, p. 78.

8. Bacon, *The Translation of Certain Psalmes into English Verse*, pp. A3, A3V.

9. The question of the circulation of the Latin poetry is much more vexed than one would expect, given the assertions of Charles and Kelliher that the Latin poems were clearly more public than the English verse. In the three collections of Latin poetry unpublished during Herbert's lifetime, *Musae Responsoriae*, *Lucus*, and *Passio Discerpta*, there is explicit evidence of circulation of only two poems, "Epigram XXV" originating in *Musae Responsoriae* but finally appearing in *Lucus*, and "Triumphis Mortis" in *Lucus*. Kelliher in fact believes that "Epigram XXV" circulated on its own. Just as occurs for the English lyrics, there is no evidence of references in commonplace books or in manuscript miscellanies during Herbert's lifetime to any other poem in *Musae Responsoriae* or *Lucus*, and none at all to the poems in *Passio Discerpta*. It is assumed that *Musae* circulated because of the public nature of the subject matter and Herbert's dedications to King James, Prince Charles, and Bishop Andrewes. Certainly, this suggests that the English lyrics might also have circulated without references in commonplace books, especially given the signs of coterie influence. See Kelliher, p. 39. See also Hutchinson's comments in Herbert's *Works*, pp. 384–439.

10. Wilcox, pp. 43–45. Wilcox concludes, "Our knowledge of how Herbert performed his poems, or intended them for performance, is likely to remain speculative."

11. Saintsbury, p. 303.

12. George Herbert, *Select Hymns*, p. A2.

13. Aubrey, *Brief Lives*, p. 137.

14. Aubrey, "Description and model of Sir John Danvers' Garden," Aubrey 2 MS, fols. 53, 56, Bodleian Library (Aubrey describes the musical evenings at the house in Chelsea in fol. 56). See also Tuve, "'Sacred Parody'."

15. Walter R. Davis has argued that, in the history of music, the sev-

enteenth-century lyric sung by an individual represents a move away from the group activity of the madrigal to the "private" world of "the isolated self observed" ("The Musical Career of Thomas Campion," paper presented at the 1996 meeting of the Modern Language Association). I would argue that the solo lyric sung before an audience is an intermediate step between the social ritual of the madrigal and private meditative poetry. I thank Professor Davis for sharing his paper with me.

16. I owe these points about Marvell and the commonplace books to Ann Baynes Coiro, who has examined Milton's relationship to coterie circulation and publication in "Milton and Class Identity."

17. *The Index of English Literary Manuscripts* lists a copy of Herbert's "A Parodie" in a manuscript volume of Donne's poetry, collected "c. 1632," but the poem in the manuscript is actually Pembroke's "Soule's Joy," which Herbert imitated. The *Index* also lists a copy of Herbert's "The 23rd Psalm" with musical setting in Henry Lawes's autograph songbook, compiled in the mid–seventeenth century. Since Lawes came from Wilton, was Pembroke's client, and set his poetry to music, it is quite possible that Lawes knew George Herbert's poem from musical evenings at Wilton and provided his own musical setting. See Beal, *Index of English Literary Manuscripts*, vol. 1, pt. 2, pp. 203, 208. On Lawes, see n. 19, this chapter.

18. Love, pp. 43–44, 70–72.

19. On upper-class poetic exchange, see n. 2, this chapter, including Hart, p. 21, and Saunders, *Profession*, pp. 41–44. Evans discusses Lawes and Pembroke, pp. 23–24, 35–46. Clients of William Herbert also included Thomas Adams, Christopher Brooke, William Browne, Samuel Daniel (his tutor), John Earle, Ben Jonson, William Shakespeare, and George Wither. Pembroke inherited the patronage networks established by his mother, Mary Sidney Herbert, and to some extent, those developed by the Earl of Leicester, the Earl of Essex, and Sir Philip Sidney. On these circles, see Hannay, Lamb, O'Farrell, and Brennan. The patronage circle around Lucy, Countess of Bedford is analogous; see Ben Jonson's poem "To Lucy, Countess of Bedford, with Mr. Donne's Satires."

20. For commentary on the accuracy of the text of William Herbert's *Poems*, see the edition of Gary E. Onderwyzer. See Tuve, "'Sacred Parody'," p. 208, and Marotti, *John Donne: Coterie Poet*, pp. 18 and 333, for information on the attribution of "Soules Joy" to William Herbert, and on the appearance of poems by William Herbert, Rudyerd, and Donne in other manuscripts. William Herbert also exchanged answer-poems with Drummond, and Herbert's poetry seems to have been well known to his client-poets, who praised it highly (O'Farrell, pp. 199–206, 226–28).

21. Herbert, William, *Poems*, p. 38.

22. O'Farrell, pp. 143–45, 153–58, 163–74; Brennan, pp. 155–56, 166, 173, 180, 187; Rudyerd, pp. 18–23, 28. George Herbert writes that he plans to correspond with "my Lord, or Sir Benjamin Ruddyard" to help him secure the position of Cambridge orator. The "Lord" is almost certainly Pembroke (370).

23. Pebworth identifies the members of this coterie and states that Pembroke became patron to several members after 1601 (pp. 62–63). Donne sought Pembroke's assistance in obtaining the deanship of St. Paul's in 1621 through a poem in praise of Sidney and his sister, but it is unclear whether Donne received the support he was seeking. Despite Donne's patronage by Magdalene Herbert by 1607, he was never an explicit client of Pembroke's. On Donne's relationship with William and Magdalene Herbert, see Novarr, pp. 150–57; Marotti, pp. 186, 284–85; and O'Farrell, pp. 214–15. Given Donne's great financial need and his exchange of verse with Pembroke, the lack of a client-relationship is surprising. The scandal of Donne's marriage may have deterred Pembroke, although Pembroke's affairs were far more disreputable. It is possible that Pembroke became a patron to Donne after the "cleansing" experience of ordination.

24. Marotti, p. 333.

25. From "Poems attributed to John Donne," in *Poems*, vol. 1, pp. 429–30. I quote from this text because the text in Pembroke's *Poems* is shortened and garbled (p. 24). See Tuve, "'Sacred Parody'," pp. 239–40. Strier calls Pembroke's poem "a valediction forbidding mourning" but does not claim that the two poems influenced each other (*Love Known*, p. 239).

26. The same question of precedence arises in terms of Donne's sonnet, "Death Be Not Proud," and the poem by his patron, Lucy, Countess of Bedford: "Death be not proud, thy hand gave not this blow." Marotti argues that Donne's valediction poems might have been shown to a few friends, like other poems of mutual love, but that they primarily represent Donne's relationship with his wife (p. 169). I cannot agree; the clear connections between "Valediction: Forbidding Mourning" and "Soules Joy" imply quite strongly that these were not private accounts of experience but coterie performances and perhaps even answer-poems.

27. Sidney, *Astrophil and Stella*, #105, #106, in *Poems*. On Hoskyns's "Absence," see Finkelpearl, pp. 73–74.

28. See Edward Herbert's "To Her Eyes," "To Her Hair," "Sonnet of Black Beauty," and "Another Sonnet to Black It Self" in his *Poems*, pp. 54–59. There is a poem of this kind in the Pembroke–Rudyerd collection, identified with Rudyerd, but actually by another author; for a correction to the original attributions, see Onderwyzer, pp. x–xi. On the exchange between Donne and Edward Herbert, see Marotti, pp. 195–202, and Eu-

gene Hill, pp. 66–103. Hill points out the link between "The Progress of the Soul" and "State-Progress of Ill" (pp. 67–69), and argues that Herbert's "An Ode upon a Question Moved" followed and commented upon Donne's "Exstacie" (pp. 95–103). Hutchinson associates "The Church Militant" with Donne's "The Progress of the Soul" (p. 543). On Magdalene Herbert's patronage of Donne, see Novarr, p. 89, and Marotti, pp. 343–44. Later in his life, the tables turned and Donne lent money to Sir John Danvers (Gosse, p. 248).

29. Edward Herbert, *Poems*, "Ditty," pp. 1, 12, 40, 41, 44, 47, 84; "Echo" poems, pp. 40, 69, 70, 72.

30. William Herbert, *Poems*, pp. 8, 13.

31. Ibid., p. 13.

32. Ibid., pp. 53–55.

33. On the disputed question, see Altman and the "General Introduction" in Donne, *Paradoxes and Problems*, pp. xxviii–xxxviii.

34. From the official schedule for Eton and Westminster during this period, quoted by Baldwin, vol. 1, p. 358. See also Altman, pp. 43–53.

35. Curtis, pp. 88–90; O'Day, p. 112.

36. Rudyerd, *Memoirs*, p. 12. See also Finkelpearl, pp. 48–61. Rudyerd's phrase, "Fustian Answer," suggests that "answering" originated in debate and was not restricted to "answer-poems."

37. Herbert's gift of his early sonnets to his mother does not take them out of the network of patronage and poetic exchange; he refers to her as "My clan's / especial guardian" in *Memoriae Matris Sacrum* (McCloskey, p. 139). For a different interpretation of this gift, see Pearlman's excellent essay.

38. Altman, pp. 41–42, 49–50; Donne, *Paradoxes and Problems*, pp. 21–22, 89–90.

39. Edward Herbert, *Poems*, pp. 76–77.

40. Donne, *The Elegies*, p. 27, lines 1–2, 37–40, 43.

41. I am indebted to Kevin Dunn, who pointed out to me the wit displays about women in Donne's *Paradoxes and Problems*, which, like the poems, work out positions in the debate about women. Discussing the issue was a social pastime much like the answer-poem; see Donne, *Paradoxes*, xxxi–xxxvi, and Ben Jonson's poem, "That Women are but Mens Shaddowes," written, according to Drummond, because of a debate between Pembroke and his wife: "Pembrooke and his Lady discoursing, the Earl said, That woemen were mens shadowes, and she maintained them. Both appealing to Jonson, he affirmed it true; for which my Lady gave a pennance to prove it in verse, hence his epigram" (quoted in Jonson, *The Complete Poetry*, p. 93). On rhetorical debate and the controversy about women, see Woodbridge and the introduction to Tilney, pp. 1–93.

42. Ong, "Latin Language," and *Fighting for Life*.

43. Donne, *Divine Poems*, pp. 52–53, 111–12, 138–47. See also Novarr, pp. 103–7. Neither Gardner nor Novarr conclude that Donne's poem could have been written with patronage in mind; I think it is unwise to discount it, given the prestige of the Herbert family and Donne's difficult financial situation. Novarr does conclude that Donne sought patronage even after his ordination (pp. 150–57).

44. Donne, *Divine Poems*, p. 112.

45. Ibid., pp. 144–45. On Donne's use of Latin, see Novarr, p. 106.

46. Gardner suggests that Herbert may have written the translation, which appeared, along with the Latin poem, in Walton's *Life of Herbert* (1658). Both Gardner and Novarr discuss the conceited wit of Donne's poem; Gardner points out in Herbert's verses a change in form, tone, and style between what she sees as a part written in 1615 (an "obscurely worded conceit") and a section written after Donne's death in 1631 ("warm in tone; they reveal a deep affection," pp. 146–47). Such a change is analogous to the transition in style I am describing in this essay.

47. Featley, *The Grand Sacrilege* (1630) is quoted in O'Farrell, p. 246. Chapman is quoted in Brennan, p. 121. For Thomas Moffet's work, see his *Nobilis*. On Edward's political adherence to Protestantism, see Eugene Hill, pp. 9–13. Edward wrote an "Epitaph on Sir Philip Sidney" in *Poems* (p. 80).

48. Wayne, "Jonson's Sidney." David Rigg considers Jonson's relationship to William Herbert and his political faction (pp. 179–87, 226, 231–32).

49. See Martz, *The Poetry of Meditation*, pp. 259–82; and Joseph Summers, "Sidney and Herbert," pp. 207–17.

50. Sidney, *Apology*, pp. 137–38.

51. Ibid., pp. 137–38.

52. See pp. 54–55.

53. I do not agree with Tuve's conclusion that "Herbert's title will not bear the meaning which the word *parody* has in seventeenth-century dictionaries of the learned or vernacular tongues. . . . These, like our own use of the word, stress the element of mockery, burlesque or at the least some sidelong denigrating comment on the original author's sense" ("'Sacred Parody'," pp. 208–9). Tuve claims that the word is used only in a musical sense, to refer to "'replacement of text for a known tune,'" (p. 212), and that the poems by Pembroke and Herbert were sung to the same music. It is clear, however, from Herbert's early sonnets that he was quite proficient at denigrating love poets. I believe that he uses the term in order to evoke expectations of aggressive satire in order to deflate them. See the discussion of this issue in Gottlieb, "The Two Endings," p. 75, n. 21.

54. Pearlman considers Herbert's turn from masculine to feminine models of behavior (p. 101).

55. Strier notices the significant placement of these two poems (*Love Known*, 239).

56. Chartier, pp. 231–33.

57. On "Jordan," see especially Tuve, *A Reading of George Herbert*, p. 194–96; and Fish, *Self-Consuming Artifacts*, pp. 156–223, still among the best discussions of the dynamics of Herbert's verse.

58. I use the word "device" in order to suggest that "Jordan," though associated with religious purity, was nevertheless a witty invention, and that it was meant to represent Herbert personally, just as mottos or emblems were used to represent other members of the upper classes.

59. Shuger offers an intriguing analysis of the structure of *The Temple* in terms of William Perkins's notion of dual persons, a split between a private self and a public persona (pp. 91–119).

60. "Invention" became "Jordan" (II); both are elaborate imitations of the first poem of Sidney's *Astrophil and Stella*. In the *W* manuscript, "Invention" precedes "Perfection," the original version of "The Elixir," and both poems come before the sequence on "last things" that ends "The Church." In the later *B* manuscript, the combination of "Invention" and "Perfection" is revised into "The Posie," "A Parodie," "The Elixir," and "A Wreath," all of which comment on the earthly things of poetry and performance. For a different account of these manuscript revisions, see Gottlieb, "The Two Endings," pp. 57–76.

## CHAPTER 3, *Gentility and Vocation in the Original 'Temple'*

1. According to Hutchinson, the Williams manuscript contains an earlier version of *The Temple* than the one printed in 1633. The Williams manuscript is in the hand of an amanuensis but includes corrections in Herbert's handwriting. The 1633 text of *The Temple* prints these poems in their corrected form. Also, several more poems have been added (see George Herbert, *Works*, pp. lii–lvi, lxx–lxxii). For a discussion of the dating of the Williams and the Bodleian manuscripts, see Chapter 4, n. 11. I am arguing here that the Williams manuscript had a structure that represented the relationship between Herbert's devotional and social lives, but that the structure and meaning changed significantly when he revised the manuscript into the shape of the Bodleian manuscript. Other accounts of the revisions are primarily aesthetic or religious. These include Vendler's argument that the later poems are less self-abasing (pp. 231–76); Gottlieb's similar claim in "The Two Endings" that the revised ending sequence includes a new emphasis on religious confidence; Charles's view that the re-

vised manuscript reveals Herbert's poetic maturity and a new sense that "immediate achievement" is not possible to a Christian ("The Williams Manuscript," p. 422); and Lull's thorough consideration of the lyrics. Lull argues that in his revisions Herbert intended to develop the similarity between the reading experience of "The Church" and the Bible, to give up the illusion of poetic and personal creativity, and to increase the number of resemblances and connections between different poems. For arguments that the revisions introduce aesthetic improvements, see White; Molesworth; Stein, pp. 139–43; and Rickey.

2. Thomas Adams, *The Temple*, p. 64.

3. There are numerous arguments about "The Church-porch," primarily in terms of the structure of the collection, and most are theological or ecclesiastical; see the summary in Fish, *The Living Temple*, pp. 8–10. Schoenfeldt reads the lyrics in the context of the courtiership in "The Church-porch," and argues that "shrewd advice on social comportment is contiguous with rather than divorced from the sacred lyrics it introduces" (p. 5). I hope to show that the doctrine of vocation explains this coordination of social advice and devotional lyrics. I disagree with Schoenfeldt's implication that this coordination erases the difference between devotion and social role (pp. 5–6). Singleton has a useful account of the internalizing emphasis in "The Church-porch," although she does not discuss vocation (p. 164–73).

4. Strier, "Sanctifying the Aristocracy," pp. 55–56. See also "George Herbert and the World" and *Resistant Structures*, pp. 83–117. I believe that all of these essays reveal Strier's assumption that Reformation theology is responsible for Herbert's religious lyrics but not for his accounts of social experience (*Resistant Structures*, p. 108; "Sanctifying the Aristocracy," p. 57). He therefore assumes that the self-interest of "The Church-porch" is a form of elitism on the part of Herbert instead of the result of the literature of vocation, which includes a similar mix of worldliness and sincere religiosity. Strier's analysis inaccurately flattens out this mixture in order to produce a self-serving text. There is a Protestant ethic throughout the poem, rather than "moments of high ethical humanism" in the first third ("George Herbert and the World," p. 227). I agree with Strier that Herbert does not have the attitude toward the world implicit in Christian humanism, but Strier's consideration of "The Church-porch" and "The Elixir" in the context of humanism rather than the doctrine of vocation allows him to exaggerate Herbert's ultimate "retreat from the world" ("George Herbert and the World," pp. 223–25, 232). See the discussion later in this chapter about the relationship between Herbert's class position and the self-interest in "The Church-porch."

5. Shuger, *Habits of Thought*, pp. 93, 95. I disagree with Shuger's account of privacy; see Conclusion, n. 47.

6. Perkins, *Treatise*, pp. 729–31, 733–34.

7. Strier's discussion of cunning in "The Church-porch" alerted me to the importance of this term for Herbert, although Strier does not consider its role in the Bible and the significance of these Biblical passages to Herbert. See n. 4.

8. Harrison describes gentility as a matter of "port, change and countenance" rather than a matter of birth (pp. 113–14; see also Whigham, pp. 1–61). Schoenfeldt has analyzed the influence of the strategies for seeking preferment on Herbert's work, pp. 19–113.

9. See n. 7, this chapter.

10. Strier, "Sanctifying the Aristocracy," p. 45; Hutchinson, in *George Herbert, Works*, p. 480. Herbert uses rather explicitly Bacon's essays "On Discourse" and "Of Anger."

11. Thomas Adams, *The Two Sonnes*, in *Works*, p. 427; *Certaine Sermons or Homilies*, p. 250.

12. Brathwait, *The English Gentleman*, pp. 115, 118. There are many similarities in the comments on vocation in Brathwait and Herbert's *Country Parson*.

13. Sanderson, p. 212; *Certaine Sermons or Homilies*, p. 250.

14. George Herbert, *The Country Parson,* in *Works*, p. 274; Brathwait, *English Gentleman*, p. 103.

15. Donne, "To Mr. Tilman after he had taken orders," line 30; George Herbert, "The Church-porch," line 80; and *The Country Parson*, in *Works*, p. 277.

16. Sanderson, p. 212.

17. Brathwait, *The English Gentleman*, p. 105. See also pp. 133–34.

18. I disagree with Strier, who dismisses this passage as counseling the gentry simply to be ambitious and proud. He admits that there is something "serious" here, but his insistence that the poem is relentlessly worldly obscures from view the doctrine of vocation and turns upper-class work into a form of glory-seeking (*Resistant Structures*, pp. 97–98). Therefore, he can claim that "the poem contains no vision of community" (p. 103) despite Herbert's urging the upper-classes to adopt the doctrine of vocation in order the improve the nation. See George Herbert's comments on the aristocrat's "debt to our Countrey" in *The Country Parson* (*Works*, p. 274–5).

19. In "'The Church-porch' and George Herbert's Family Advice," Powers-Beck places Herbert's poem in the context of the advice manuals of other members of his family, and argues that whereas Edward's advice

is less concerned with the Protestant ethic, Henry's manual voices the same insistence on the need for employment (*Writing*, pp. 59–95).

20. Singleton comments on this contrast in the poem between "the substance of true worth and the mere appearance of it" and finds it similar to "the disintegration of the ideal lamented in other seventeenth-century sources" (pp. 166–73).

21. I therefore disagree with Strier that "'Solid Braverie' is the ideal" of the poem ("Sanctifying the Aristocracy," p. 47).

22. Strier, "Sanctifying the Aristocracy," p. 49; "George Herbert and the World," p. 227.

23. Strier condemns Herbert for "strategic humility" and again considers it as simply materialistic rather than the result of the problematic requirement within vocation to be both engaged in the world but unaffected by it ("Sanctifying the Aristocracy," p. 48). Schoenfeldt has shown that such strategic humility was not a personal failing on Herbert's part, but necessary for courtiership.

24. Thomas Adams, *The Temple*, pp. 57–59.

25. Ibid., p. 48. For similar discussions of the inner temple, see Featley, p. 224; Hall, "The Temple," p. 1156–59, and Lewalski, pp. 100–104.

26. Charles and others have suggested that "The Church-porch" was written around 1614, and therefore that Herbert changed his views later, perhaps after he was ordained in 1624 (Charles, *A Life*, pp. 77–78; Hutchinson, in George Herbert, *Works*, p. 482; Strier, "Sanctifying the Aristocracy," pp. 56–58). But this event neither committed him to a clerical life nor removed the necessity for obtaining patronage. Schoenfeldt quotes Maycock: "Many men, in the ordinary course, entered the diaconate without any intention of becoming priests" (p. 36). The rest of Schoenfeldt's discussion is also pertinent (pp. 36–37). See also Maycock, p. 120. A transmuted sense of this division between reputation and devotion appears in a letter written by Herbert in 1631 to Arthur Woodnoth:

> As in things inwardly good to have an eye to the world may be pharisaicall: so in things naturally visible and apparent, as the course of our life and the changes thereof, we are to regard others, and neither to scandalize them, nor wound our owne reputation." (380)

This comment is more charitable than "The Church-porch" in its attention to the feelings of others, but reputation is still a primary concern.

27. Perkins, *Treatise*, pp. 729–31, 733–34.

28. See "The Church-porch": "Thou, whose sweet youth and early hopes inhance / Thy rate and price, and mark thee for a treasure" (1–2). Cf. "Easter-Wings":

> Lord, who createdst man in wealth and store,
> Though foolishly he lost the same,
> Decaying more and more,
> Till he became
> Most poore
> · · ·

(1–5)

29. Davison, p. 81; "Corona Dedicatoria," (lines 13–14) in Sylvester, vol. 2, p. 888.

30. Whereas I focus on the distinctions Herbert makes between his dedications to God and his dedication to patrons, Schoenfeldt discusses the similarities.

31. Luther, "On Secular Authority," p. 28.

32. Dickson, pp. 88–94; Schoenfeldt, pp. 161–67.

33. I therefore disagree with Strier's claim that the poem finally "puts human art in its place by decisively turning away from it" because the word altar in the last line refers only to the heart (*Love Known*, p. 195).

34. Sylvester, p. 898; Davison, p. "B."

35. Dickinson, *The King's Right* (London, 1619), quoted in O'Farrell, p. 243.

36. See Chapter 2. The poem, "Had I loved butt att that rate," is quoted by Waller, pp. 177–78. According to Waller, the poem not only appeared in manuscripts with Pembroke's name but was also published in Mary Wroth's continuation of *Urania* and attributed to the character based on Pembroke (see Wroth, pp. 217–18). The "language of love," as Nestrick puts it, in the words "mine" and "thine" becomes severely religious in "The Sacrifice," in which Christ's refrain, "Was ever grief like mine," opens up a chasm between human and divine and breaks the facile dreams of unity imagined by the speaker of "The Altar." The rest of "The Church" works out the implication that, unlike human love, the communion between God and man cannot be mutual. Although I believe the use of art in "The Altar" is justified by the Biblical passages it alludes to, the speaker's misguided desire to imitate Christ's "blessed SACRIFICE" (line 15) is not. See Nestrick's "'Mine and Thine' in *The Temple*."

37. Translators McCloskey and Murphy show that *Lucus* must have been written after August 1623 (p. 178).

38. On the Reformation Protestantism of Herbert's devotional poems, see Introduction, n. 15. On "The Thanksgiving," see Lewalski, p. 171; Strier, *Love Known*, pp. 49–54; Bell, pp. 219–41; and the excellent essay by Nestrick, "George Herbert—The Giver and the Gift."

39. Schoenfeldt, pp. 40–43. See especially his discussion of imitation as both religious and rhetorical.

40. Thomas Adams, *The Temple*, p. 63.

41. Herbert's poem, "Judgement," toward the end of "The Church," develops and resolves the interest of the opening sequence in what is "mine" and "thine," especially in reference to literary imitation. Like "The Thanksgiving," "Judgement" contrasts "ev'ry mans peculiar book" to the New Testament, and claims that what is "mine," however original or meritorious, can never save one from sin.

42. McCloskey, p. 165. The poem is not dated, but the translators agree with Hutchinson that it was probably written in 1618 "since it reflects Herbert's earlier style" (p. 181). Hutchinson lists the years when the two dates coincided: 1607, 1618, 1629 (George Herbert, *Works*, p. 596). "On the concurrence of a birthday and Good Friday" appears in its original Latin and is not translated in the Hutchinson edition of George Herbert's *Works*. The following discussion is based on the McCloskey translation and all in-text line numbers refer to this translation.

43. See Dickson's very useful and convincing discussion of the entrance of a new member into the Church and the opening sequence of Herbert's "Church" (pp. 87–98).

44. See n. 1, this chapter.

45. See Hutchinson's footnotes on *The Temple* in George Herbert, *Works*, for the revisions to the *W* manuscript. The "Easter" poem that precedes this one in both *W* and *B* may refer to justification, the stage in salvation that preceded sanctification: "His life may make thee gold, and much more, just" ("Easter" [I], 6). The line refers to the faith made possible through the Resurrection, and therefore, the justification by faith alone required of all Protestants. For the pattern of salvation—election, vocation, justification, sanctification, glorification—see "The Calling of the Saints," in Haller, pp. 83–91. Herbert's revisions suggest that originally this pattern was made much more explicit in *The Temple*. "H. Baptisme" (I), included in the later *B* manuscript, contains this line, "You taught the Book of Life my name" (12), but this is not the same as the possibility offered in "Easter" in *W*, that the birth of the new man could be dated from the moment the speaker is taught "to sing thy praise" on Easter. Also, such a dating of the life of the new man differs from the sense of advance rather than rebirth in "Easter-Wings."

46. Stein comments on this shift away from self-reference in "Easter": "The major structural change is to move the 'I' of the poem out of the last stanza" (p. 142). See also Lull's comment that Herbert's "revised lyric sequence moves toward an ideal vision of human character in which the individual personality would be indistinguishable from that of Christ" (p. 52). Neither critic notices the biographical or textual significance of the

similarity between the earlier version of "Easter" and "On the concurrence of a birthday and Good Friday."

CHAPTER 4, *'The Temple' Revised: "Selfnesse" and Pollution*

1. Defoe, *The Compleat English Gentleman*, pp. 45–46. Defoe wrote the manuscript in the 1720s, but never completed it; it was first published in 1890. On the significance of the work, see Shinagel, pp. 233–45. On the redefinition of gentility, see Shinagel and also Ustick.

2. See the Introduction.

3. Donne, "To Mr. George Herbert, with my Seal, of the Anchor and Christ," lines 23–24. See the discussion of this poem in Chapter 2. Helen Gardner posits a date for the poem in *Divine Poems*, p. 141.

4. It could be argued that Herbert's sources of gentility were unquestionable, since he was a son of a gentleman and had attended the university. Technically, this was so, but his experience belied it. As a younger son, he did not receive the land or money necessary to maintain the lifestyle of a gentleman, and his employment as a member of the clergy associated him with a group never clearly enough placed within the gentry category. Christopher Hill (*Economic Problems of the Church*, pp. 202–10), Curtis ("Alienated Intellectuals"), and Stone ("Social Mobility," pp. 17–20) all provide evidence of the low status of the clergy during this time. Stone does not include the clergy or any profession within the status group of gentleman but argues that the professions were "semi-independent occupational hierarchies," never clearly included in the overall status system. Laslett, however, categorizes the clergy as gentlemen, but places them just above the line between gentry and commoner (p. 38). He, like many others, assumes that the famous comments of William Harrison and Thomas Smith on university-acquired gentility inevitably include all members of the clergy (Laslett, p. 33; Harrison, pp. 113–14; Thomas Smith, pp. 71–72). Thomas Wilson, unlike Harrison and Smith, explicitly includes the clergy as members of the minor nobility (p. 23). Cressy concludes that, although people at the time saw clergy as gentry and part of the ruling minority, the clergy were in fact not in this group, but "had a service relationship to it, reinforcing its hegemony" (p. 37). I do not agree that contemporary commentary proves that the clergy were considered members of the gentry (see Christopher Hill and Curtis), nor do I agree that Harrison's and Smith's account of university-acquired gentility inevitably extended to all parish clergy. In their comments, the clergy are never explicitly mentioned, and gentility is not obtained until sufficient money is expended to live the life of a gentleman and to purchase a title. The effect of membership in the clergy on Herbert's upper-class status is evident in the contemporary com-

ment that "he did not manage his brave parts to his best advantage and preferment, but lost himself in an humble way" (Oley, p. M3).

5. On the patronage-seeking courtier who had to finesse the cultural distinction between leisured gentlemen and those who work for a living, see Montrose, "Of Gentlemen and Shepherds" (pp. 433–48), and Whigham. Schoenfeldt's analysis stems from his understanding of Herbert's uneasy status position and dependence on courtesy for success, although Schoenfeldt does not explicitly discuss those strategies as a form of labor (see pp. 25–26). For an anthropological analysis of pollution beliefs as a response to a mixture of social categories, see "Ritual Uncleanness" and "Secular Defilement" in Douglas, pp. 1–40, especially pp. 35–36. The Jordan complex of meaning includes this mixture of social categories, since it seeks to purify not only the "workmans tool" but also the pride of high status through its reference to Naaman, the Syrian official who must learn humility before he can be cleansed of his leprosy by bathing in the waters of the Jordan. It is this combination of aristocratic pride in superiority and the workmanship needed to produce it that suggested pollution to Herbert.

6. Douglas, p. 38. Much of Douglas's analysis of the anomaly is relevant to the position of the younger son, whose placelessness disrupts and threatens the coherence of the status system (pp. 5, 37–40). See also her discussion of beliefs about persons in a marginal state (pp. 94–113). My analysis differs from hers because she treats pollution beliefs as largely a conservative defense of traditional categories.

7. I take this reassertion of the status system to be the implication of the arguments by Montrose and Whigham: the courtier without title or estate does not challenge but lays claim to gentility through the pastoral he writes or the upper-class behavior he adopts. See Montrose, "Of Gentlemen and Shepherds," p. 446, and Whigham, pp. 32–34.

8. McKeon calls the marginal position of the younger son "status inconsistency," and claims that it led to a significant questioning of the hierarchical system. See the chapter on "The Destabilization of Social Categories," including the consideration of status and class (pp. 131–75), and the discussion of younger sons (pp. 218–23). Hexter claims to have dispelled the myth of the rise of the middle class during this period, and Laslett argues for the concept of a "one-class society" for pre-industrial England (pp. 23–54), but Herbert was unstably positioned between two distinguishable social rankings, whether they are called status groups or classes. Although Hexter and Laslett have argued fairly persuasively that there were no clearly shared interests among those of middle status, and therefore no shared ideology, these historians themselves acknowledge that the nobility and gentry had

quite a precise sense of what distinguished them from those below them, and that this included manual labor and commercial trade. Though Hexter shows that aristocrats at times engaged in commercial projects, he admits that the middle classes were the ones vilified for them (p. 95). These well-known differences between those who were gentlemen and those who were not are the distinctions that I am claiming Herbert's experience disrupted. His vocational labors, his pursuit of financial gain, and his poverty relative to gentry status associated him with what had been traditionally defined as non-genteel. Wayne has traced the emerging ideology of merit in the work of Jonson (*Penshurst*, pp. 150–65), and Shinagel displays its full-blown appearance in the "middle-class gentility" in the works of Defoe. In both cases this ideology is not exclusively connected to the middle classes but complexly mixed with upper-class values. The tendency of Herbert's critics to identify self with achievement or merit is discussed fully in the Conclusion. These critics include Stanley Fish (*Self-Consuming Artifacts*, pp. 156–223 and *The Living Temple*), Marcus (*Childhood and Cultural Despair*, pp. 94–120), Harman (*Costly Monuments*), and, to some extent, Schoenfeldt (*Prayer and Power*). It would be appropriate to ask to what extent Herbert associated self with merit or achievement, but this association is in no way inevitable in the seventeenth century.

9. Sanderson, p. 230. Sanderson also comments:

> demean my self in thy *particular* calling, as that thou do nothing but what may stand with the *general* calling . . . do not think he hath called you . . . to *Simplicity* in the one, and to *Dissimulation* in the other; to *Holiness* in the one, and to *Prophaneness* in the other. (p. 230)

See also Perkins, *Treatise*, pp. 733–34; and Brathwait, *The English Gentleman*, p. 135.

10. George Herbert, *Works*, p. 228. For Herbert's admonitions against the pursuit of promotion in *The Country Parson*, see pp. 226, 230, 238, 264.

11. Hutchinson discusses the *W* and *B* manuscripts in George Herbert, *Works* (pp. i–lvi); see especially his list of poems in *W* (pp. liv–lv). His footnotes throughout his edition, describing the original *W* poems and the revisions made to them, are invaluable. Charles considers the dating of the *W* manuscript in *A Life* (pp. 78–87). She claims that "virtually nothing in *W* refers directly to contemporary events," but she does not recognize the links between "Affliction" (I) and *Memoriae Matris Sacrum*. She concludes that *W* was written during Herbert's years at Cambridge (1610–24). This conclusion is motivated, I believe, by her desire to prove that Herbert's commitment to church employment was firm almost from the start, and that his anxieties about finding a place were merely a problem of his youth

(*A Life*, pp. 87–89). George Herbert Palmer dates "Affliction" (I), as I do, around 1627, but for different reasons. He concludes that the Williams manuscript was not completed until 1629, which seems rather late to me. Also, his division of the poems into chronological sections of Herbert's life is not trustworthy. Nevertheless, he does accurately point out that the *W* manuscript includes no poems written from the perspective of an established clergyman, whereas the *B* manuscript includes several, and some like "The Priesthood," in which the speaker is "still hesitating about taking orders" (pp. 183–87).

12. *Memoriae Matris Sacrum*, #19, in McCloskey, p. 145.

13. *Aeneid*, bk. IV.441–49.

14. I include my own translation of this crucial line, since that of McCloskey and Murphy is rather free.

15. Gottlieb considers the revised version of this set of poems in "'Content' to 'Affliction' (III)." Gottlieb practices what we might call cluster analysis by considering a group of sequential poems in relation to each other, an approach quite appropriate to Herbert's ordering principles in *The Temple*. I do the same in this chapter.

16. Charles points out that this new sequence in the *B* manuscript focuses on sin, affliction, and God's merciful love ("The Williams Manuscript," p. 423).

17. #61, quoted from the Ringler edition of Sidney's poems. All subsequent citations from Sidney's poetry will be to this edition.

18. For a discussion of these lines in relation to Sidney's life and career, see McCoy, pp. 69–109.

19. I owe this point to William Nestrick.

20. See the analysis of "Employment" (II) in Chapter 6, and of "Paradise" in Chapter 7.

21. McCloskey, *Memoriae Matris Sacris*, #11, p. 145.

22. The most famous of these is the one-line reversal in Sonnet #71: "But ah, Desire still cries, give me some food." See also Sonnets #5, #11, #18, #32, #52, and #76.

23. This quite consciously structured autobiographical story is analyzed by Tuve in *A Reading of George Herbert* (pp. 187–93) and Fish in *Self-Consuming Artifacts* (pp. 193–99). Joseph Summers notices the link between "Miserie" and "Jordan" (II) in *George Herbert* (p. 110), and Strier in *Love Known* (p. 39). Strier discusses the "important connection between ingenuity, elaborate craft, and egotistical selfhood" in several poems, including "Sinnes Round" and "Jordan" (II) (pp. 31–40). None of these critics notice how the revisions emphasize this connection and produce the autobiographical story of the Jordan poems.

24. See Greenblatt, *Renaissance Self-Fashioning*, and "A Mint of Phrases," in Halpern, pp. 19–60. Sidney Gottlieb considers Herbert in the light of self-fashioning in "'Content' to 'Affliction' (III)."

25. On Sidney's concept of *energia*, see *Apology*, pp. 137–38.

26. The original poem "Invention" had from the outset defined verbal elaboration as a religious problem. But "Jordan" (II) defines it as a form of self-fabrication. "Invention" focuses on the indirect methods of the poet: "As flames do work and winde, when they ascend, / So I bespoke me much insinuation" (13–14 in *W*). Insinuation refers to indirection used to ingratiate, and to an exordium or preface designed to win over the hearers, or, as it was put in 1616, "a cunning speech to creep into one's favor" (*OED* 3b). These definitions emphasize preliminary strategies in rhetoric (as opposed to forthright statement), strategies associated with the long "preparation" criticized in "Invention." But "Jordan" (II) turns this cunning literary indirection into an indirect self, forged in the process of coterie poetry, polluting pure expression through competitive imitation.

27. Quoted from Booth's edition of the sonnets, #21. For a discussion of the unproven thesis that William Herbert is the "W.H." to whom Shakespeare's sonnets are dedicated, see Dick Taylor. The famous dedication of the *First Folio* in 1623 to William Herbert and his brother Philip speaks of the great favor shown to Shakespeare by both men (see Brennan, pp. 94–95, 105, 141–42, 176; O'Farrell, pp. 265–67). George Herbert's knowledge of and allusion to Shakespeare's sonnets before 1633 may be evidence of the involvement of both men in William Herbert's coterie, since the sonnets were first published in 1609 and not again until 1640. Herbert may have had access to a purchased copy, or he may have read the manuscripts circulating "among [Shakespeare's] private friends," as Francis Meres put it (see Bevington's edition of Shakespeare's works, p. 1612). I am indebted to Richard Dutton for pointing out this possibility to me.

28. I am indebted to my student Mark Gwinn, who pointed out this veiled reference to Stella in Shakespeare's sonnet.

29. Castiglione, p. 43. See also Montrose, "Of Gentlemen and Shepherds"; Whigham, *Ambition and Privilege*, pp. 93–95; and Schoenfeldt, who discusses "sacred *sprezzatura*" (p. 164).

30. Harington, p. 320.

31. Edward Herbert, *Autobiography*, p. 27.

32. Patterson, *Hermogenes and the Renaissance*, pp. 53–56, 123–26.

33. Castiglione, p. 43.

34. See n. 26, this chapter.

35. In the *W* manuscript, "Jordan" (I) is in close proximity to "Employment" (II) (with only "Denial" and "Ungratefulness" in between), whereas

in the *B* manuscript, "Jordan" (I) immediately precedes "Employment" (I). This suggests that Herbert considered sacred parody in conjunction with employment, as if both required the same purification of motive. The combination of "Invention" and "Perfection" suggests that Herbert also believed that purification of motive could lead to social advancement. This belief would be quite understandable if, as I argued in Chapter 2, the "Jordan" poems were performed before or read by Herbert's patrons, especially William Herbert.

36. Passages from "The Church-porch" and *The Country Parson* can clarify the change in Herbert's attitude toward status. In a stanza in "The Church-porch" on the importance of cleanliness for the young gentleman, Herbert uses the model of the inner/outer self inherent in his works from the beginning: "Affect in things about thee cleanlinesse. . . . Let thy mindes sweetnesse have his operation / Upon thy body, clothes, and habitation" (367–72). *The Country Parson* reproduces this passage but in a revised way: "The Parsons yea is yea, and nay nay; and his apparell plaine, but reverend, and clean, without spots, or dust, or smell; the purity of his mind breaking out, and dilating it selfe even to his body, cloaths, and habitation" (228). The phrase "body, cloaths, and habitation" reveals that the same issues are at stake in the two passages: both gentleman and parson display and protect their cultural position of authority through a freedom from dirt, perhaps in both cases associated with those manual laborers who till the soil. But the second passage suggests a much more extensive personal program, as well as a deep desire to demolish the boundary between the inside and the outside: "the purity of the mind breaking out" fractures the difference model upon which the original *Temple* was built and dreams of an unmediated transparency in public performance. Just as God "sees hearts as we see faces," so Herbert's advice to ministers attempts to project the heart and mind into the social arena. As "Jordan" (II) puts it, the Parson must "copie out only" an inward spirituality before his parishioners. Whereas the words of the whispering friend in "Invention" could primarily be an elegant allusion to Sidney's first and third poems in *Astrophil and Stella*, "Jordan" (II) turns the poem into another manifesto for the "character" of holiness, in which a plain style of language becomes the model for a purified style of life. Tuve also interprets the ending of "Jordan" (II) as calling for a different style of life, as well as a different style of poetry in "Herbert and Caritas" (pp. 175–76).

37. Sidney, *Astrophil and Stella*, #21. Also see #18, #23, and #27.

38. The first example for this meaning, 12b in the *OED*, is dated 1679, but it seems likely that the use of the word in "The Rose" includes this significance, especially given the poem "The Size," which compares human

and divine estates: "Content thee, greedie heart. / Modest and moderate joys to those, that have / Title to more hereafter when they part, / Are passing brave" (1–4).

39. Thomas Adams, *The Temple*, pp. 48–53.

40. See Kerrigan, p. 77.

41. See the discussion of "The Altar" in Chapter 3.

42. The *OED* advises that the word *mate* is "now only in working-class use," and it quotes examples in which the word refers to a companion from the upper classes, but it also defines the word as "used as a form of address by sailors, labourers, etc." during the seventeenth century (1b).

43. Charles, *A Life*, p. 42.

44. "Praise" (I) itself differs in the *W* and the *B* manuscripts, reflecting a change from unemployment to employment. In the last stanza in *B*, the bees remind the speaker that he has "a work, as well as they," whereas the earlier *W* manuscript builds a contrast between the busy spider and the useless fly:

> O raise me then: for if a Spider may
> Spin all the day:
> Not flyes, but I shall bee his prey
> Who doe no more.
>
> (17–20 in *W*, quoted in George Herbert, *Works*, p. 61)

The association between being raised by God and obtaining a position in society is even more explicit in the earlier manuscript.

45. See "The Protestant Concept of Wealth" in Charles George and Katherine George, pp. 122–26.

46. Perkins comments in his *Treatise*:

> They profane their lives and callings that imploy them to get honours, pleasures, profites, worldly commodities etc. for thus we live to another end then God hath appointed, and thus we serve ourselves, and consequently, neither God, nor man. . . . Now the works of every calling, when they are performed in a holy manner, are done in faith and obedience, and serve notably for Gods glory. (*Works*, vol. 1, pp. 756–57)

47. The revised "Elixir" also emphasizes the importance of purifying labor through the figure of the servant: "Who sweeps a room, as for thy laws, / Makes that and th'action fine" (17–20). I am indebted to Sidney Gottlieb for this point.

CHAPTER 5, *The Character of Holiness in 'The Temple'*

1. The emphasis on sin despite entrance into the church is also deepened by "Nature," the first poem in *B* after the Baptism poems.

"Nature" immediately refers again to the image of the hard heart as a stone, used throughout the opening sequence in both manuscripts, but which in *W* does not reappear until "Prayer" ("Church-lock and key"), nine poems after "H. Baptism" (II), and the original "Nature," twenty poems later. On the imagery of the heart as a stone, see Dickson, especially pp. 80–123.

2. Augustine, *Confessions*, bk. 10, chapter 8, p. 216. See Petrarch's use of the same passage in the *Confessions* to mark his conversion experience in "The Ascent of Mont Ventoux." Herbert perhaps alludes to Petrarch as well as Augustine in order to signal that "The Agonie" is a conversion poem, but, if so, it is quite an impersonal one.

3. Augustine, *Confessions*, bk. 10, chapter 8, pp. 215–16.

4. Ibid., bk. 10, chapter 8, p. 215.

5. Ibid., bk. 10, chapter 17, p. 224.

6. See Martz, *The Poetry of Meditation*, pp. 25–32; and Lewalski.

7. Strier notes that "the word 'fiction' here is the culmination of the associations between human art, craft, or ingenuity and evading, lying, or constructing pretenses" (*Love Known*, pp. 31–32).

8. Charles tells of the "canopied tomb" built by Magdalene Herbert in Montgomery in 1600 to commemorate her husband Richard, father to George. It includes "the recumbent figures of man and wife and representations of eight of their ten children" (*A Life*, p. 33). Palmer prints a picture of this tomb next to "Church-monuments," vol. 2, between pp. 200 and 201. Herbert was not buried in the family tomb but in the church at Bemerton. His burial is marked by a small plaque on the wall with the inscription "G.H., 1632."

9. Vendler notices this significant change in the terms of the metaphor and sees it as the result of a sense of unworthiness that the poet battles throughout the poem (pp. 80–83).

10. Augustine, *On Christian Doctrine*, bk. 3, sec. 5, pp. 83–84.

11. See Kronenfeld's excellent account of the metaphor of the stained-glass window and the use of the word "within." See, especially, pp. 75–76: "It is only in a very mental or conceptual way that the preacher may be said to contain the image of Christ, to be a stained-glass window in himself."

12. Williams, *The Country and the City*, p. 32.

13. For critical analyses of the Reformation Protestantism of Herbert's poems, see the Introduction, n. 15. For critics who describe the poetry as dramatizing a loss of self, see Chapter 4, n. 8.

14. See Williams's classic formulation of this position in *The Country and the City* (pp. 1–54). Critics who apply this approach, although in mod-

ified form, include Montrose, "Of Gentlemen and Shepherds," and Whigham, *Ambition and Privilege.*

15. See Chapter 4, n. 8.

16. In *Purity and Danger*, Douglas argues that whatever disrupts traditional categories can be characterized as either polluted or sacred.

17. Fish does not argue that the self is reduced in this poem, but traces a movement from diminishment to "the growth of the preacher." He does say that the poem requires the poet to resign all claims to responsibility for his work (*The Living Temple*, pp. 79–81, 167). Schoenfeldt sees the poem as requiring "absolute subordination in order to allow God's light and life to show through" (*Prayer and Power*, pp. 179–80).

18. For a definition and historical account of the "general calling" and "particular calling," see the Introduction, pp. 3–5.

19. Gottlieb, "'Content' to 'Affliction' (III)," pp. 473–74.

20. Singleton, p. 179.

## CHAPTER 6, *Pastoral, Vocation, and "Private Benefit"*

1. Empson, *Some Versions of Pastoral*, p. 23. I am also indebted to Williams, *The Country and the City*, and his essay, "Ideas of Nature," in *Problems in Materialism and Culture*, pp. 67–85. See also Montrose, "Of Gentlemen and Shepherds," and Wayne, *Penshurst.*

2. See, especially, Vendler, pp. 49–50.

3. Strier glosses these lines: "This voice is obsessed with its own effort and longing, and seems unaware of the almost cavalier quality with which, in Luther's phrase, it confides in its own contrition" (*Love Known*, p. 249).

4. See the discussion of Weber's theory in the Introduction, pp. 11–12 and n. 18, and in Chapter 1, n. 30.

5. Perkins, *Treatise*, pp. 727–28. Subsequent page numbers will appear in the text.

6. See MacPherson. He claims that individual property rights are characteristic of market society and that seventeenth-century writers begin to develop the political theories that can justify such rights. On the other hand, Macfarlane argues that the conditions that many historians have identified with market society—the nuclear family, social and geographical mobility, a market system, and absolute, individualistic property rights—actually existed in 1300. Many reviewers have countered Macfarlane by arguing that, whereas he shows that there was always a brisk market in land, nevertheless he does not consider several restrictions on land ownership: "royal proclamations, statutes of the realm, customs of the manor, and municipal regulations" (see Joyce Appleby, review of *The Origins of English Individualism* by Alan Macfarlane, *American Historical Review* 84, no. 4

(1979): 1047). Lordship, seignorial exploitation, and serfdom are not taken into account, nor are the customs surrounding the common fields (see Paul R. Hyams, book review, *English Historical Review* 96, no. 380 (1981): 606; and Christopher Dyer, book review, *Economic History Review* 32, no. 4 (1979): 606). In addition, Macfarlane does not consider cultural ideology in relation to the practices he identifies. It is significant that the sermons on vocation in the seventeenth century specifically advocate against individualistic thinking, accumulation, and social mobility. It is this cultural and intellectual history that MacPherson studies. McKeon makes an illuminating distinction between the "isolated existence of attitudes and activities within a context that channels and contains them" in the earlier period, and "the full exploitation of those elements as the vital constituents of their context, as that which renders it systematic" in the later period (p. 165).

7. See Chapter 4, n. 11 on dating the revisions.

8. The placement of "Employment" (I) in the revised *B* manuscript emphasizes the pastoral imagery of the last stanza, since the poem now follows "Jordan" (I), which refers wittily to lyric, court, and anti-court pastoral. The sequence of "Jordan" (I) and "Employment" (I) suggests not only that Herbert associated sacred parody with employment, since both require a purification of motive, but that when Herbert made these revisions, the plain style announced in "Jordan" (I) no longer referred to the poem's condensed style but to a willingness to accept "one strain" for "my poore reed"—that is, the poem now referred to a humbler style associated with a humbler position of employment. Notice that the placing of "Jordan" (I) after "Temper" (I) and (II) also reduces the possibility that "My King" in "Jordan" (I) refers to the Stuart monarch, since "Temper" (II) makes a strong distinction between "thy chair of grace" and "the grosser world" (5–6), and the sequence calls attention to the linked phrases "thy chair of grace" and the "painted chair" of secular authority ("Jordan" [I], 5).

9. See accounts of these revisions in Lull, who argues that they emphasize "the sexual aggressiveness concealed in the desire to 'rise,' 'spredd,' and 'swell' in the service of God," and that such striving is always represented as self-serving (p. 35); and in Vendler, who sees in them a decision to replace active service with stasis and speech (pp. 249–51).

10. See the analysis of the Wiltshire regions of the "chalk" and "cheese" countries in Underdown, especially the chapter entitled "Regional Cultures" (pp. 74–105).

11. See, especially, Kerridge, "Agriculture," "The Floating of the Wiltshire Watermeadows," "The Sheepfold in Wiltshire and the Floating of the Water Meadows," and *Surveys*.

12. See Thirsk, "Enclosing and Engrossing."

13. On "good neighborhood," see Underdown, p. 18; and Marcus, *Childhood and Cultural Despair*, p. 6.

14. Montrose, "'The Place of a Brother,'" p. 35; Cressy, p. 37. The difference between Herbert's resistance to Pembroke in *The Country Parson* and the ideology of power as love in the poetry is crucial, since that ideology makes possible the social obedience that was distasteful for Herbert because of his upper-class status. "The Flower" implies that Herbert would have preferred to develop his own estate rather than serve as chaplain to Pembroke. See the discussion later in the chapter on the socializing role of Christ as "Master" in the literature on vocation. The same coordination of power and love occurs in "The Temper" (I), which also describes the soul as rising and falling. Like "The Flower," it imagines but denies to the speaker a form of non-transgressive development through the image of the nestling bird (17–20). Like "The Flower," both movement and discipline become acceptable by linking power with love. Unlike "The Flower," the sequence of "Temper" (I) and (II) may acknowledge to some extent that the coordination of power and love is a form of human ideology, since the resolution dissolves immediately at the beginning of the second poem.

15. See Mark 2:15–17; Mark 15:27–28; Luke 23:32–43; and John 18:30.

16. I agree with Strier that the Crucifixion "violates decorum in a fundamental way," and that the poem reenacts this violation, at least to some extent (*Love Known*, p. 57). But Strier implies that the terms of the poem are wholly concocted by the speaker and represent his "world view," which is subsequently demolished. Christ, however, speaks the same language of hierarchy, kingship, and aristocracy ("*Your suit is granted,*" [14]) and the poem needs the metaphoric link between Biblical covenants and tenant leases in order to make sense.

17. "The Thomistic estimation of the worth of labor is inextricably intertwined with considerations of differing levels of social or institutional status and differing degrees of occupational dignity" (Charles George and Katherine George, p. 138; see also pp. 82, 131).

18. Strier claims that "devout humanism" was "a way of defusing the democratic and anti-elitist strains in Protestantism," but the sermons on vocation frequently did the same thing, including those by the Puritans Perkins, Dod, and Cleaver ("Sanctifying the Aristocracy," p. 37).

19. For comments on equality, see Tyndale, "The Parable of the Wicked Mammon" (1527), pp. 98, 100–102; Latimer, "Sermon of the Plough" (1548) and "A Sermon made on Christmas-Day" (1552), pp. 60, 93; Perkins, *Treatise*, p. 735. For the reintroduction of hierarchy, see Perkins, *Treatise*, pp. 731–32, and Sanderson, p. 205. On Christ as the

Master, see Tyndale, p. 101–2; Perkins, *Treatise*, p. 734; Sanderson, p. 205. Also, see George and George, pp. 131, 138. The book by the Georges is invaluable; nevertheless, they ignore the limits on this vocational egalitarianism. Wright interprets "the doctrine of contentment" as no "mere resignation to fate"; God may call a Christian "to better things" (p. 172).

20. Latimer, "A Sermon made on Christmas-Day," pp. 84–95; subsequent page numbers will appear in the text.

21. For an interpretation of Herbert's "assertion of dependence" in terms of the rituals of deference, see "'Subject to Ev'ry Mounters Bended Knee': Herbert and Authority," in Schoenfeldt. Strier has argued that Protestant political theory included both a doctrine of non-obedience and active resistance, but I have found that only the former shows up, and this rarely, in sermons on vocation, which consider social rather than political obedience (*Resistant Structures*, pp. 170–75).

22. Kerridge, "Agriculture," pp. 48, 60; *Surveys*; "Movement of Rent."

23. Sanderson, p. 212. Also see *Certaine Sermons or Homilies*, p. 250; and Thomas Adams, "The Two Sonnes," in *Works*, p. 427.

24. Tyndale, "The Parable of the Wicked Mammon," p. 98.

25. On the "magical extraction of labor," see Williams, The *Country and City*, p. 32; Wayne, pp. 126–27.

26. Dod and Cleaver, pp. 102, 105. Subsequent quotations from this work will be indicated by page numbers in the text.

27. Ben Jonson, "To Penshurst," lines 49–50.

28. Protestant and Puritan preachers mount vociferous attacks on immersion in earthly affairs and the profit-seeking that they see as its result; nevertheless, it is more the rule than the exception for devotional industry to be modeled on social engagement and for the desire for spiritual profit to be structured according to the pursuit of secular success. In a sermon on *The Fruitful Labour for Eternal Food* (1630), Richard Sibbes takes his cue from Isaiah 55:2 by urging his audience to "labour not for the meate that perisheth," but sacred work is understood in terms of secular business:

> Hope stirreth up endeavor, as we see in marchandizing, though when we venter beyond the seas we commit all to winde and water (as they say) and it is doubtfull what the issue may be, yet we hope, and that sets us on worke; so the poore Husbandman, but that he hopes to have a comfortable issue, to have a harvest, he would never set himselfe to worke. (199)

The "hope" and "endeavor" required for religious dedication takes its shape from the rich merchant or "the poore Husbandman"; the second example seems to be offered in order to counteract both the uncertainty and the potential opulence associated with commercial investment. The agricultural harvest as a metaphor for religious growth receives full authorization from the Bible, but it also regulates and limits achievement according to the natural cycle of the seasons and the unpretentious status of the rural laborer. The "issue" becomes "comfortable" rather than risky or prodigal. Like "Love unknown," which revises the promise of an "inheritance" into leased land, Sibbes uses the agrarian analogy in order to articulate both the differences and the similarities between religious and worldly achievement.

29. Thomas Adams, *Works*, p. 420.

30. Sanderson, p. 204.

31. Weber, p. 85; also see pp. 214–15, n. 19 and n. 20.

32. Sibbes, *Commentary*, p. 257; Perkins, *Treatise*, p. 734. Strier comments on Sibbes's reference to alchemy in "George Herbert and the World" (p. 224) and *Love Known* (p. 208).

33. On the psychic and cultural implications of reactions to dirt and disorder, see Douglas. Strier considers the passage quoted as an example of how *The Country Parson* appropriates only for the minister the spiritual value given to work by the doctrine of vocation, and not for the work of any Christian, like the laborers in the cottage ("George Herbert and the World," p. 225).

34. Marcus describes Herbert's poetry and this poem as re-creating a nearly extinct social institution, the "late-feudal household, with its cores of retainers, magnificent shows of hospitality, and great hall where everyone from the lord and lady down to the lowliest guest dined communally" (in *Childhood and Cultural Despair*, p. 114). For a different interpretation of the sociological implications of this poem, see "Standing on Ceremony: The Comedy of Manners in Herbert's 'Love (III),'" in Schoenfeldt.

35. "An Homilie of the worthy receiving and reverend esteeming of the Sacrament of the body and blood of Christ," from *Certaine Sermons or Homilies*, p. 200.

## CHAPTER 7, *Religion and Enterprise*

1. "Paradise" has never received the attention it deserves, in part because of its deceptively simple language and exceedingly artificial form, and in part because few have recognized the centrality of the poem to Herbert's program of religious self-improvement, and no one has recognized the resonance of the gardening metaphor for Herbert and his family. The best discussion of "Paradise" is found in Stewart, pp. 51–59. Also useful are the analyses by Bloch, pp. 300–302; Rickey, pp. 171–72; Joseph Summers, *George Herbert*, pp. 138–39; and Vendler, pp. 219–22. My analysis is indebted to these discussions as well as to the work of

Williams, who argues that ideas of nature necessarily include attitudes toward society: see "Ideas of Nature" in *Problems in Materialism and Culture*, pp. 67–85. But unlike Williams, I argue that "the new morality of improvement" was celebrated long before the eighteenth century and Pope's country-house poems; it in fact appeared in the complex and elaborate literature on gardening developing in the sixteenth and seventeenth centuries (see *Country and City*, pp. 27, 59–60).

2. Schoenfeldt argues that the imagery of torture in Herbert's poetry produces a recognition of divine power analogous to the reverence produced for the monarch by coercive governmental acts of punishment (pp. 117–53). I believe this power operates in Herbert's poetry for the sake of a larger cultural and economic process of transition.

3. Quoted in Eyler, p. 55.

4. Pope, p. 193, lines 117–18. Further quotations from this edition will be indicated by line or page numbers in the text.

5. I disagree with Strier's argument that Herbert considered artistic representation as of little importance in comparison with sincere feeling (*Love Known*, pp. 175, 188–217). See my comments on this in the Conclusion.

6. See Stewart and Lewalski, pp. 97–99.

7. Stewart, pp. 51–59.

8. According to the *OED*, "start" does not mean "to begin" until the eighteenth century (I.12).

9. Strong, p. 176; Hunt, p. 126. Although Strong's source is Aubrey's description of the garden written in 1691, when the Chelsea estate was in the hands of Danvers's second daughter, nevertheless Strong assumes that the order and statuary of the garden were in place by the mid-1620s, especially given Nicholas Stone's work on the statuary.

10. *Memoriae Matris Sacrum*, #3, #4, and perhaps #7, in McCloskey, pp. 122–55.

11. Quoted in Strong, p. 178.

12. Aubrey 2 MS, fols. 56r–59r; Strong, pp. 176–81; Hunt, pp. 126–30.

13. Aubrey 2 MS, fol. 56r.     14. Aubrey 2 MS, fol. 58v.

15. Aubrey 2 MS, fol. 56v.     16. Bush, p. 295.

17. Bacon, *Of the Advancement of Learning*, pp. 296–97. Aubrey refers to Bacon's visits to the house in Chelsea, which make his comments on gardens particularly relevant (see Aubrey 2 MS, fol. 53r).

18. Montrose, "Of Gentlemen and Shepherds," pp. 431–32.

19. Richard Mulcaster's *Positions* (1581), quoted by Montrose, p. 428.

20. Danby was also an innovator in Renaissance gardens. He began the Oxford Botanic Gardens in 1621, and his brother John's garden at

Chelsea, one of the first of the Italian variety in England, was laid out in 1622. See the *DNB* for Danvers's involvement in the court.

21. Danvers to Duke of Buckingham, 2 February 1619, Fortescue State Papers, #294, Bodleian Library.

22. John Taylor, p. 37.

23. Strong, p. 20.

24. Aubrey 2 MS, fol. 44r. John Taylor, p. 37. Gilbert's term for William Herbert's garden would be a remarkable link to George Herbert's poem, if it were not the case that nearly every garden during this period was called a "paradise." The word itself comes from the Persian for enclosure or park and can mean "walled garden." Nevertheless, George Herbert must have been familiar with the "delicate orchard" on his aristocratic relative's estate and with its name.

25. Strong, pp. 147–64.

26. George Herbert refers to this innovation in "The Invitation" (24) and *The Country Parson* (275).

27. Kerridge, "The Floating of the Wiltshire Watermeadows," pp. 105, 113, and "The Sheepfold in Wiltshire and the Floating of the Water Meadows." A contemporary treatise on the subject was dedicated to Philip's brother William (Rowland Vaughan, *Most Approved, and Long experienced Water-Workes*).

28. Underdown, pp. 106–45; Kerridge, "The Revolts in Wiltshire"; Buchanan Sharpe, *In Contempt of All Authority*, pp. 170–82, 194–96, 202–12; Barnes, pp. 150–61. George Herbert refers quite positively to the benefits of enclosure in *The Country Parson*, p. 275.

29. Kerridge, "Agriculture," pp. 58, 64; "The Floating of the Wiltshire Watermeadows," p. 113.

30. Quoted in Kerridge, "The Revolts in Wiltshire," p. 64.

31. Aubrey mentions the "handsome wall about Rowlington-Park [which adjoins the Garden]" designed by Wilton's gardener Adrian Gilbert in the 1620s (Aubrey 2 MS, fol. 44v).

32. John Taylor, p. 37.

33. The history of the relationship between changing attitudes toward skilled labor in the Renaissance and the use of the dichotomy of art and nature remains to be written. In the Middle Ages and the Renaissance, the word *art* could refer to manual, professional, or liberal arts, but modern studies of the issue largely focus on the philosophical and aesthetic significance of the dichotomy (see Tayler). Nevertheless, it seems likely that the figure of the gardener and the willingness of aristocrats to identify themselves as gardeners could have revised status notions about the "baseness" of manual work and authorized the "arts" of commercial industry.

34. Benson, p. 93.

35. Whitaker, p. 22.

36. Cotton, p. 16. Leo Marx argues that initial European responses to the New World ranged between the extreme of the image of the Garden of Eden, and therefore of "immediate joyous fulfillment," and the extreme of the "hideous wilderness," an image that constituted America as "a field for the exercise of power" (pp. 42–43). But the accounts of several writers co-ordinate these images, since their American garden is one of European making. See, especially, Johnson. See also Jones, pp. 185–93; and Chiapelli.

37. Whitaker, p. 44.

38. Ibid., p. 33.

39. Ibid., p. 22.

40. For discussions of the sexual and psychoanalytic implications of "Paradise," see Vendler (p. 295 n) and the chapter "'That Ancient Heat'; Sexuality and Spirituality in *The Temple*," in Schoenfeldt. For a compelling psychoanalytic account of Herbert's family relations, see Pearlman.

41. *A Sermon Preached to the Honorable Company of the Virginia Plantation, 13 November 1622*, in Donne, *Sermons*, vol. 4, no. 10, p. 269.

42. "And where of old the Empire and the Arts / Ushered the Gospel ever in men's hearts, / Spain hath done one; when Arts perform the other, / The Church shall come, and Sin the Church shall smother" (263–66).

43. See Stewart for a full account of this tradition; Lewalski comments on it as well (pp. 97–99).

44. It could be argued that the poem's apparent authorization of the colonial project is undermined by the figure of "Sinne" that dogs the "Church" in this poem; Herbert may be acknowledging the inevitable en-tangling of religious motives with the pursuit of gain and the acquisition of property. In addition, the poem's rather negative vision of the future, an apocalyptic last judgment rather than a successful conquest of the world, makes it impossible to claim that Herbert in this poem imagines infinite expansion as the goal of Protestant improvement. Nevertheless, this dis-tinction between "Sinne" and "The Church" obscures from view the ex-tent to which the missionary zeal of Protestantism itself, not just mercenary motives, robs native populations of their lands as well as their gold. Reli-gion, in this case, does not side "with povertie" (252) but with empire, as the poem makes clear.

## CONCLUSION

1. Harmon, pp. 83–84.

2. Vendler, p. 7.

3. Although Vendler uses the language of "The Elixir" in this passage,

she is not discussing the poem, but rather her claim that Herbert's goal in writing is "fidelity to experience." Her close analysis of "The Elixir" is far more complex, yet it still privileges "repudiation of both religious cliché and intellectual self-absorption" over the concern about "action" in the poem (pp. 269–73).

4. For an overview of this social change, see Wrightson.

5. Agnew discusses the character genre, the "growing obscurity of new commercial relationships" (p. 71), and the social emphasis on scutinizing personal motives (pp. 57–100). On the transformation of honor from land-based aristocratic concepts to personal credit or reputation, see Agnew (p. 175), Watson, and James.

6. Wordworth, "Preface" (1800), in *Lyrical Ballads*, p. 173.

7. Wordsworth, *Lyrical Ballads*, p. 157.

8. Post-structuralist theories provide help in demystifying the mythology of personality, especially in the concept of de-centering the subject. Nevertheless, this helpfulness is limited by the frequent dependence of these theories on psychoanalysis, which writes back into them an emphasis on the bourgeois nuclear family and reconfirms modern notions of selfhood as domestic, even private. One of the axioms of psychoanalysis is the fundamental power of the distinction between inside and out, infant desire and "the reality principle," a horizontal distinction whose cultural significance was only coming into being in the seventeenth century through works like *The Temple*. For these reasons, I find psychoanalysis inherently incapable of illuminating hierarchical culture as well as Herbert's role in historical change. See Greenblatt, "Psychoanalysis and Renaissance Culture." See also the fascinating discussion of these issues in the work of Nancy Selleck. On de-centering the subject, see Belsey, p. 48.

9. Althusser, p. 170.
10. Trilling, pp. 15–16.
11. Ibid., pp. 12–13.
12. Ibid., p. 9.
13. Ibid., pp. 93, 99–100.

14. Targoff argues forcefully that most twentieth-century critics have created a false distinction between sincerity and the public or social ("The Poetics of Common Prayer," pp. 2–4; see also "The Performance of Prayer"). She offers a definition of sincerity that acknowledges the power of liturgical practices to create devotion.

15. Empson, *Seven Types of Ambiguity*, pp. 226–33; Tuve, *A Reading of George Herbert*, pp. 19–99; Strier, *Love Known*, p. 152, n. 28. See Althusser on the interpellation of the subject, in "Ideology and Ideological State Apparatuses," p. 170.

16. Tuve, *A Reading of George Herbert*, p. 117, 194.

17. Joseph Summers, *George Herbert*, p. 84.

18. Ibid., p. 11, and "Sidney and Herbert," pp. 213–14.

19. Joseph Summers, "Sidney and Herbert," p. 214.

20. Vendler, p. 5.

21. Strier, "'Humanizing' Herbert," pp. 78–79, 81.

22. Strier, *Love Known*, p. 151.

23. In his chapter, "The Limits of Experience," Strier clarifies: "The Christian who is feeling deserted by heaven has, as we have seen, the right to complain. What he cannot properly do is draw conclusions on the basis of his feelings" (*Love Known*, p. 219).

24. Strier, *Love Known*, p. 217.

25. Ibid., p. 199–200.

26. The difference between Herbert's and Strier's attitudes toward feeling can be illuminated through the following passage from Herbert's *Brief Notes on Valdesso's Considerations*. Herbert is considering Valdesso's comparison of faith produced through human as opposed to divine influence:

> He often useth this manner of speech *Beleeving by Revelation, not by relation*, whereby I understand he meaneth only the effectuall operation or illumination of the holy spirit, testifying, and applying the revealed truth of the Gospell; and not any private Enthusiasmes, or Revelations: As if he should say: A generall apprehension, or assent to the promises of the Gospell by heare-say, or relation from others, is not that which filleth the heart with joy and peace in believing; but the spirits bearing witness with our spirit, revealing and applying the generall promises to every one in particular with such syncerity and efficacy, that it makes him godly, righteous, and sober all his life long; this I call *beleeving by Revelation, and not by Relation*. (308–9)

Strier uses this passage to demonstrate the importance of "a feeling faith," to Herbert and Protestantism (p. 145). But the passage also suggests that "the heart alone" is dangerous business, especially when given to "private Enthusiasmes, or Revelations," whether shared with others as "hearsay" or not. When Herbert speaks of "syncerity" here, he refers not to a pure feeling of the heart, but to a visitation of the holy spirit: "the spirits bearing witness with our spirit, revealing and applying the generall promises to every one in particular with such syncerity and efficacy." The word "syncerity" carries its older meaning of purity of the gospel, unadulterated by human opinion, and therefore full of power.

27. Strier, *Love Known*, p. 146.

28. I therefore also disagree with Strier that Herbert rejected artistic representation as of no importance in relation to the heart's experience

(*Love Known*, pp. 188–217). It is also inaccurate to state that "Herbert never held that anything intellectual, visible, or external was essential to salvation. What was essential was conative and 'within,' a matter of the heart" (*Love Known*, p. 217). See Herbert's letter to his mother for his own sense of the requirement "to perform those Offices for which I came into the world, and must yet be kept in it" (373). I find compelling Strier's claim that the "I–thou" relationship determining some poems in *The Temple* conflicts with the full hierarchical cosmos or the great chain of being emphasized in others (*Love Known*, p. 168). Nevertheless, it is the case that the particular calling in the doctrine of vocation was meant to deal with this very problem. Tuve puts it this way: "We do not need *The Country Parson* to know that Herbert's theories on love and gratitude for it extend straight *through* a social philosophy which negates the idea of a 'private good'" ("Herbert and Caritas," p. 189). Therefore, I find unpersuasive Strier's claim that "Employment" (I) undermines this hierarchy, since it is one poem among many in *The Temple* that consider the general and the particular calling simultaneously (*Love Known*, pp. 172–73).

   29.  See Fish's comments on this issue in *The Living Temple*:

> Underlying the debate over how to characterize Herbert's poetry is the familiar opposition between art and sincerity. If Herbert is a craftsman, he cannot mean what he is saying because the changes he reports cannot really be occurring (they are faked, or staged, or recollected in tranquility); and if he means what he says, he isn't functioning as a craftsman because the changes are simply reported as they occur (he is a transcriber or tape-recorder). . . . The contradiction disappears, however, if the two intuitions are parceled out; that is, if they are not assumed to be the exclusive property either of a formal structure or of a single personality, but of a *situation*. Herbert's theory of catechizing provides a way of doing just that, and thus makes it possible to acknowledge both his art and his sincerity without compromising either. Indeed they become interdependent: rather than being a sincere report of a mind in the act of changing, the poem is a sincere effort on the part of the poet-catechist to change his reader-pupil's mind. Sincerity is thus not a bodiless interior phenomenon in relation to which a poem is merely a transcription; sincerity is inseparable from an intention in relation to which a poem (or some other act) is an implementation. (8, 26)

Fish restores the social and didactic dimension to Herbert's poetry by defining sincerity not as emanating through the voice of a "single personality" but as part of a public act. I would add that the catechizing Fish describes occurred not simply between poet and anonymous reader, but between Herbert and the members of his poetic coterie, including his patrons.

30. Fish, "Letting Go: The Dialectic of the Self in Herbert's Poetry," in *Self-Consuming Artifacts*, pp. 156–223.

31. Ibid., pp. 156–57.

32. Fish, *The Living Temple*, pp. 133, 135.

33. Fish, *Self-Consuming Artifacts*, p. 158.

34. Foucault, p. 141.

35. Goldberg, pp. 107–8.

36. Marcus, *Childhood and Cultural Despair*, pp. 95, 101.

37. See Chapter 1, n. 48.

38. Schoenfeldt, pp. 10, 11.

39. Ibid., p. 10. Shuger addresses the need for contemporary scholars to give more attention to the role of religion in dominant culture, pp. 1–16.

40. Schoenfeldt, p. 215.

41. Ibid., pp. 18, 13.        42. Harmon, pp. 43.

43. Ibid.                     44. Harmon, p. 47.

45. Greenblatt, *Renaissance Self-Fashioning*, pp. 1–9.

46. Shuger, pp. 4, 6.

47. I disagree with Shuger's account of privacy in the Protestant notion of the dual person. She claims that in the spiritual regimen, the self is "dependent, passive, and private" (p. 93). However, it is not clear that Reformation theologians considered the spiritual regiment to be private, according to our meaning of the term. Tyndale's account suggests that, in the spiritual regiment, social differences are not replaced by personal privacy, but by another kind of community:

> Ye must understand that there be two states or degrees in this world: the kingdom of heaven, which is the regiment of the gospel; and the kingdom of this world, which is the temporal regiment. In the first state there is neither father, mother, son, daughter; neither master, mistress, maid, man-servant, nor husband, nor wife, nor lord, nor subject, nor man, nor woman, but Christ is all; each to other is Christ himself. There is none better than other; but all like good, all brethren, and Christ only is Lord over all. ("Exposition," p. 238)

The spiritual regiment includes both Christ as lord and all Christians as brethren. This notion of community underlies the central uses of this doctrine made by the theologians: Christians are not to resist evil in their personal relations with others, but if that Christian has a secular position of authority, evildoers must be punished. The idea of the two regiments does foreshadow our sense of privacy: Luther uses the terms "outward" and "inward" to refer to the two realms, and he asserts that inwardly a Christian owes no allegiance to any temporal authority ("On Secular Authority," pp. 19–23). Nevertheless, the invisible rule of Christ includes its own notion of community, requiring certain modes of behavior towards others. Not only individual prayer, but preaching itself is categorized as part of the spiritual regiment ("On Secular Authority," p. 19). A passage by Tyndale can clarify the difference between early modern notions of privacy and our own:

> In the first state [the spiritual] . . . there thou must love, and of love do, study, and enforce; yea, and suffer all things (as Christ did) to make peace. . . . 'Blessed be the peacemakers, for they shall be the children of God.' If thou suffer and keepest peace in thyself only, thy blessing is the possession of this world. But if thou so love the peace of thy brethren, that thou leave nothing undone or unsuffered to further it, thy blessing is, thou shalt be God's son, and consequently possess heaven. But in the worldly state, where thou art no private man, but a person in respect of other, thou not only mayest, but also must, and art bound under pain of damnation to execute thine office. ("Exposition," p. 239)

Tyndale uses the term "private man" to refer to the spiritual self, but this private man cannot be identified with personal autonomous states ("if thou suffer and keepest peace in thyself only, thy blessing is the possession of this world"), and this private man is expected to perform actions influencing others ("thou [must] leave nothing undone or unsuffered to further it"). The term "private" seems to refer to experiences with others that are not defined by one's recognized position in society; it is not synonymous with personal meditation. I agree with Shuger's implication that *The Temple* contributes to "an intensification of private spirituality split off from a historicized and rationalized account of social and political behavior" (p. 105), but not with her argument that *The Temple* is an example of this private spirituality. On the contrary, Herbert and the doctrine of vocation are explicitly interested in weaving the spiritual and the temporal parts of the self together.

# Bibliography

Adams, Simon. "Foreign Policy and the Parliaments of 1621 and 1624."
In *Faction and Parliament: Essays on Early Stuart History*, ed. Kevin
Sharpe. London: Methuen, 1978.

Adams, Thomas. *Mystical Bedlam, or the World of Mad-Men*. London:
G. Purslowe for C. Knight, 1615.

———. *The Temple: A Sermon Preached at Pauls Crosse the fifth of
August, 1624*. London: A. Mathews for J. Grismand, 1624.

———. *Works*. London: Thomas Harper, 1629.

Agnew, Jean-Christophe. *Worlds Apart: The Market and the Theater in
Anglo-American Thought, 1550–1750*. Cambridge: Cambridge
University Press, 1986.

Alpers, Paul. *What Is Pastoral?* Chicago: University of Chicago Press, 1996.

Althusser, Louis. "Ideology and Ideological State Apparatuses." In *Lenin
and Philosophy and Other Essays*. New York: Monthly Review Press,
1971.

Altman, Joel. *The Tudor Play of Mind: Rhetorical Inquiry and the Development of Elizabethan Drama*. Berkeley: University of California Press,
1978.

Appleby, Joyce. *Economic Thought and Ideology in Seventeenth Century
England*. Princeton, N.J.: Princeton University Press, 1978.

Aristotle. *Nichomachean Ethics*. Trans. H. Rackham. Cambridge: Harvard
University Press, 1939.

Armstrong, Nancy. *Desire and Domestic Fiction: A Political History of the
Novel*. Oxford: Oxford University Press, 1987.

Aubrey, John. *Brief Lives*. Ed. Oliver Lawson Dick. London: Secker and
Warburg, 1949.

———. Description and model of Sir John Danvers' Garden. Aubrey 2
MS. Bodleian Library.

Augustine. *Confessions*. Trans. R. S. Pine-Coffin. Harmondsworth:
Penguin Books, 1981.

———. *On Christian Doctrine*. Trans. D. W. Robertson, Jr. Indianapolis: Bobbs-Merrill, 1958.

Bacon, Francis. *Of the Advancement of Learning*, bk. 1. In *The Works of Francis Bacon*, vol. 3, ed. James Spedding. New York: Garrett Press, 1870.

———. *The Translation of Certain Psalmes into English Verse*. London, 1625.

Baldwin, T. W. *William Shakspere's Small Latine and Lesse Greeke*. 2 vols. Urbana: University of Illinois Press, 1944.

Barnes, Thomas. *Somerset, 1625–1640*. Cambridge: Harvard University Press, 1961.

Barthes, Roland. *Mythologies*. New York: Hill and Wang, 1972.

Baxter, Richard. *Poetical Fragments: Heart-Imployment with God and It Self*. London, 1681.

Beal, Peter. *Index of English Literary Manuscripts*. 4 vols. London: Mansell; New York: Bowker, 1980–1997.

Bell, Ilona. "'Setting Foot into Divinity': George Herbert and the English Reformation." *Modern Language Quarterly* 38 (Sept. 1977): 219–41.

Belsey, Catherine. "Constructing the Subject: Deconstructing the Text." In *Feminist Criticism and Social Change*, ed. Judith Newton and Deborah Rosenfelt. London: Methuen, 1985.

Benet, Diana. "Herbert's Experience of Politics and Patronage in 1624." *George Herbert Journal* 10, nos. 1 and 2 (1986/87): 33–45.

———. *Secretary of Praise: The Poetic Vocation of George Herbert*. Columbia: University of Missouri Press, 1984.

Benson, George. *A Sermon Preached at Paules Crosse the Seaventh of May, 1608*. London: 1609.

Bloch, Chana. *Spelling the Word: George Herbert and the Bible*. Berkeley: University of California Press, 1985.

Bouwsma, William. "Anxiety and the Formation of Early Modern Culture." In *After the Reformation*, ed. Barbara Malament. Philadelphia: University of Pennsylvania Press, 1980.

Brathwait, Richard. *The English Gentleman*. London: John Haviland, 1630.

Brennan, Michael G. *Literary Patronage in the English Renaissance*. London: Routledge, 1988.

Brooks, Peter. *The Novel of Worldliness*. Princeton: Princeton University Press, 1969.

Bush, Douglas. *Mythology and the Renaissance Tradition in English Poetry*. Rev. ed. New York: W. W. Norton, 1963.

Castiglione, Baldesar. *The Book of the Courtier*. New York: Anchor Books, 1959.

*Certaine Sermons or Homilies appointed to be read in Churches*. London: John Bill, 1623.

Charles, Amy. *A Life of George Herbert*. Ithaca: Cornell University Press, 1977.

———. "The Williams Manuscript and *The Temple*." In *Essential Articles for the Study of George Herbert*. Hamden, Conn.: Archon Books, 1979.

Chiapelli, Fredi, ed. *First Images of America: The Impact of the New World on the Old*. Berkeley: University of California Press, 1970.

Cogswell, Thomas. "England and the Spanish Match." In *Conflict in Early Stuart England*, ed. Richard Cust and Ann Hughes. London: Longman, 1989.

Cohen, Walter. "Political Criticism of Shakespeare." In *Shakespeare Reproduced: The Text in History and Ideology*, ed. Jean E. Howard and Marion F. O'Connor. London: Methuen, 1987.

Coiro, Ann Baynes. "Milton and Class Identity: The Publication of *Areopagitica* and the 1645 *Poems*." *Journal of Medieval and Renaissance Studies* 22 (spring 1992): 261–89.

Cotton, John. *Gods Promise to His Plantation*. London, 1630.

Crashaw, William. *A Sermon Preached in London*. . . . London, 1610.

Craven, Wesley F. *Dissolution of the Virginia Company*. Oxford: Oxford University Press, 1932.

Cressy, David. "Describing the Social Order of Elizabethan and Stuart England." *Literature and History* 3 (March 1976): 29–42.

Curtis, Mark H. "Alienated Intellectuals of Early Stuart England." *Past and Present* 23 (1962): 25–43.

———. *Oxford and Cambridge in Transition, 1558–1642*. Oxford: Clarendon Press, 1959.

Cust, Richard. *The Forced Loan and English Politics, 1626–1628*. Oxford: Clarendon Press, 1987.

Cust, Richard, and Ann Hughes, eds. *Conflict in Early Stuart England: Studies in Religion and Politics, 1603–1642*. London: Longman, 1989.

Davies, Godfrey. *The Oxford History of England: The Early Stuarts: 1603–1660*. Oxford: Clarendon Press, 1937.

Davison, Francis. *Davison's Poetical Rhapsody*. Ed. A. H. Bullen. London: George Bell and Sons, 1890.

Defoe, Daniel. *The Compleat English Gentleman*. Ed. Karl D. Bulbring. Folcroft, Pa.: Folcroft Library Editions, 1972.

Dickson, Donald R. *The Fountain of Living Waters: The Typology of the Waters of Life in Herbert, Vaughan, and Traherne.* Columbia: University of Missouri Press, 1987.

Dod, John, and Richard Cleaver. *Ten Sermons tending chiefly to the fitting of men for the worthy receiving of the Lords Supper.* London, 1611.

Dollimore, Jonathan. "Introduction: Shakespeare, Cultural Materialism, and the New Historicism." In *Political Shakespeare: New Essays in Cultural Materialism,* ed. Jonathan Dollimore and Alan Sinfield. Ithaca, N.Y.: Cornell University Press, 1985.

Donne, John. *Divine Poems.* Ed. Helen Gardner. Oxford: Clarendon Press, 1952.

————. *The Elegies and the Songs and Sonnets.* Ed. Helen Gardner. Oxford: Clarendon Press, 1965.

————. *Paradoxes and Problems.* Ed. Helen Peters. Oxford: Clarendon Press, 1980.

————. *The Poems of John Donne.* 2 vols. Ed. Herbert J. C. Grierson. Oxford: Oxford University Press, 1912.

————. *Sermons.* 10 vols. Ed. George Potter and Evelyn Simpson. Berkeley: University of California Press, 1953–62.

Douglas, Mary. *Purity and Danger: An Analysis of the Concepts of Pollution and Taboo.* London: Routledge and Kegan Paul, 1966.

Du Bartas, Guillaume de Saluste. *The Divine Weeks and Works of Guillaume de Saluste Sieur du Bartas.* Trans. Joshua Sylvester; ed. Susan Snyder. Oxford: Clarendon Press, 1979.

Dutton, Richard. *Mastering the Revels: The Regulation and Censorship of English Renaissance Drama.* Iowa City: University of Iowa Press, 1991.

Earle, John. *Micro-cosmographie: Or a Peece of the World Discovered.* London, 1628.

Elias, Norbert. *The Civilizing Process: The History of Manners.* Trans. Edmund Jephcott. New York: Urizen Books, 1978.

Empson, William. *Seven Types of Ambiguity.* 1930. Reprint, New York: New Directions, 1947.

————. *Some Versions of Pastoral.* 1935. Reprint, New York: New Directions, 1950.

Evans, Willa M. *Henry Lawes: Musician and Friend of Poets.* New York: Modern Language Association, 1941.

Eyler, Ellen C. *Early English Gardens and Garden Books.* Ithaca, N.Y.: Cornell University Press, 1963.

Featley, Daniel. *The Living Temple.* In *Clavis Mystica.* 1636.

Ferguson, Margaret. "Sidney's *A Defence of Poetry*: A Retrial." *Boundary 2* 7, no. 2 (winter 1979): 61–95.

Fincham, Kenneth. "Prelacy and Politics: Archbishop Abbot's Defence of Protestant Orthodoxy." *Historical Research* 61 (1988): 36–64.

Finkelpearl, Philip J. *John Marston of the Middle Temple*. Cambridge: Harvard University Press, 1969.

Fish, Stanley. *The Living Temple: George Herbert and Catechizing*. Berkeley: University of California Press, 1978.

———. *Self-Consuming Artifacts*. Berkeley: University of California Press, 1972.

Foucault, Michel. "What is an Author?" In *Textual Strategies*, ed. Josue V. Harari. Ithaca, N.Y.: Cornell University Press, 1979.

Gardiner, Samuel R. *History of England from the Accession of James I to the Outbreak of the Civil War, 1603–1642*, vol. 5. London: Longmans, Green, 1883.

Gataker, Thomas. *Certaine Sermons*. London, 1637.

George, Charles H., and Katherine George. *The Protestant Mind of the English Reformation, 1570–1640*. Princeton: Princeton University Press, 1961.

Goldberg, Jonathan. *Voice Terminal Echo: Postmodernism and English Renaissance Texts*. London: Methuen, 1986.

Gosse, Edmund. *The Life and Letters of John Donne*. Gloucester, Mass.: Peter Smith, 1959.

Gottlieb, Sidney. "'Content' to 'Affliction' (III): Herbert's Anti-Court Sequence." *English Literary Renaissance* 23 (fall 1993): 472–89.

———. "The Social and Political Backgrounds of George Herbert's Poetry." In *"The Muses Common-weale": Poetry and Politics in the Seventeenth Century*, ed. Claude Summers and Ted-Larry Pebworth. Columbia: University of Missouri Press, 1988, 107–18.

———. "The Two Endings of George Herbert's 'The Church.'" In *A Fine Tuning: Studies of the Religious Poetry of Herbert and Milton*, ed. Mary A. Maleski. Binghamton, N.Y.: Medieval and Renaissance Texts and Studies, 1989.

Gottlieb, Sidney, and Jonathan F. S. Post, eds. *George Herbert in the Nineties: Reflections and Reassessments*. Fairfield, Conn.: George Herbert Journal Publishers, 1995.

Greenblatt, Stephen. "Psychoanalysis and Renaissance Culture." In *Literary Theory/Renaissance Texts*, ed. Patricia Parker and David Quint. Baltimore: Johns Hopkins University Press, 1986.

———. *Renaissance Self-Fashioning, From More to Shakespeare*. Chicago: University of Chicago Press, 1980.

————. *Sir Walter Ralegh: The Renaissance Man and His Roles.* New Haven: Yale University Press, 1973.

Grierson, Sir Herbert. "Bacon's Poem, *The World*: Its Date and Relation to Certain Other Poems." In *Cross-Currents in Seventeenth-Century Literature.* New York: Harper, 1958.

Grosart, Alexander B., ed. *The Complete Works in Verse and Prose of George Herbert,* vol. 3. Fuller Worthies' Library. London: Robson, 1874.

Halewood, William. *The Poetry of Grace: Reformation Themes and Structures in English Seventeenth-Century Poetry.* New Haven: Yale University Press, 1970.

Hall, Joseph. *Characters of Vertues and Vices.* London, 1608.
————. "The Temple." In *Works.* London: N. Butler, 1634.

Haller, William. *The Rise of Puritanism.* Philadelphia: University of Pennsylvania Press, 1938.

Halpern, Richard. *The Poetics of Primitive Accumulation: English Renaissance Culture and the Genealogy of Capital.* Ithaca, N.Y.: Cornell University Press, 1991.

Hannay, Margaret. *Philip's Phoenix: Mary Sidney, Countess of Pembroke.* Oxford: Oxford University Press, 1990.

Harington, John. *Letters and Epigrams.* Ed. Norman Egbert McClure. New York: Octagon Books, 1977.

Harman, Barbara. *Costly Monuments: Representations of the Self in George Herbert's Poetry.* Cambridge: Harvard University Press, 1982.

Harrison, William. *The Description of England.* Trans. Georges Edelen. Ithaca, N.Y.: Cornell University Press, 1968.

Hart, E. F. "The Answer-Poem of the Early Seventeenth-Century." *Review of English Studies,* n.s., 7 (1956): 19–29.

Heller, Thomas, Morton Sosna, and David Wellbery, eds. *Reconstructing Individualism: Autonomy, Individuality, and the Self in Western Thought.* Stanford, Calif.: Stanford University Press, 1986.

Herbert, Edward. *The Autobiography of Edward Lord Herbert of Cherbury.* London: Alexander Murray, 1870.
————. *The Poems English and Latin of Edward Lord Herbert of Cherbury.* Ed. G. C. Moore Smith. Oxford: Clarendon Press, 1923.

Herbert, George. *Select Hymns, Taken out of Mr. Herbert's Temple* [1697]. Augustan Reprint Society, no. 98. Los Angeles: University of California Press, 1962.
————. *Works.* Ed. F. E. Hutchinson. Oxford: Clarendon Press, 1941.

Herbert, William. *Poems Written by the Right Honorable William Earl of Pembroke Lord Steward of his Majesties Houshold. Whereof Many of which are answered by way of Repartee, by Sr Benjamin Ruddier, Knight.* Ed. John Donne. 1660.

Hexter, J. H. "The Myth of the Middle Class in Tudor England." In *Reappraisals in History.* Chicago: University of Chicago Press, 1979.

Hill, Christopher. *Economic Problems of the Church: From Archbishop Whitgift to the Long Parliament.* Oxford: Clarendon Press, 1956.

———. *Society and Puritanism in Pre-Revolutionary England.* New York: Schocken Books, 1964.

Hill, Eugene. *Edward, Lord Herbert of Cherbury.* Boston: G. K. Hall, 1987.

Hodgkins, Christopher. *Authority, Church, and Society in George Herbert: Return to the Middle Way.* Columbia: University of Missouri Press, 1993.

Hooker, Richard. *Of the Laws of Ecclesiastical Polity.* London: John Windt, 1594.

Hughes, Lewis. *A Plaine and True Relation of the Goodness of God Toward the Summer Islands. . . .* London, 1621.

Hunt, John Dixon. *Garden and Grove: The Italian Renaissance Garden in the English Imagination, 1600–1750.* London: J. M. Dent and Sons, 1986.

James, Mervyn. *English Politics and the Concept of Honor, 1485–1642.* Past and Present Supplement 3. Oxford: Past and Present Society, 1978.

Johnson, Robert. *Nova Britannia. Offring Most Excellent fruites by Planting in Virginia.* 1609.

Jones, Howard Mumford. *O Strange New World: American Culture: The Formative Years.* New York: Viking Press, 1964.

Jonson, Ben. *The Complete Poetry.* Ed. William B. Hunter, Jr. New York: New York University Press, 1968.

Kelliher, W. Hilton. "The Latin Poetry of George Herbert." In *The Latin Poetry of English Poets*, ed. J. W. Binn. London: Routledge and Kegan Paul, 1974.

Kerridge, Eric. *Agrarian Problems of the Sixteenth Century and After.* New York: Barnes and Noble, 1969.

———. *The Agricultural Revolution.* London: Allen and Unwin, 1967.

———. "Agriculture, c. 1500–c. 1793." In *A History of the County of Wiltshire*, vol. 4, ed. Elizabeth Crittall. Oxford: Oxford University Press, 1959.

———. "The Floating of the Wiltshire Watermeadows." *Wiltshire Archaeological and Natural History Magazine* 55 (1954): 105–18.

———. "Movement of Rent, 1540–1640." *Economic History Review*, 2d ser., 6 (1953): 16–34.

————. "The Revolts in Wiltshire Against Charles I." *Wiltshire Archaeological and Natural History Magazine* 57 (1958–60): 64–75.

————. "The Sheepfold in Wiltshire and the Floating of the Water Meadows," *Economic History Review*, 2d ser., 6 (1954): 286–89.

————. *Surveys of the Manors of Philip, Fourth Earl of Pembroke, 1631–2.* Devizes, Wiltshire County, England: Wiltshire Archaeological and Natural History Society, vol. 9 (1953).

Kerrigan, William. "Ritual Man: On the Outside of Herbert's Poetry." *Psychiatry* 48 (Feb. 1985): 68–82.

Kingsbury, Susan Myra, ed. *The Records of the Virginia Company of London.* 4 vols. Washington: Government Printing Office, 1906–35.

Kitch, M. J. *Capitalism and the Reformation.* London: Longman Group, 1967.

Kollmeier, Harold H. "'A Mark To Aim At': Genre and Sensibility in George Herbert's *Country Parson.*" Ph.D. diss., State University of New York at Stony Brook, 1976. Abstract in *Dissertation Abstracts International* 37 (1976): 1566A.

Kronenfeld, Judy Z. "Probing the Relation Between Poetry and Ideology: Herbert's 'The Windows.'" *John Donne Journal* 2, vol. 1 (1983): 55–80.

Lake, Peter. "Anti-Popery: The Structure of a Prejudice." In *Conflict in Early Stuart England*, ed. Richard Cust and Ann Hughes. London: Longman, 1989.

Lamb, Mary Ellen. *Gender and Authorship in the Sidney Circle.* Madison: University of Wisconsin Press, 1990.

Laslett, Peter. *The World We Have Lost.* New York: Scribner, 1965.

Latimer, Hugh. "Sermon of the Plough" [1548], "The Sermon Preached Upon Saint Andrew's Day, 1552," and "A Sermon made on Christmas-Day" [1552]. In *Sermons and Remains.* The Parker Society. Cambridge: The University Press, 1845.

Lewalski, Barbara. *Protestant Poetics and the Seventeenth-Century Religious Lyric.* Princeton: Princeton University Press, 1979.

Lockyer, Roger. *Buckingham: The Life and Political Career of George Villiers, First Duke of Buckingham, 1592–1628.* London: Longman, 1981.

Love, Harold. *Scribal Publication in Seventeenth-Century England.* Oxford: Clarendon Press, 1993.

Low, Anthony. *The Georgic Revolution.* Princeton: Princeton University Press, 1985.

Lull, Janis. *The Poem in Time: Reading George Herbert's Revisions of 'The Church.'* Newark: University of Delaware Press, 1990.

Luther, Martin. "On Secular Authority." In *Luther and Calvin on Secular Authority*, ed. and trans. Harro Hopfl. Cambridge: Cambridge University Press, 1981.

Macfarlane, Alan. *The Origins of English Individualism: The Family, Property, and Social Transition*. Oxford: Basil Blackwell, 1978.

MacPherson, C. B. *The Political Theory of Possessive Individualism: Hobbes to Locke*. Oxford: Oxford University Press, 1962.

Marcus, Leah Sinanglou. *Childhood and Cultural Despair: A Theme and Variations in Seventeenth-Century Literature*. Pittsburgh: University of Pittsburgh Press, 1978.

————. "George Herbert and the Anglican Plain Style." In *"Too Rich to Clothe the Sunne": Essays on George Herbert*, ed. Claude Summers and Ted-Larry Pebworth. Pittsburgh: University of Pittsburgh Press, 1980.

Marotti, Arthur. *John Donne: Coterie Poet*. Madison: University of Wisconsin Press, 1986.

Martz, Louis. *The Poetry of Meditation*. New Haven: Yale University Press, 1954.

Marx, Leo. *The Machine in the Garden*. Oxford: Oxford University Press, 1964.

Maus, Katherine Elizabeth. *Inwardness and Theater in the English Renaissance*. Chicago: University of Chicago Press, 1995.

Maycock, A. L. *Nicholas Ferrar of Little Gidding*. London: Society for Promotion of Christian Knowledge; New York: Macmillan, 1938.

Mayor, J. E. B. *Nicholas Ferrar: Two Lives by His Brother John and by Dr. Jebb*. Cambridge: Cambridge University Press, 1855.

McCloskey, Mark R., and Paul R. Murphy, trans. *The Latin Poetry of George Herbert*. Athens: Ohio University Press.

McCoy, Richard. *Sir Philip Sidney: Rebellion in Arcadia*. New Brunswick, N.J.: Rutgers University Press, 1979.

McKeon, Michael. *The Origins of the English Novel, 1600–1740*. Baltimore: Johns Hopkins University Press, 1987.

Moffet, Thomas. *Nobilis, or A View of the Life and Death of Sidney*. Ed. Virgil B. Heltzel and Hoyt H. Hudson. San Marino, Calif.: The Huntington Library, 1940.

Mohl, Ruth. *The Three Estates in Medieval and Renaissance Literature*. New York: F. Ungar, 1962.

Molesworth, Charles. "Herbert's 'The Elixir': Revision Towards Action." *Concerning Poetry*, vol. 5, no. 2 (1972): 12–20.

Montrose, Louis. "Of Gentlemen and Shepherds: The Politics of Pastoral Form." *English Literary History* 50 (fall 1983): 415–59.

————. "'The Place of a Brother' in *As You Like It*: Social Process and Comic Form." *Shakespeare Quarterly* 32 (spring 1981): 28–54.

More, Thomas. *The Complete Works of St. Thomas More*. Vol. 4, *Utopia*, ed. Edward Surtz, S.J., and J. H. Hexter. New Haven: Yale University Press, 1965.

Nestrick, William. "George Herbert—The Giver and the Gift." *Ploughshares* 2, no. 4 (1975): 187–205.

————. "'Mine and Thine' in *The Temple*." In *"Too Rich to Clothe the Sunne": Essays on George Herbert*, ed. Claude J. Summers and Ted-Larry Pebworth. Pittsburgh: University of Pittsburgh Press, 1980.

Novarr, David. *The Disinterred Muse*. Ithaca, N.Y.: Cornell University Press, 1980.

O'Connell, Laura. "Anti-Entrepreneurial Attitudes in Elizabethan Sermons and Popular Literature." *Journal of British Studies* 15 (spring 1976): 1–20.

O'Day, Rosemary. *Education and Society, 1500–1800*. London: Longman, 1982.

O'Farrell, Brian. "Politician, Patron, Poet: William Herbert, Third Earl of Pembroke, 1580–1630." Ph.D. diss., University of California, Los Angeles, 1966.

Oley, Barnabas. "A Prefatory View of the Life of the Author." In *Herbert's Remains*. 1671.

Onderwyzer, Gary E. *Poems Written by the Right Honorable William Earl of Pembroke*. The Augustan Reprint Society, no. 79. Los Angeles: William Andrews Clark Memorial Library, 1959.

Ong, Walter. *Fighting for Life: Contest, Sexuality, and Consciousness*. Ithaca, N.Y.: Cornell University Press, 1981.

————. "Latin Language as a Renaissance Puberty Rite." *Studies in Philology* 56 (Apr. 1959): 103–24.

Overbury, Thomas. *The Miscellaneous Works in Prose and Verse*. Ed. Edward Rimbault. London: Reeves and Turner, 1890.

Palmer, George Herbert. *The English Works of George Herbert*. 6 vols. Boston: Houghton Mifflin, 1905.

Parfitt, George. *Ben Jonson: Public Poet and Private Man*. New York: Harper & Row, 1977.

Patterson, Annabel. M. *Hermogenes and the Renaissance: Seven Ideas of Style*. Princeton: Princeton University Press, 1970.

————. *Pastoral and Ideology: Virgil to Valéry*. Oxford: Clarendon Press, 1986.

Pearlman, E. "George Herbert's God." *English Literary Renaissance* 13 (winter 1983): 88–112.

Pebworth, Ted-Larry. "John Donne, Coterie Poetry, and the Text as Performance." *Studies in English Literature* 29 (winter 1989): 61–75.

Peck, Linda Levy. *Court Patronage and Corruption in Early Stuart England.* Boston: Unwin Hyman, 1990.

———. *Northampton: Patronage and Policy at the Court of James I.* London, Allen and Unwin 1982.

Perkins, William. *Treatise of the Vocations, or Callings of men, with the sorts and kinds of them, and the right use thereof.* In *Workes*, vol. 1. Cambridge: John Legate, 1609.

Pope, Alexander. *Poetry and Prose.* Ed. Aubrey Williams. Boston: Houghton Mifflin, 1969.

Powers-Beck, Jeffrey. "Conquering Laurels and Creeping Ivy: The Tangled Politics of Herbert's *Reditum Caroli.*" *George Herbert Journal* 17 (fall 1993): 1–23.

———. "'Proudly Mounted on the Oceans Backe': The Myth and Emblematic Method of Thomas Herbert." *English Literary Renaissance* 28 (May 1998).

———. *Writing the Flesh: The Herbert Family Dialogue.* Pittsburgh: Duquesne University Press, 1998.

Rickey, Mary Ellen. *Utmost Art: Complexity in the Verse of George Herbert.* Lexington: University of Kentucky, 1966.

Rigg, David. *Ben Jonson: A Life.* Cambridge: Harvard University Press, 1989.

Rowe, V. A. "The Influence of the Earls of Pembroke on Parliamentary Elections, 1625–41." *English Historical Review* 50 (1935): 242–56.

Rudyerd, Benjamin. *Memoirs of Sir Benjamin Rudyerd, Knt.* Ed. James Alexander Manning. London: T. & W. Boone, 1841.

Ruigh, Robert E. *The Parliament of 1624: Politics and Foreign Policy.* Cambridge: Harvard University Press, 1971.

Sanderson, Robert. *Ad Populum; The Fourth Sermon; In St. Paul's Church, London, Nov. 4, 1621.* In *XXXVI Sermons.* London: Thomas Hodgkins, 1686.

Saunders, J. W. *The Profession of English Letters.* London: Routledge and Kegan Paul, 1964.

———. "The Stigma of Print: A Note on the Social Bases of Tudor Poetry." *Essays in Criticism* 1 (Jan. 1951): 139–64.

Schoenfeldt, Michael. *Prayer and Power: George Herbert and Renaissance Courtship.* Chicago: University of Chicago Press, 1991.

Seaver, Paul S. "The Puritan Work Ethic Revisited." *Journal of British Studies* 19 (spring 1980): 35–53.

————. *Wallington's World: A Puritan Artisan in Seventeenth-Century London*. Stanford, Calif.: Stanford University Press, 1985.

*The Second Tome of Homilies Set Out by the Authority of the Late Queenes Majesties: to be read in every Parish Church agreeablie*. 1623.

Selleck, Nancy. "Shakespeare's Mirrors and Other Perspectives." In "Coining the Self: Language, Gender, and Exchange in Early Modern English Literature," Ph.D. diss., Princeton University, 1997.

Shakespeare, William. *The Complete Works of Shakespeare*. Ed. David Bevington. New York: HarperCollins, 1992.

————. *Sonnets*. Ed. Stephen Booth. New Haven: Yale University Press, 1977.

Sharpe, Buchanan. *In Contempt of All Authority: Rural Artisans and Riot in the West of England, 1580–1660*. Berkeley: University of California Press, 1980.

Sharpe, Kevin, ed. *Faction and Parliament: Essays on Early Stuart History*. London: Methuen, 1978.

Shaw, Robert B. *The Call of God: The Theme of Vocation in the Poetry of Donne and Herbert*. Cambridge, Mass.: Cowley, 1981.

Shinagel, Michael. *Daniel Defoe and Middle-Class Gentility*. Cambridge: Harvard University Press, 1968.

Shuger, Debora. *Habits of Thought in the English Renaissance: Religion, Politics, and the Dominant Culture*. Berkeley: University of California Press, 1990.

Sibbes, Richard. *Commentary on II Corinthians I*. In *The Complete Works of Richard Sibbes*, ed. Alexander Grosart, vol. 3. Edinburgh: J. Nichol, 1862.

————. *The Fruitful Labour for Eternal Food*. London, 1630.

Sidney, Philip. *An Apology for Poetry*. Ed. Geoffrey Shepherd. Manchester: Manchester University Press, 1973.

————. *Poems*. Ed. William A. Ringler, Jr. Oxford: Clarendon Press, 1962.

Singleton, Marion White. *God's Courtier: Configuring a Different Grace in George Herbert's Temple*. Cambridge: Cambridge University Press, 1987.

Smith, Paul. *Discerning the Subject*. Minneapolis: University of Minnesota Press, 1988.

Smith, Thomas. *De Republica Anglorum*. Ed. Mary Dewar. Cambridge: Cambridge University Press, 1982.

Sommerville, C. John. "The Anti-Puritan Work Ethic." *Journal of British Studies* 20 (spring 1981): 70–81.

Bibliography

Stein, Arnold. *George Herbert's Lyrics*. Baltimore: Johns Hopkins University Press, 1968.

Stewart, Stanley. *The Enclosed Garden: The Tradition and the Image in Seventeenth-Century Poetry*. Madison: University of Wisconsin Press, 1966.

Stone, Lawrence. *Crisis of the Aristocracy: 1558–1641*. Oxford: Clarendon Press, l965.

———. *The Family, Sex, and Marriage in England, 1500–1800*. London: Weidenfeld and Nicolson, 1977.

Stone, Lawrence, with Jeane C. Fawtier Stone. *An Open Elite? England, 1540–1880*. Oxford: Clarendon Press, 1984.

———. "Social Mobility in England, 1500–1700." *Past and Present* 33 (April 1966): 16–55.

Strier, Richard. "George Herbert and the World." *Journal of Medieval and Renaissance Studies* 12 (fall 1981): 211–36.

———. "'Humanizing' Herbert." *Modern Philology* 74, vol. 1 (Aug. 1976): 78–79.

———. *Love Known: Theology and Experience in George Herbert's Poetry*. Chicago: University of Chicago, 1983.

———. *Resistant Structures: Particularity, Radicalism, and Renaissance Texts*. Berkeley: University of California Press, 1995.

———. "Sanctifying the Aristocracy: 'Devout Humanism' in François de Sales, John Donne, and George Herbert." *Journal of Religion* 69 (Jan. 1989): 36–58.

Strong, Roy. *The Renaissance Garden in England*. London: Thames and Hudson, 1979.

Summers, Claude J., and Ted-Larry Pebworth. "Herbert, Vaughan, and Public Concerns in Private Modes." *George Herbert Journal* 3, nos. 1 and 2 (1979/80): 1–21.

Summers, Joseph. *George Herbert: His Religion and Art*. Cambridge: Harvard University Press, 1968.

———. "Sidney and Herbert: Sir Calidore and the Country Parson." In *Like Season'd Timber: New Essays on George Herbert*, ed. Edmund Miller and Robert DiYanni. New York: Peter Lang, 1987.

Targoff, Ramie. "The Performance of Prayer: Sincerity and Theatricality in Early Modern England." *Representations* 60 (fall 1997): 49–69.

———. "The Poetics of Common Prayer: George Herbert and the Seventeenth-Century Devotional Lyric." *English Literary Renaissance* (forthcoming).

Tawney, R. H. *Religion and the Rise of Capitalism*. London: John Murray, 1954.

Tayler, Edward. *Nature and Art in Renaissance Literature.* New York: Columbia University Press, 1964.

Taylor, Dick, Jr. "The Earl of Pembroke and the Youth of Shakespeare's Sonnets." *Studies in Philology* 56, no. 1 (Jan. 1959): 26–54.

Taylor, John. *A New Discovery by Sea: With a Wherry from London to Salisbury.* London: 1623.

Theophrastus. *Characters.* Trans. J. M. Edmonds. London, 1929.

Thirsk, Joan. "Enclosing and Engrossing." In *The Agrarian History of England and Wales*, vol. 4, *1500–1640*, ed. Joan Thirsk. Cambridge: Cambridge University Press, 1967.

———. "Younger Sons in the Seventeenth Century." *History* 54 (1969): 358–77.

Thompson, E. N. S. *Literary Bypaths of the Renaissance.* New Haven: Yale University Press, 1924.

Thompson, E. P. "The Moral Economy of the English Crowd in the Eighteenth Century." *Past and Present* 50 (Feb. 1971): 76–136.

Tilney, Edmund. *The Flower of Friendship: A Renaissance Dialogue Contesting Marriage.* Ed. Valerie Wayne. Ithaca, N.Y.: Cornell University Press, 1992.

Trachtenberg, Alan. "Man and Tradition: Land and Landscape." *Yale Review* 63 (summer 1974): 610–19.

Travers, William. *A Directory of Church Government Anciently Contended For.* Trans. Thomas Cartwright. Printed in Daniel Neal, *History of the Puritans*, vol. 2. New York: Harper and Brothers, 1844.

Trilling, Lionel. *Sincerity and Authenticity: The Charles Eliot Norton Lectures, 1969–1970.* Cambridge: Harvard University Press, 1971.

Tuve, Rosemund. "Herbert and Caritas." In *Essays by Rosemund Tuve*, ed. Thomas P. Roche, Jr. Princeton: Princeton University Press, 1970.

———. *A Reading of George Herbert.* London: Faber & Faber, 1952.

———. "'Sacred Parody' of Love Poetry, and Herbert." In *Essays by Rosemund Tuve*, ed. Thomas P. Roche, Jr. Princeton: Princeton University Press, 1970.

Tyndale, William. "Exposition upon the Fifth, Sixth and Seventh Chapters of Matthew." In *The Works of William Tyndale*, ed. G. E. Duffield. The Courtenay Library of Reformation Classics. Applefield, Berkshire, England: The Sutton Courtenay Press, 1969.

———. "The Parable of the Wicked Mammon" [1527]. In *Doctrinal Treatises and Introductions to Different Portions of the Holy Scriptures.* The Parker Society. Cambridge: The University Press, 1848.

Underdown, David. *Revel, Riot, and Rebellion: Popular Politics and*

*Culture in England, 1603–1660.* Oxford: Oxford University Press, 1987.

Ustrick, W. Lee. "Changing Ideals of Aristocratic Character and Conduct in Seventeenth-Century England." *Modern Philology* 30 (Nov. 1932): 147–66.

Vaughan, Rowland. *Most Approved, and Long experienced Water-Workes.* London, 1610.

Veith, Gene Edward, Jr. *Reformation Spirituality: The Religion of George Herbert.* London: Associated University Presses, 1985.

Vendler, Helen. *The Poetry of George Herbert.* Cambridge: Harvard University Press, 1975.

Waller, Gary. *The Sidney Family Romance: Mary Wroth, William Herbert, and the Early Modern Construction of Gender.* Detroit: Wayne State University Press, 1993.

Walton, Isaak. *Lives.* London, 1670.

———. *The Lives of John Donne, Sir Henry Wotton, Richard Hooker, George Herbert, and Robert Sanderson,* ed. George Saintsbury. Oxford: Oxford University Press, 1927.

Watson, Curtis Brown. *Shakespeare and the Renaissance Concept of Honor.* Princeton: Princeton University Press, 1960.

Wayne, Don. "Jonson's Sidney: Legacy and Legitimation in *The Forrest.*" In *Sir Philip Sidney's Achievements,* ed. M. J. B. Allen, Dominic Baker-Smith, Arthur Kinney, and Margaret Sullivan. New York: AMS Press, 1990.

———. *Penshurst: The Semiotics of Landscape and the Poetics of History.* Madison: University of Wisconsin Press, 1984.

Weber, Max. *The Protestant Ethic and the Spirit of Capitalism.* Trans. Talcott Parsons. New York: Charles Scribner's Sons, 1958.

Whigham, Frank. *Ambition and Privilege: The Social Tropes of Elizabethan Courtesy Theory.* Berkeley: University of California Press, 1984.

Whitaker, Alexander. *Good Newes from Virginia.* London, 1613.

White, Helen C. *The Metaphysical Poets.* New York: Macmillan, 1936.

Wilcox, Helen. "Herbert's Musical Contexts: From Countrey-Aires to Angels Musick." In *Like Season'd Timber: New Essays on George Herbert,* ed. Edmund Miller and Robert DiYanni. New York: Peter Lang, 1987.

Williams, Raymond. *The Country and the City.* Oxford: Oxford University Press, 1973.

———. *Marxism and Literature.* Oxford: Oxford University Press, 1977.

———. *Problems in Materialism and Culture.* London: Verso, 1980.

Wilson, Thomas. *The State of England, Anno-dom. 1600.* Ed. F. J. Fisher and reprinted in *Camden Miscellany*, vol. 16. Royal Historical Society's Publications, Camden 3d series, vol. 52. London: Offices of the Society, 1936.

Woodbridge, Linda. *Women and the English Renaissance: Literature and the Nature of Womankind, 1540–1620*. Urbana: University of Illinois Press, 1984.

Woodnoth, Arthur. *A Short Collection of the Most Remarkable Passages from the originall to the dissolution of the Virginia Company*. 1651.

Wordsworth, William. *Lyrical Ballads*. Ed. W. J. B. Owen. Oxford: Oxford University Press, 1969.

Wright, Louis B. *Middle-Class Culture in Elizabethan England*. Chapel Hill: University of North Carolina Press, 1935.

———. *Religion and Empire: The Alliance Between Piety and Commerce in English Expansion, 1558–1625*. Chapel Hill: University of North Carolina Press, 1943.

Wrightson, Keith. *English Society, 1580–1680*. London: Hutchinson, 1982.

Wroth, Mary. *Poems*. Ed. Josephine A. Roberts. Baton Rouge: Louisiana State University Press, 1983.

Zagorin, Perez. *The Court and the Country*. New York: Atheneum, 1970.

# General Index

In this index an "f" after a number indicates a separate reference on the next page, and an "ff" indicates separate references on the next two pages. A continuous discussion over two or more pages is indicated by a span of page numbers, e.g., "57–59." *Passim* is used for a cluster of references in close but not consecutive sequence.

# Index of Works
## by George Herbert

In this index an "f" after a number indicates a separate reference on the next page, and an "ff" indicates separate references on the next two pages. A continuous discussion over two or more pages is indicated by a span of page numbers, e.g., "57–59." *Passim* is used for a cluster of references in close but not consecutive sequence.

Library of Congress Cataloging-in-Publication Data

Malcolmson, Cristina.
    Heart-work : George Herbert and the Protestant ethic / Cristina
Malcolmson.
        p.   cm.
    Includes bibliographical references and index.
    ISBN 0-8047-2988-3 (alk. paper)
    1. Herbert, George, 1593–1633—Criticism and interpretation.
2. Protestant work ethic—England—History—17th century.
3. Protestantism and literature—History—17th century.
4. Christian poetry, English—History and criticism.   5. Herbert,
George, 1593–1633—Religion.   6. Christian ethics in literature.
7. Protestantism in literature.   I. Title.
PR3508.M29   1999
821'.3—dc21                                          99-39448

⊗   This book is printed on acid-free, archival quality paper.

Original printing 1999

Last figure below indicates the year of this printing:
08   07   06   05   04   03   02   01   00   99

Designed by James P. Brommer
Typeset in 10/14 Zaph Humanist and Stuyvesant display